Oracle Coherence 3.5

Create Internet-scale applications using
Oracle's high-performance data grid

Aleksandar Seović

Mark Falco

Patrick Peralta

PUBLISHING

BIRMINGHAM - MUMBAI

Oracle Coherence 3.5

First published: April 2010

Production Reference: 1240310

Published by Packt Publishing Ltd.
32 Lincoln Road
Olton
Birmingham, B27 6PA, UK.

ISBN 978-1-847196-12-5

www.packtpub.com

Cover Image by Vinayak Chittar (vinayak.chittar@gmail.com)

Credits

Authors

Aleksandar Seović

Mark Falco

Patrick Peralta

Reviewers

Rob Harrop

Jimmy Nilsson

Patrick Peralta

Steve Samuelson

Robert Varga

Acquisition Editor

James Lumsden

Development Editor

Dilip Venkatesh

Technical Editor

Arani Roy

Indexer

Rekha Nair

Editorial Team Leader

Mithun Sehgal

Project Team Leader

Lata Basantani

Project Coordinator

Srimoyee Ghoshal

Proofreader

Chris Smith

Graphics

Geetanjali Sawant

Production Coordinator

Shantanu Zagade

Cover Work

Shantanu Zagade

Foreword

There are a few timeless truths of software development that are near-universally accepted, and have become the basis for many a witty saying over the years. For starters, there's Zymurgy's First Law of Evolving Systems Dynamics, which states:

> *Once you open a can of worms, the only way to re-can them is to use a bigger can.*

And Weinberg's Second Law, which postulates that,

> *If builders built buildings the way that programmers wrote programs, the first woodpecker to come along would destroy civilization.*

There is true brilliance in this timeless wit, enjoyed and appreciated by generation after generation of software developers.

The largest set of challenges that the modern programmer faces, and thus the source of most of the wit that we as programmers revel in, revolves around the seemingly boundless growth of complexity. Hardware becomes more complex. Operating systems become more complex. Programming languages and APIs become more complex. And the applications that we build and evolve, become more and more complex.

The complexity of a system always seems to hover ever so slightly on the far side of manageable, just slightly over the edge of the cliff. And while our work reality is a world full of complexity — or perhaps because of that complexity — we gravitate toward the pristine and the simple. While our day-to-day lives may be focused on diagnosing failures in production systems, our guiding light is the concept of continuous availability. While we may have to manually correct data when things go wrong, our aspirations remain with data integrity and information reliability. While the complexity of the legacy applications that we manage forces us to adopt the most expensive means of adding capacity, our higher thoughts are focused on commodity scale-out and linear scalability. And while the complex, layered, and often twisted system designs result in hopelessly slow responses to user actions, we fundamentally believe that users should experience near-instant responses for almost any conceivable action they take.

In a word, we believe in the *ilities*.

Availability. Reliability. Scalability. Performance. These are attributes that we wish to endow each and every one of our systems with. If a system lacks continuous availability, its users will be directly impacted by failures within the system. If a system lacks information reliability, then users will never know if the information they are using can be trusted. If a system lacks scalability, its growing popularity will overwhelm and kill it—it will fail just as it begins to succeed! If a system lacks performance, it will inflict a dose of pain upon its users with each and every interaction.

We wish to achieve these *ilities* because we wish for our labors to be beneficial to others, and we hope that the value that we provide through these systems endures far longer than the passing whims and fads of technology and industry.

Perhaps no greater revolution has occurred in our industry than the World Wide Web. Suddenly, the systems we provide had a limitless audience, with instant access to the latest and greatest versions of our software. Users are so accustomed to instant responses from one application that failure to achieve the same will cause them to quickly abandon another. Downtime no longer represents an inconvenience—for major websites, their online foibles have become headline news on the printed pages of the Wall Street Journal!

At the same time, the competitive landscape has forced companies, and thus their IT departments, to act and react far more quickly than before. The instant popularity of a particular good, service, or website can bring mind-boggling hordes of unexpected—though generally not undesired—users. Companies must be able to roll out new features and capabilities quickly, to grow their capacity dynamically in order to match the increase in users, and to provide instantaneous responsiveness with correct and up-to-date information to each and every user.

These are the systems that Oracle Coherence was designed to enable. These are the systems that this book will help you build.

If there was only one piece of advice that I could instill into the mind of a software architect or developer responsible for one of these systems, it would be this: architecture matters, and in systems of scale and systems that require availability, architecture matters absolutely! Failure to achieve a solid architecture will doom in advance any hope of significant scalability, and will leave the effects of failure within the system to pure chance.

No amount of brilliant programming can make up for a lack of architectural foresight. Systems do not remain available by accident, nor do they scale by accident. Achieving information reliability in a system that remains continuously available and provides high performance under varying degrees of load and scale is an outcome that results only when a systematic and well-conceived architecture has been laid down. Availability, reliability, scalability, and performance must be the core tenets of an architecture, and they must be baked into and throughout that architecture.

If there were a second piece of advice that I could confer, it would be this: as a craftsman or craftswoman, know your tools, and know them well. Using Oracle Coherence as part of a system does not ensure any of the *ilities* by itself; it is simply a powerful tool for simultaneously achieving those *ilities* as part of a great architecture. This book is an effort to condense a huge amount of experience and knowledge into a medium of transfer that you can rehydrate into instant knowledge for yourself.

And the last piece of advice is this: don't believe it until you see it; make sure that you push it until it fails. While testing, if you don't overload the system until it breaks, then you can't be certain that it will work. If you don't pull the plug while it's running, then you can't be certain that it will handle failure when it truly matters. Don't be satisfied until you understand the limits of your systems, and until you appreciate and understand what lies beyond those boundaries.

A word about the author

I first met Aleks Seović in 2005. I was attending the Javapolis (now Devoxx) conference in Antwerp with the express purpose of persuading Aleks to create the .NET implementation of Coherence. I had known of him through his work in creating the Spring.NET framework, and knew that there was only one person whom I wanted to lead the creation of our own product for .NET. As they say, the rest is history: We hit it off smashingly, and found a great deal of common ground in our experiences with enterprise systems, the challenges of distributed computing, architecting for scalable performance and high availability, and the need for seamless and reliable information exchange between Java and .NET applications.

Aleks has such a great ability to understand complex systems, and such a compelling manner of reducing complexity into simple concepts, that I was ecstatic when he told me that he was writing this book. Starting a book is no challenge at all, but *finishing* a book is a great feat. Many years of work have gone into these pages. May you enjoy and profit from this book as deeply as I have enjoyed and profited from my conversations with Aleks over these past years.

Cameron Purdy
Lexington, MA
January 2010

About the author

Aleksandar Seović is the founder of and managing director at S4HC, Inc., where he leads professional services practice. He works with customers throughout the world to help them solve performance and scalability puzzles and implement innovative solutions to complex business and technical problems.

Aleksandar lead the implementation of Oracle Coherence for .NET, a client library that allows applications written in any .NET language to access data and services provided by an Oracle Coherence data grid. He was also one of the key people involved in the design and implementation of Portable Object Format (POF), a platform-independent object serialization format that allows seamless interoperability of Coherence-based Java, .NET, and C++ applications.

Aleksandar is Oracle ACE Director for Fusion Middleware, and frequently speaks about and evangelizes Coherence at conferences, Java and .NET user group events, and Coherence SIGs. He blogs about Coherence and related topics at http://coherence.seovic.com.

Acknowledgements

First and foremost, I'd like to thank Cameron Purdy and Alex Gleyzer for giving me the opportunity to work on Coherence. It has been quite a journey—I still remember the day when we got a .NET application to connect to the cluster for the first time. Guys, it has been a privilege working with you all these years to make a great product even better.

I've heard many times that a book is never a single person's creation. Only now, after I have written one myself, I truly understand what that means.

I cannot thank enough my co-authors, Mark Falco and Patrick Peralta, members of the Coherence engineering team, who contributed two great chapters to the book. Patrick's chapter covers pretty much everything you need to know in order to integrate Coherence with persistent data sources. As for Mark's chapter on using the Coherence C++ client, well, let's just say that I would've had a *really* hard time writing that one myself ☺.

The sample application for the book is the result of the hard work of my colleagues from Solutions for Human Capital: Ivan Cikić, Nenad Dobrilović, Marko Dumić, and Aleksandar Jević. They managed to deliver (once again) on a very tight schedule, and I am very proud of the final result. Thank you for all the help and for putting up with my last minute change requests—I know it wasn't easy at times, but you have done a wonderful job.

I can honestly say (and everyone who saw the first draft is my witness) that this book was significantly improved based on the feedback from many reviewers. The official reviewers for the book were Rob Harrop, Jimmy Nilsson, Patrick Peralta, Steve Samuelson, and Robert Varga, but Mark Falco, Cameron Purdy, Cristobal Soto, Phil Wheeler, and Andrew Wilson also provided invaluable feedback. Jimmy, it is mostly your "fault" that there is a sample application now demonstrating (among other things) how to build a clean, testable domain model that works well with Coherence.

Many members of Coherence engineering and Oracle's Architecture team were only an e-mail or phone call away when I had questions: Noah Arliss, Simon Bisson, Gene Gleyzer, Jason Howes, Rob Misek, Andy Nguyen, Brian Oliver, Jon Purdy, and Randy Stafford all helped at one point or another, whether they know it or not. Thank you for that, and thank you for building such a great product.

James Lumsden, Dilip Venkatesh, Rajashree Hamine, and Srimoyee Ghoshal from Packt Publishing provided necessary support when I needed it and helped me reach the finish line. James, I know the journey was much longer than either of us expected. Thank you for believing in me even when I didn't.

My partners at Solutions for Human Capital, Snejana Sevak, Aleksandar Jević, and Nebojša Peruničić, helped more than they realize by shielding me from the daily disturbances of running a business and allowing me to focus my energy on writing, and I thank them for that.

I would also like to thank all the clients and colleagues I worked with over the years. I learned something new from each one of you, and for that I am grateful.

Most importantly, I would like to thank my family. My wife Marija supported me from the moment I decided to work on this book, even though she knew that my already busy schedule would only get busier because of it. People who think astronauts' wives have it rough have never met the wife of a traveling geek who decides to write a book. Хвала, љубави.

To my children, Ana Maria and Novak, I am sorry I couldn't play with you as much as we all wanted, and promise to make it up to you. You are too young to understand why daddy was sleeping during the day and working at night, but that doesn't matter now. Daddy is back and loves you both very much!

About the co-authors

Mark Falco is a Consulting Member of Technical Staff at Oracle. He has been part of the Coherence development team since 2005 where he has specialized in the areas of clustered communication protocols as well as the Coherence for C++ object model. Mark holds a B.S. in computer science from Stevens Institute of Technology.

> I would like to thank Aleks for the opportunity to contribute to this book and Tangosol for the years of fun and interesting work. Thank you Otti, Erika, and Mia for your encouragement and support.

Patrick Peralta is a Senior Software Engineer for Oracle (formerly Tangosol) specializing in Coherence and middleware Java. He wears many hats in Coherence engineering, including development, training, documentation, and support. He has extensive experience in supporting and consulting customers in fields such as retail, hospitality, and finance.

As an active member of the Java developer community he has spoken at user groups and conferences across the US including Spring One and Oracle Open World. Prior to joining Oracle, Patrick was a senior developer at Symantec, working on Java/J2EE based services, web applications, system integrations, and Swing desktop clients. Patrick has a B.S. in computer science from Stetson University in Florida.

He currently maintains a blog on Coherence and other software development topics at http://blackbeanbag.net.

> I would like to express my appreciation and gratitude to those that provided valuable feedback, including Aleks Seović, Gene Gleyzer, Andy Nguyen, Pas Apicella, and Shaun Smith. Many thanks as well to my family, including my parents, siblings, and especially my wonderful wife Maria and son Isaac for providing me with joy and perspective on what is truly important in life.

About the reviewers

Rob Harrop is a respected speaker, author, entrepreneur, and technologist.

As Lead Engineer of SpringSource dm Server, Rob is driving SpringSource's enterprise middleware product line and ensuring that the company continues to deliver high-performance, highly scalable enterprise solutions.

With a thorough knowledge of both Java and .NET, Rob has successfully deployed projects across both platforms. He has extensive experience across a variety of sectors, in particular banking, retail, and government. Prior to joining SpringSource, he co-founded the UK-based software company Cake Solutions Limited and worked as a Lead Developer for a successful dotcom start-up.

Rob is the author of five books, including *Pro Spring*, a widely acclaimed, comprehensive resource on the Spring Framework.

Jimmy Nilsson has been working as a developer/architect for over 20 years.

He has authored *Applying Domain-Driven Design and Patterns* and *.NET Enterprise Design*.

Steve Samuelson has worked in IT for over 20 years across various industries including home building, finance, and education. Although experienced with Windows deployment and hardware, Steve prefers custom software development. Currently, Steve is the Chief Architect for an international education provider where he works with multiple technologies running under Unix and Windows. Steve's primary interest lies in Microsoft .NET development and tools, but he makes sure to keep up on emerging Java and Oracle technologies among others.

Robert Varga is a Lead Software Engineer at EPAM Systems. He has worked in various roles from Developer to Enterprise Architect on several large projects for various customers, mostly in the areas of insurance, online betting, online auctions, and finance. He is also an Oracle ACE since 2008.

Robert has worked on Java-based enterprise systems since 1998 and on various projects with the Coherence data grid since 2005. He is among the most active contributors to the Oracle Coherence support forums helping developers with questions about Oracle Coherence.

Table of Contents

Preface

As an architect of a large, mission-critical website or enterprise application, you need to address at least three major non-functional requirements: *performance*, *scalability*, and *availability*.

Performance is defined as the amount of time that an operation takes to complete. In a web application, it is usually measured as "time to last byte" (**TTLB**) — the amount of time elapsed from the moment the web server received a request, until the moment the last byte of response has been sent back to the client. Performance is extremely important, because experience has shown us that no matter how great and full-featured an application is, if it is slow and unresponsive, the users will hate it.

Scalability is the ability of the system to maintain acceptable performance as the load increases, or to support additional load by adding hardware resources. While it is relatively simple to make an application perform well in a single-user environment, it is significantly more difficult to maintain that level of performance as the number of simultaneous users increases to thousands, or in the case of very large public websites, to tens or even hundreds of thousands. The bottom line is, if your application doesn't scale well, its performance will degrade as the load increases and the users will hate it.

Finally, **availability** is measured as the percentage of time an application is available to the users. While some applications can crash several times a day without causing major inconvenience to the user, most mission-critical applications simply cannot afford that luxury and need to be available 24 hours a day, every day. If your application is mission critical, you need to ensure that it is highly available or the users will hate it. To make things even worse, if you build an e-commerce website that crashes during the holiday season, your investors will hate you as well.

The moral of the story is that in order to keep your users happy and avoid all that hatred, you as an architect need to ensure that your application is fast, remains fast even under heavy load, and stays up and running even when the hardware or software components that it depends on fail. Unfortunately, while it is relatively easy to satisfy any one of these three requirements individually and not too difficult to comply with any two of them, it is considerably more difficult to fulfill all three at the same time.

Introducing Oracle Coherence

Over the last few years, **In-Memory Data Grids** have become an increasingly popular way to solve many of the problems related to performance and scalability, while improving availability of the system at the same time.

Oracle Coherence is an In-Memory Data Grid that allows you to eliminate *single points of failure* and *single points of bottleneck* in your application by distributing your application's objects and related processing across multiple physical servers.

There are several important points in the definition above:

- Coherence manages *application objects*, which are ready for use within the application. This eliminates the need for repeated, and often expensive, loading and transformation of the raw data into objects.

- Coherence distributes application objects *across many physical servers* while ensuring that a coherent, **Single System Image** (**SSI**) is presented to the application.

- Coherence ensures that *no data or in-flight operations are lost* by assuming that any node could fail at any time and by ensuring that every piece of information is stored in multiple places.

- Coherence *stores data in memory* in order to achieve very high performance and low latency for data access.

- Coherence allows you to distribute not only application objects, but also *the processing* that should be performed on these objects. This can help you eliminate single points of bottleneck.

The following sections provide a high-level overview of Coherence features; the remainder of the book will teach you "how", and more importantly, "when" to use them.

Distributed caching

One of the easiest ways to improve application performance is to bring data closer to the application, and keep it in a format that the application can consume more easily.

Most enterprise applications are written in one of the object-oriented languages, such as Java or C#, while most data is stored in relational databases, such as Oracle, MySQL or SQL Server. This means that in order to use the data, the application needs to load it from the database and convert it into objects. Because of the impedance mismatch between tabular data in the database and objects in memory, this conversion process is not always simple and introduces some overhead, even when sophisticated O-R mapping tools, such as Hibernate or EclipseLink are used.

Caching objects in the application tier minimizes this performance overhead by avoiding unnecessary trips to the database and data conversion. This is why all production-quality O-R mapping tools cache objects internally and short-circuit object lookups by returning cached instances instead, whenever possible.

However, when you scale out your application across multiple servers, you will start running into cache synchronization issues. Each server will cache its own copy of the data, and will have no way of knowing if that same data has been changed on another server—in this case, the locally cached copy should be invalidated and evicted from the cache.

Oracle Coherence solves this problem by allowing you to distribute your cache across a cluster of machines, while providing a unified, fully coherent view of the data. This means that you can configure Coherence as an L2 cache for Hibernate or EclipseLink, and forget about distributed cache synchronization!

If this was all Coherence did, it would be impressive enough. However, it actually does so much more that I don't recommend using it purely as an L2 cache, unless you have an existing application that you need to scale out. While Coherence works like a charm as an L2 cache behind an O-R mapper, this architecture barely scratches the surface of what Coherence can do. It is like "killing an ox for a pound of meat", as the Serbian proverb says.

It is much more powerful to use Coherence as a logical persistence layer of your application, which sits between the application logic and the physical data store. Whenever the application needs data, it asks Coherence for it. If the data is not already in the cache, Coherence will transparently load it from the data store, cache it, and return it to the application. Similarly, when the application needs to store data, it simply puts objects into the cache, and Coherence updates the underlying data store automatically.

This architecture is depicted in the following diagram and is the basis for the architecture we will use throughout the book:

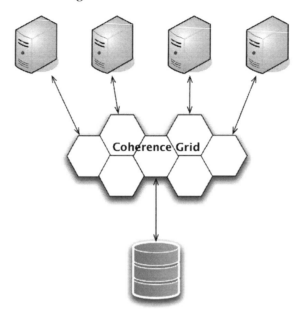

Although Coherence is not really a *persistent* store in the preceding scenario, the fact that the application *thinks* that it is decouples the application from the data store and enables you to achieve very high scalability and availability. You can even configure Coherence so the application will be isolated from a complete data store failure.

Distributed queries

Having all the data in the world is meaningless unless there is a way to find the information you need, when you need it. One of the many advantages of In-Memory Data Grids over clustered caches, such as Memcached, is the ability to find data not just by the primary key, but also by executing queries and aggregations against the cache.

Coherence is no exception—it allows you to execute queries and aggregations in parallel, across all the nodes in the cluster. This allows for the efficient processing of large data sets within the grid and enables you to improve aggregation and query performance by simply adding more nodes to the cluster.

In-place and parallel processing

In many situations, you can improve performance enormously if you perform the processing where the data is stored, instead of retrieving the data that needs to be processed. For example, while working with a relational database, you can use bulk update or a stored procedure to update many records without moving any data across the network.

Coherence allows you to achieve the same thing. Instead of retrieving the whole dataset that needs to be processed and iterating over it on a single machine, you can create an *entry processor*—a class that encapsulates the logic you want to execute for each object in a target dataset. You can then submit an instance of the processor into the cluster, and it will be executed locally on each node. By doing so, you eliminate the need to move a large amount of data across the network. The entry processor itself is typically very small and allows processing to occur in parallel.

The performance benefit of this approach is tremendous. Entry processors, just like distributed queries, execute in parallel across grid nodes. This allows you to improve performance by simply spreading your data across more nodes.

Coherence also provides a grid-enabled implementation of CommonJ Work Manager, which is the basis for JSR-237. This allows you to submit a collection of work items that Coherence will execute "in parallel" across the grid. Again, the more nodes you have in the grid, the more work items can be executed in parallel, thereby improving the overall performance.

Cache events

In many applications, it is useful to know when a particular piece of data changes. For example, you might need to update a stock price on the screen as it changes, or alert the user if a new workflow task is assigned to them.

The easiest and the most common solution is to periodically poll the server to see if the information on the client needs to be updated. This is essentially what Outlook does when it checks for new e-mail on the POP3 mail server, and you (the user) control how often the polling should happen.

The problem with polling is that the more frequently it occurs, the more load it puts on the server, decreasing its scalability, even if there is no new information to be retrieved.

On the other hand, if the server knows which information you are interested in, it can push that information to you. This is how Outlook works with Exchange Server—when the new mail arrives, the Exchange Server notifies Outlook about this event, and Outlook displays the new message in your inbox.

Coherence allows you to register interest in a specific cache, a specific item, or even a specific subset of the data within the cache using a query. You can specify if you are interested in cache insertions, updates or deletions only, as well as whether you would like to receive the old and the new cache value with the event.

As the events occur in the cluster, your application is notified and can take the appropriate action, without the need to poll the server.

Coherence within the Oracle ecosystem

If you look at Oracle marketing material, you will find out that Coherence is a member of the Oracle Fusion Middleware product suite. However, if you dig a bit deeper, you will find out that it is not just another product in the suite, but a foundation for some of the high-profile initiatives that have been announced by Oracle, such as Oracle WebLogic Application Grid and Complex Event Processing.

Coherence is also the underpinning of the "SOA grid"—a next-generation SOA platform that David Chappell, vice president and chief technologist for SOA at Oracle, wrote about for *The SOA Magazine* [SOAGrid1&2].

I believe that over the next few years, we will see Coherence being used more and more as an enabling technology within various Oracle products, because it provides an excellent foundation for fast, scalable, and highly-available solutions.

Coherence usage scenarios

There are many possible uses for Coherence, some more conventional than the others.

It is commonly used as a mechanism to off-load expensive, difficult-to-scale backend systems, such as databases and mainframes. By fronting these systems with Coherence, you can significantly improve performance and reduce the cost of data access.

Another common usage scenario is **eXtreme Transaction Processing (XTP)**. Because of the way Coherence partitions data across the cluster, you can easily achieve throughput of several thousand transactions per second. What's even better is that you can scale the system to support an increasing load by simply adding new nodes to the cluster.

As it stores all the data in memory and allows you to process it in-place and in parallel, Coherence can also be used as a computational grid. In one such application, a customer was able to reduce the time it took to perform risk calculation from eighteen hours to twenty minutes.

Coherence is also a great integration platform. It allows you to load data from multiple data sources (including databases, mainframes, web services, ERP, CRM, DMS, or any other enterprise system), providing a uniform data access interface to client applications at the same time.

Finally, it is an excellent foundation for applications using the Event Driven Architecture, and can be easily integrated with messaging, ESB, and **Complex Event Processing** (CEP) systems.

That said, for the remainder of the book I will use the "conventional" web application architecture described earlier, to illustrate Coherence features—primarily because most developers are already familiar with it and also because it will make the text much easier to follow.

Oracle Coherence editions

Coherence has three different editions—Standard, Enterprise, and Grid Editions. As is usually the case, each of these editions has a different price point and feature set, so you should evaluate your needs carefully before buying.

The Coherence client also has two different editions—Data Client and Real-Time Client. However, for the most part, the client edition is determined by the server license you purchase—Standard and Enterprise Edition give you a Data Client license, whereas the Grid Edition gives you a Real-Time Client license.

A high-level overview of edition differences can be found at `http://www.oracle.com/technology/products/coherence/coherencedatagrid/coherence_editions.html`, but you are likely to find the following documents available in the Coherence Knowledge Base much more useful:

- *The Coherence Ecosystem*, available at `http://coherence.oracle.com/display/COH35UG/The+Coherence+Ecosystem`
- *Coherence Features by Edition*, available at `http://coherence.oracle.com/display/COH35UG/Coherence+Features+by+Edition`

Throughout the book, I will assume that you are using the Grid Edition and Real-Time Client Edition, which provide access to all Coherence features.

The important thing to note is that when you go to Oracle's website to download Coherence for evaluation, you will find only one download package for Java, one for .NET, and one for each supported C++ platform. This is because all the editions are included into the same binary distribution; choosing the edition you want to use is simply a matter of obtaining the appropriate license and specifying the edition in the configuration file.

By default, Grid Edition features are enabled on the server and Real-Time Client features on the client, which is exactly what you will need in order to run the examples given in the book.

What this book covers

Chapter 1, Achieving Performance, Scalability, and Availability Objectives discusses obstacles to scalability, performance, and availability and also some common approaches that are used to overcome these obstacles. It also talks about how these solutions can be improved using Coherence.

Chapter 2, Getting Started teaches you how set up Coherence correctly in a development environment, and the basics of how to access Coherence caches, both by using the supplied command-line client and programmatically.

Chapter 3, Planning Your Caches covers various cache topologies supported by Coherence and provides guidance on when to use each one and how to configure them.

Chapter 4, Implementing Domain Objects introduces the sample application we will be building throughout the book and shows you how to design your domain objects to take full advantage of Coherence.

Chapter 5, Querying the Data Grid teaches you how to use Coherence queries and aggregators to retrieve data from the cache in parallel.

Chapter 6, Parallel and In-Place Processing covers Coherence features that allow you to perform in-place or parallel processing within a data grid.

Chapter 7, Processing Data Grid Events shows you how to use powerful event mechanisms provided by Coherence.

Chapter 8, Implementing Persistence Layer discusses options for integration with various data repositories, including relational databases.

Chapter 9, Bridging Platform and Network Boundaries covers the Coherence*Extend protocol, which allows you to access a Coherence cluster from remote clients and from platforms and languages other than Java, such as .NET and C++.

Chapters 10, Accessing Coherence from .NET and *Chapter 11, Accessing Coherence from C++* teach you how to access Coherence from .NET and C++ clients, respectively.

Chapter 12, The Right Tool for the Job, provides some parting thoughts and reiterates practices you should apply when building scalable applications.

Appendix, Coherent Bank Sample Application, describes how to set up the sample application that accompanies the book in your environment.

The main goal of this book is to provide the missing information that puts various Coherence features into context and teaches you when to use them. As such, it does not cover every nook and cranny Coherence has to offer, and you are encouraged to refer to the Coherence product documentation [CohDoc] for details.

On the other hand, real-world applications are not developed using a single technology, no matter how powerful that one technology is. While the main focus of the book is Coherence, it will also discuss how Coherence fits into the overall application architecture, and show you how to integrate Coherence with some popular open source frameworks and tools.

You are encouraged to read this book in the order it was written, as the material in each chapter builds on the topics that were previously discussed.

What you need for this book

In addition to some spare time, an open mind, and a desire to learn, you will need to have Java SDK 1.5 or higher in order to run Coherence and the examples given in this book. While Coherence itself will run just fine on Java 1.4, the examples use some features that are only available in Java 1.5 or higher, such as enums and generics.

To run .NET examples from Chapter 10, you will need .NET Framework 3.5 and Visual Studio 2008. Although you can access Coherence using .NET Framework 1.1 and higher, the examples use features such as generics and Windows Presentation Foundation, which are only available in the more recent releases of the .NET Framework.

Finally, to run the C++ examples from Chapter 11, you need an appropriate version of the C++ compiler and related tools depending on your platform (for details check `http://download.oracle.com/docs/cd/E14526_01/coh.350/e14513/cpprequire.htm#BABDCDFG`), a fast machine to compile and link examples on, and a lot of patience!

Who this book is for

The primary audience for this book is experienced architects and developers who are interested in, or responsible for, the design and implementation of scalable, high-performance systems using Oracle Coherence.

However, Coherence has features that make it useful even in smaller applications, such as applications based on Event Driven Architecture, or Service Oriented Applications that would benefit from the high-performance, platform-independent binary protocol built into Coherence.

Finally, this book should be an interesting read for anyone who wants to learn more about the implementation of scalable systems in general, and how Oracle Coherence can be used to remove much of the pain associated with the endeavor.

Who this book is not for

This book is not for a beginner looking forward to learning how to write computer software. While I will try to introduce the concepts in a logical order and provide background information where necessary, for the most part I will assume that you, the reader, are an experienced software development professional with a solid knowledge of object-oriented design, Java, and XML.

Conventions

In this book, you will find a number of styles of text that distinguish between different kinds of information. Here are some examples of these styles, and an explanation of their meaning.

Code words in text are shown as follows: "As a matter of fact, such a class already exists within `coherence.jar`, and is called `AbstractEvolvable`".

A block of code is set as follows:

```
public interface QueryMap extends Map {
  Set keySet(Filter filter);
  Set entrySet(Filter filter);
  Set entrySet(Filter filter, Comparator comparator);
  ...
}
```

When we wish to draw your attention to a particular part of a code block, the relevant lines or items are set in bold:

```
Filter filter = new BetweenFilter(
                    new PropertyExtractor("time"),
                    from, to);
```

Any command-line input or output is written as follows:

```
$ . bin/multicast-test.sh -ttl 0
```

New terms and **important words** are shown in bold. Words that you see on the screen, in menus or dialog boxes for example, appear in the text like this: "clicking the **OK** button finishes the installation".

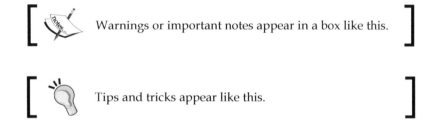

Warnings or important notes appear in a box like this.

Tips and tricks appear like this.

Reader feedback

Feedback from our readers is always welcome. Let us know what you think about this book—what you liked or may have disliked. Reader feedback is important for us to develop titles that you really get the most out of.

To send us general feedback, simply send an e-mail to feedback@packtpub.com, and mention the book title via the subject of your message.

If there is a book that you need and would like to see us publish, please send us a note in the **SUGGEST A TITLE** form on www.packtpub.com or e-mail to suggest@packtpub.com.

If there is a topic that you have expertise in and you are interested in either writing or contributing to a book on, see our author guide on www.packtpub.com/authors.

Customer support

Now that you are the proud owner of a Packt book, we have a number of things to help you to get the most from your purchase.

Downloading the example code for the book

Visit `http://www.packtpub.com/files/code/6125_Code.zip` to directly download the example code.

The downloadable files contain instructions on how to use them.

Errata

Although we have taken every care to ensure the accuracy of our content, mistakes do happen. If you find a mistake in one of our books—maybe a mistake in the text or the code—we would be grateful if you would report this to us. By doing so, you can save other readers from frustration and help us improve subsequent versions of this book. If you find any errata, please report them by visiting `http://www.packtpub.com/support`, selecting your book, clicking on the **let us know** link, and entering the details of your errata. Once your errata are verified, your submission will be accepted and the errata will be uploaded on our website, or added to any list of existing errata, under the Errata section of that title. Any existing errata can be viewed by selecting your title from `http://www.packtpub.com/support`.

Piracy

Piracy of copyright material on the Internet is an ongoing problem across all media. At Packt, we take the protection of our copyright and licenses very seriously. If you come across any illegal copies of our works, in any form, on the Internet, please provide us with the location address or website name immediately so that we can pursue a remedy.

Please contact us at `copyright@packtpub.com` with a link to the suspected pirated material.

We appreciate your help in protecting our authors, and our ability to bring you valuable content.

Questions

You can contact us at `questions@packtpub.com` if you are having a problem with any aspect of the book, and we will do our best to address it.

1
Achieving Performance, Scalability, and Availability Objectives

Building a highly available and scalable system that performs well is no trivial task. In this chapter, we will look into the reasons why this is the case, and discuss what can be done to solve some of the problems.

I will also explain how Coherence can be used to either completely eliminate or significantly reduce some of these problems and why it is a great foundation for scalable applications.

Achieving performance objectives

There are many factors that determine how long a particular operation takes. The choice of the algorithm and data structures that are used to implement it will be a major factor, so choosing the most appropriate ones for the problem at hand is important.

However, when building a distributed system, another important factor we need to consider is network latency. The duration of every operation is the sum of the time it takes to perform the operation, and the time it takes for the request to reach the application and for the response to reach the client.

In some environments, latency is so low that it can often be ignored. For example, accessing properties of an object within the same process is performed at in-memory speed (nanoseconds), and therefore the latency is not a concern. However, as soon as you start making calls across machine boundaries, the laws of physics come into the picture.

Dealing with latency

Very often developers write applications as if there is no latency. To make things even worse, they test them in an environment where latency is minimal, such as their local machine or a high-speed network in the same building.

When they deploy the application in a remote datacenter, they are often surprised by the fact that the application is much slower than what they expected. They shouldn't be, they should have counted on the fact that the latency is going to increase and should have taken measures to minimize its impact on the application performance early on.

To illustrate the effect latency can have on performance, let's assume that we have an operation whose actual execution time is 20 milliseconds. The following table shows the impact of latency on such an operation, depending on where the server performing it is located. All the measurements in the table were taken from my house in Tampa, Florida.

Location	Execution time (ms)	Average latency (ms)	Total time (ms)	Latency (% of total time)
Local host	20	0.067	20.067	0.3%
VM running on the local host	20	0.335	20.335	1.6%
Server on the same LAN	20	0.924	20.924	4.4%
Server in Tampa, FL, US	20	21.378	41.378	51.7%
Server in Sunnyvale, CA, US	20	53.130	73.130	72.7%
Server in London, UK	20	126.005	146.005	86.3%
Server in Moscow, Russia	20	181.855	201.855	90.1%
Server in Tokyo, Japan	20	225.684	245.684	91.9%
Server in Sydney, Australia	20	264.869	284.869	93.0%

As you can see from the previous table, the impact of latency is minimal on the local host, or even when accessing another host on the same network. However, as soon as you move the server out of the building it becomes significant. When the server is half way around the globe, it is the latency that pretty much determines how long an operation will take.

Of course, as the execution time of the operation itself increases, latency as a percentage of the total time will decrease. However, I have intentionally chosen 20 milliseconds for this example, because many operations that web applications typically perform complete in 20 milliseconds or less. For example, on my development box, retrieval of a single row from the MySQL database using **EclipseLink** and rendering of the retrieved object using **FreeMarker template** takes 18 milliseconds on an average, according to the **YourKit Profiler**.

On the other hand, even if your page takes 700 milliseconds to render and your server is in Sydney, your users in Florida could still have a sub-second response time, as long as they are able to retrieve the page in a single request. Unfortunately, it is highly unlikely that one request will be enough. Even the extremely simple Google front page requires four HTTP requests, and most non-trivial pages require 15 to 20, or even more. Each image, external CSS style sheet, or JavaScript file that your page references, will add latency and turn your sub-second response time into 5 seconds or more.

You must be wondering by now whether you are reading a book about website performance optimization and what all of this has to do with Coherence. I have used a web page example in order to illustrate the effect of extremely high latencies on performance, but the situation is quite similar in low-latency environments as well.

Each database query, each call to a remote service, and each Coherence cache access will incur some latency. Although it might be only a millisecond or less for each individual call, it quickly gets compounded by the sheer number of calls.

With Coherence for example, the actual time it takes to insert 1,000 small objects into the cache is less than 50 milliseconds. However, the elapsed wall clock time from a client perspective is more than a second. Guess where the millisecond per insert is spent.

This is the reason why you will often hear advice such as "make your remote services coarse grained" or "batch multiple operations together". As a matter of fact, batching 1,000 objects from the previous example, and inserting them all into the cache in one call brings total operation duration, as measured from the client, down to 90 milliseconds!

The bottom line is that if you are building a distributed application, and if you are reading this book you most likely are, you need to consider the impact of latency on performance when making design decisions.

Minimizing bandwidth usage

In general, bandwidth is less of an issue than latency, because it is subject to Moore's Law. While the speed of light, the determining factor of latency, has remained constant over the years and will likely remain constant for the foreseeable future, network bandwidth has increased significantly and continues to do so.

However, that doesn't mean that we can ignore it. As anyone who has ever tried to browse the Web over a slow dial-up link can confirm, whether the images on the web page are 72 or 600 DPI makes a big difference in the overall user experience.

So, if we learned to optimize the images in order to improve the bandwidth utilization in front of the web server, why do we so casually waste the bandwidth behind it? There are two things that I see time and time again:

- The application retrieving a lot of data from a database, performing some simple processing on it, and storing it back in a database.

- The application retrieving significantly more data than it really needs. For example, I've seen large object graphs loaded from database using multiple queries in order to populate a simple drop-down box.

The first scenario above is an example of the situation where moving the processing instead of data makes much more sense, whether your data is in a database or in Coherence (although, in the former case doing so might have a negative impact on the scalability, and you might actually decide to sacrifice performance in order to allow the application to scale).

The second scenario is typically a consequence of the fact that we try to reuse the same objects we use elsewhere in the application, even when it makes no sense to do so. If all you need is an identifier and a description, it probably makes sense to load only those two attributes from the data store and move them across the wire.

In any case, keeping an eye on how network bandwidth is used both on the frontend and on the backend is another thing that you, as an architect, should be doing habitually if you care about performance.

Coherence and performance

Coherence has powerful features that directly address the problems of latency and bandwidth.

First of all, by caching data in the application tier, Coherence allows you to avoid disk I/O on the database server and transformation of retrieved tabular data into objects. In addition to that, Coherence also allows you to cache recently used data in-process using its near caching feature, thus eliminating the latency associated with a network call that would be required to retrieve a piece of data from a distributed cache.

Another Coherence feature that can significantly improve performance is its ability to execute tasks in parallel, across the data grid, and to move processing where the data is, which will not only decrease latency, but preserve network bandwidth as well.

Leveraging these features is important. It will be much easier to scale the application if it performs well—you simply won't have to scale as much.

Achieving scalability

There are two ways to achieve scalability: by **scaling up** or **scaling out**.

You can scale an application up by buying a bigger server or by adding more CPUs, memory, and/or storage to the existing one. The problem with scaling up is that finding the right balance of resources is extremely difficult. You might add more CPUs only to find out that you have turned memory into a bottleneck. Because of this, the law of diminishing returns kicks in fairly quickly, which causes the cost of incremental upgrades to grow exponentially. This makes scaling up a very unattractive option, when the cost-to-benefit ratio is taken into account.

Scaling out, on the other hand, implies that you can scale the application by adding more machines to the system and allowing them to share the load. One common scale-out scenario is a farm of web servers fronted by a load balancer. If your site grows and you need to handle more requests, you can simply add another server to the farm. Scaling out is significantly cheaper in the long run than scaling up and is what we will discuss in the remainder of this section.

Unfortunately, designing an application for scale-out requires that you remove all single points of bottleneck from the architecture and make some significant design compromises. For example, you need to completely remove the **state** from the application layer and make your services **stateless**.

Stateless services do not exist

Well, I might have exaggerated a bit to get your attention. It is certainly possible to write a completely stateless service:

```
public class HelloWorldService {
  public String hello() {
    return "Hello world!";
  }
}
```

However, most "stateless" services I've seen follow a somewhat different pattern:

```
public class MyService {
  public void myServiceMethod() {
    loadState();
    doSomethingWithState();
    saveState();
  }
}
```

Implementing application services this way is what allows us to scale the application layer out, but the fact that our service still needs state in order to do anything useful doesn't change. We haven't removed the need—we have simply moved the responsibility for state management further down the stack.

The problem with that approach is that it usually puts more load on the resource that is the most difficult and expensive to scale—a relational database.

Scaling a database is hard

In order to provide **ACID** (**atomicity**, **consistency**, **isolation**, and **durability**) guarantees, a relational database needs to perform quite a bit of locking and log all mutating operations. Depending on the database, locks might be at the row level, page level, or even table level. Every database request that needs to access locked data will essentially have to wait for the lock to be released.

In order to improve concurrency, you need to ensure that each database write is committed or rolled back as fast as possible. This is why there are so many rules about the best ways to organize the disk subsystem on a database server. Whether it's placing log files on a different disk or partitioning large tables across multiple disks, the goal is to optimize the performance of the disk I/O as it should be. Because of durability requirements, database writes are ultimately disk bound, so making sure that the disk subsystem is optimally configured is extremely important.

However, no matter how fast and well-optimized your database server is, as the number of users increases and you add more web/application servers to handle the additional load, you will reach a point where the database is simply overwhelmed. As the data volume and the number of transactions increase, the response time will increase exponentially, to the point where your system will not meet its performance objectives anymore.

When that happens, you need to scale the database.

The easiest and the most intuitive approach to database scaling is to scale up by buying a bigger server. That might buy you some time, but guess what—if your load continues to increase, you will soon need an even bigger server. These big servers tend to be very expensive, so over time this becomes a losing proposition. One company I know of eventually reached the point where the incremental cost to support each additional user became greater than the revenue generated by that same user. The more users they signed up, the more money they were losing.

So if scaling up is not an answer, how do we scale the database out?

Database scale-out approaches

There are three main approaches to database scale-out: **master-slave replication**, **clustering**, and **sharding**. We will discuss the pros and cons of each in the following sections.

Master-slave replication

Master-slave replication is the easiest of the three to configure and requires minimal modifications to application logic. In this setup, a single **master** server is used to handle all write operations, which are then replicated to one or more **slave** servers asynchronously, typically using log shipping:

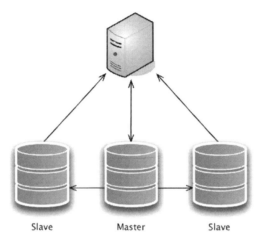

| Slave | Master | Slave |

This allows you to spread the read operations across multiple servers, which reduces the load on the master server.

From the application perspective, all that you need to do is to modify the code that creates the database connections to implement a load balancing algorithm. Simple round-robin server selection for read operations is typically all you need.

However, there are two major problems with this approach:

- There is a lag between a write to the master server and the replication. This means that your application could update a record on the master and immediately after that read the old, incorrect version of the same record from one of the slaves, which is often undesirable.

- You haven't really scaled out. Although you have given your master server some breathing room, you will eventually reach the point where it cannot handle all the writes. When that happens, you will be on your vendor's website again, configuring a bigger server.

Database clustering

The second approach to database scale-out is **database clustering**, often referred to as the **shared everything approach**. The best known example of a database that uses this strategy is Oracle RAC.

This approach allows you to configure many database instances that access a shared storage device:

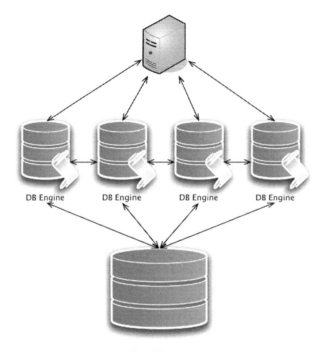

Shared Storage

In the previous architecture, every node in the cluster can handle both reads and writes, which can significantly improve throughput.

From the application perspective, nothing needs to change, at least in theory. Even the load balancing is automatic.

However, database clustering is not without its own set of problems:

- Database writes require synchronization of in-memory data structures such as caches and locks across all the nodes in the cluster. This increases the duration of write operations and introduces even more contention. In the worst-case scenario, you might even experience negative scalability as you add nodes to the cluster (meaning that as you add the nodes, you actually decrease the number of operations you can handle).

- It is difficult to set up and administer, and it requires an expensive SAN device for shared storage.
- Even read operations cannot be scaled indefinitely, because any shared disk system, no matter how powerful and expensive it is, will eventually reach its limit.

In general, database clustering might be a good solution for read-intensive usage scenarios, such as data warehousing and **BI (Business Intelligence)**, but will likely not be able to scale past a certain point in write-intensive **OLTP (online transaction processing)** applications.

Database sharding

The basic idea behind **database sharding** is to partition a single large database into several smaller databases. It is also known as a **shared nothing approach**.

It is entirely up to you to decide how to actually perform partitioning. A good first step is to identify the groups of tables that belong together based on your application's querying needs. If you need to perform a join on two tables, they should belong to the same group. If you are running an e-commerce site, it is likely that you will end up with groups that represent your customer-related tables, your product catalog-related tables, and so on.

Once you identify table groups, you can move each group into a separate database, effectively partitioning the database by functional area. This approach is also called **vertical partitioning**, and is depicted in the following diagram:

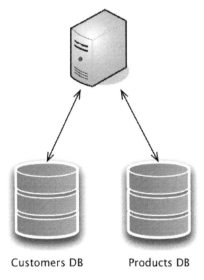

Customers DB   Products DB

Unfortunately, vertical partitioning by definition is limited by the number of functional areas you can identify, which imposes a hard limit on the number of shards you can create. Once you reach the capacity of any functional shard, you will either need to scale up or partition data horizontally.

This means that you need to create multiple databases with identical schemas, and split all the data across them. It is entirely up to you to decide how to split the data, and you can choose a different partitioning strategy for each table. For example, you can partition customers by state and products using modulo of the primary key:

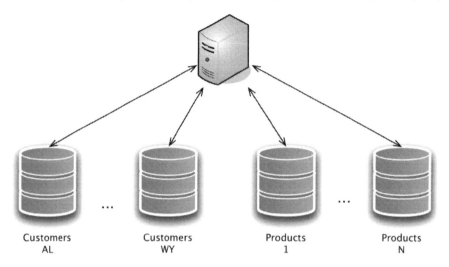

| Customers | Customers | Products | Products |
| AL | WY | 1 | N |

Implemented properly, database sharding gives you virtually unlimited scalability, but just like the other two strategies it also has some major drawbacks:

- For one, sharding significantly complicates application code. Whenever you want to perform a database operation, you need to determine which shard the operation should execute against and obtain a database connection accordingly. While this logic can (and should) be encapsulated within the Data Access Layer, it adds complexity to the application nevertheless.

- You need to size your shards properly from the very beginning, because adding new shards later on is a major pain. Once your data partitioning algorithm and shards are in place, adding a new shard or a set of shards requires you not only to implement your partitioning algorithm again, but also to undertake the huge task of migrating the existing data to new partitions, which is an error-prone and time-consuming process.

- Queries and aggregations that used to be simple are not so simple anymore. Imagine your customers are partitioned by state and you want to retrieve all female customers younger than 30, and sort them by the total amount they spent on makeup within the last six months. You will have to perform a distributed query against all the shards and aggregate the results yourself. And I hope you kept track of those makeup sales within each customer row, or you might spend a few long nights trying to collect that information from a partitioned orders table.

- It is likely that you will have to denormalize your schema and/or replicate reference data to all the shards in order to eliminate the need for cross-shard joins. Unless the replicated data is read-only, you will have the same consistency issues as with master-slave setup when it gets updated.

- Cross-shard updates will require either distributed (XA) transactions that can significantly limit the scalability, or compensating transactions that can significantly increase application complexity. If you avoid distributed transactions and implement your own solution, you will also run into data consistency issues, as updates to one shard will be visible before you update the others and complete a logical transaction.

- Failure of any single shard will likely render the whole system unusable. Unfortunately, the probability that one shard will fail is directly proportional to the number of shards. This means that you will have to implement an **HA (High Availability)** solution for each individual shard, effectively doubling the amount of hardware and the cost of the data layer.

Even with all these drawbacks, sharding is the approach used by some of the largest websites in the world, from Facebook and Flickr, to Google and eBay. When the pain is great, any medicine that reduces it is good, regardless of the side effects.

In the next section we will look at the fourth option for database scaling—removing the need to scale it at all.

Return of the state

As I mentioned earlier, removal of the state from the application has a significant increase in database load as a consequence. This implies that there is a simple way to reduce the database load—put state back into the application.

Of course, we can't really put the state back into our **stateless** services, as that would make them **stateful** and prevent them from scaling out. However, nothing prevents us from introducing a new data management layer between our stateless application logic and the database. After all, as professor Bellovin said, "any software problem can be solved by adding another layer of indirection".

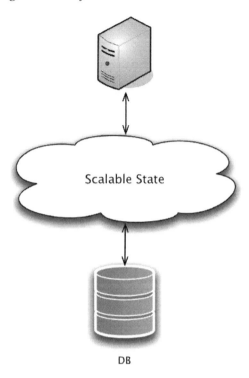

Ideally, this new layer should have the following characteristics:

- It should manage data as objects, because objects are what our application needs
- It should keep these objects in memory, in order to improve performance and avoid the disk I/O bottlenecks that plague databases
- It should be able to transparently load missing data from the persistent store behind it
- It should be able to propagate data modifications to the persistent store, possibly asynchronously
- It should be as simple to scale out as our stateless application layer

As you have probably guessed, Coherence satisfies all of these requirements, which makes it a perfect data management layer for scalable web applications.

Using Coherence to reduce database load

Many database queries in a typical application are nothing more than primary key-based lookups. Offloading only these lookups to an application-tier cache would significantly reduce database load and improve overall performance.

However, when your application-tier cache supports propagate queries and can also scale to support large datasets across many physical machines, you can offload even more work to it and let the database do what it does best—persist data and perform complex queries.

The company I mentioned earlier, which was at risk of going bankrupt because of the high cost of scaling up their database, saw database load drop more than 80% after they introduced Coherence into the architecture.

Furthermore, because they didn't have to block waiting for the response from the database for so long, their web servers were able to handle twice the load. In combination, this effectively doubled the capacity and ensured that no database server upgrades would be necessary in the near future.

This example is somewhat extreme, especially because in this case it literally meant the difference between closing the shop and being profitable, but it is not uncommon to see a 60% to 80% reduction in database load after Coherence is introduced into the architecture, accompanied with an increased capacity in the application layer as well.

Coherence and master-slave databases

Coherence effectively eliminates the need for master-slave replication, as it provides all of its benefits without any of the drawbacks.

Read-only slaves are effectively replaced with a distributed cache that is able to answer the vast majority of read operations. On the other hand, updates are performed against the cached data and written into the database by Coherence, so there is no replication lag and the view of the data is fully coherent at all times.

Coherence and database clusters

By significantly reducing the total load on the database, Coherence will give your database cluster some breathing space and allow you to handle more users, or to reduce the size of the cluster.

In the best-case scenario, it might eliminate the need for the database cluster altogether, allowing you to significantly simplify your architecture.

Coherence and database sharding

This is by far the most interesting scenario of the three. Just like with database clustering, you might be able to completely eliminate the need for sharding and simplify the architecture by using a single database.

However, if you do need to use shards, Coherence allows you to eliminate some of the drawbacks we discussed earlier.

For one, distributed queries and aggregations are built-in features, not something that you need to write yourself. Finding all female customers younger than 30 is a simple query against the customers cache. Similarly, aggregating orders to determine how much each of these customers spent on makeup becomes a relatively simple parallel aggregation against the orders cache.

Second, Coherence allows you to protect the application against individual shard failures. By storing all the data within the grid and configuring Coherence to propagate data changes to the database asynchronously, your application can survive one or more shards being down for a limited time.

Coherence and scalability

Coherence is an ideal solution for scalable data management. Scaling both capacity and throughput can be easily achieved by adding more nodes to the Coherence cluster.

However, it is entirely possible for an application to introduce contention and prevent scalability, for example, by using excessive locking. Because of this, care should be taken during application design to ensure that artificial bottlenecks are not introduced into the architecture.

Achieving high availability

The last thing we need to talk about is **availability**. At the most basic level, in order to make the application highly available we need to remove all single points of failure from the architecture. In order to do that, we need to treat every single component as unreliable and assume that it will fail sooner or later.

It is important to realize that the availability of the system as a whole can be defined as the product of the availability of its tightly coupled components:

$$AS = A1 * A2 * ... * An$$

For example, if we have a web server, an application server, and a database server, each of which is available 99% of the time, the expected availability of the system as a whole is only 97%:

$$0.99 * 0.99 * 0.99 = 0.970299 = 97\%$$

This reflects the fact that if any of the three components should fail, the system as a whole will fail as well. By the way, if you think that 97% availability is not too bad, consider this: 97% availability implies that the system will be out of commission 11 days every year, or almost one day a month!

We can do two things to improve the situation:

- We can add redundancy to each component to improve its availability.
- We can decouple components in order to better isolate the rest of the system from the failure of an individual component.

The latter is typically achieved by introducing asynchrony into the system. For example, you can use messaging to decouple a credit card processing component from the main application flow—this will allow you to accept new orders even if the credit card processor is temporarily unavailable.

As mentioned earlier, Coherence is able to queue updates for a failed database and write them asynchronously when the database becomes available. This is another good example of using asynchrony to provide high availability.

Although the asynchronous operations are a great way to improve both availability and scalability of the application, as well as perceived performance, there is a limit to the number of tasks that can be performed asynchronously in a typical application. If the customer wants to see product information, you will have to retrieve the product from the data store, render the page, and send the response to the client synchronously.

To make synchronous operations highly available our only option is to make each component redundant.

Adding redundancy to the system

In order to explain how redundancy helps improve availability of a single component, we need to introduce another obligatory formula or two (I promise this is the only chapter you will see any formulas in):

$$F = F1 * F2 * ... * Fn$$

Where F is the likelihood of failure of a redundant set of components as a whole, and F1 through Fn are the likelihoods of failure of individual components, which can be expressed as:

$$Fc = 1 - Ac$$

Going back to our previous example, if the availability of a single server is 99%, the likelihood it will fail is 1%:

$$Fc = 1 - 0.99 = 0.01$$

If we make each layer in our architecture redundant by adding another server to it, we can calculate new availability for each component and the system as a whole:

$$Ac = 1 - (0.01 * 0.01) = 1 - 0.0001 = 0.9999 = 99.99\%$$

$$As = 0.9999 * 0.9999 * 0.9999 = 0.9997 = 99.97\%$$

Basically, by adding redundancy to each layer, we have reduced the application's downtime from 11 days to approximately two and a half hours per year, which is not nearly as bad.

Redundancy is not enough

Making components redundant is only the first step on the road to high availability. To get to the finish line, we also need to ensure that the system has enough capacity to handle the failure under the peak load.

Developers often assume that if an application uses scale-out architecture for the application tier and a clustered database for persistence, it is automatically highly available. Unfortunately, this is not the case.

If you determine during load testing that you need N servers to handle the peak load, and you would like the system to remain operational even if X servers fail at the same time, you need to provision the system with N+X servers. Otherwise, if the failure occurs during the peak period, the remaining servers will not be able to handle the incoming requests and either or both of the following will happen:

- The response time will increase significantly, making performance unacceptable
- Some users will receive "500 - Service Busy" errors from the web server

In either case, the application is essentially not available to the users.

To illustrate this, let's assume that we need five servers to handle the peak load. If we provision the system with only five servers and one of them fails, the system as a whole will fail. Essentially, by not provisioning excess capacity to allow for failure, we are turning "application will fail if all 5 servers fail" into "application will fail if any of the 5 servers fail". The difference is huge—in the former scenario, assuming 99% availability of individual servers, system availability is almost 100%. However, in the latter it is only 95%, which translates to more than 18 days of downtime per year.

Coherence and availability

Oracle Coherence provides an excellent foundation for highly available architecture. It is designed for availability; it assumes that any node can fail at any point in time and guards against the negative impact of such failures.

This is achieved by data redundancy within the cluster. Every object stored in the Coherence cache is automatically backed up to another node in the cluster. If a node fails, the backup copy is simply promoted to the primary and a new backup copy is created on another node.

This implies that updating an object in the cluster has some overhead in order to guarantee data consistency. The cache update is not considered successful until the backup copy is safely stored. However, unlike clustered databases that essentially lock the whole cluster to perform write operations, the cost of write operations with Coherence is constant regardless of the cluster size. This allows for exceptional scalability of both read and write operations and very high throughput.

However, as we discussed in the previous section, sizing Coherence clusters properly is extremely important. If the system is running at full capacity, failure of a single node could have a ripple effect. It would cause other nodes to run out of memory as they tried to fail over the data managed by the failed node, which would eventually bring the whole cluster down.

It is also important to understand that, although your Coherence cluster is highly available that doesn't automatically make your application as a whole highly available as well. You need to identify and remove the remaining single points of failure by making sure that your hardware devices such as load balancers, routers, and network switches are redundant, and that your database server is redundant as well. The good news is that if you use Coherence to scale the data tier and reduce the load on the database, making the database redundant will likely be much easier and cheaper.

As a side note, while there are many stories that can be used as a testament to Coherence's availability, including the one when the database server went down over the weekend without the application users noticing anything, my favorite is an anecdote about a recent communication between Coherence support team and a long-time Coherence user.

This particular customer has been using Coherence for almost 5 years. When a bug was discovered that affects the particular release they were using, the support team sent the patch and the installation instructions to the customer. They received a polite reply:

> *You have got to be kidding me!? We haven't had a second of downtime in the last 5 years. We are not touching a thing!*

Putting it all together

Coherence can take you a long way towards meeting your performance, scalability, and availability objectives, but that doesn't mean that you can simply add it to the system as an afterthought and expect that all your problems will be solved.

Design for performance and scalability

Achieving performance, scalability, and availability goals requires you to identify bottlenecks and single points of failure in the application and to eliminate them. Doing this requires careful consideration of the problems and evaluation of the alternatives.

Unfortunately, way too often developers have "one true way" of building applications, typically reflected in the choice of the same tool stack and a "carbon copy" architecture across their projects. While this approach might work for small, departmental applications, it will not work for large, high-load, mission-critical systems. I mean, I love Spring as much as the next guy, but I tend to use it more within the architecture than as the architecture.

Another problem that I see from time to time is that people tend to misinterpret the famous quote attributed to Donald Knuth:

Premature optimization is the root of all evil.

Stated like that, this quote can be used as an excuse to avoid all kinds of hard work. The problem is that it is taken completely out of context. The full quote is:

We should forget about small efficiencies, say about 97% of the time: premature optimization is the root of all evil.

With that I agree, we should forget about **small** efficiencies. Trying to minimize the impact of a reflective method call when the method itself performs a database query or invokes a web service makes no sense.

However, the latency and scalability issues I described in this chapter are anything but small and need to be taken into account and addressed early on—addressing them later will vary from extremely hard to impossible. To quote Randy Shoup, distinguished architect at eBay:

Scalability is a prerequisite to functionality, a priority-0 requirement, if ever there was one.

Ignorance is the root of all evil. Premature optimization is not even a close second.

Set performance goals at each level

In order to know when you are done, you need to set performance goals. Most often people set a performance goal such as "end-user response time of 2 seconds or less".

Even though this is a good start, it is not nearly enough, because it doesn't tell you how much time the application can spend where. What you need to do is define some more specific requirements, such as "end-user response time of 2 seconds or less and time-to-last-byte of 1 second or less".

Now we are getting somewhere. This tells us that we can spend one second on the backend, collecting data, executing business logic, rendering the response, and sending it to the browser. And one second on the frontend, downloading HTML, CSS, JavaScript files, images, and rendering the page.

Of course, you can (and probably should), break this down even further. Your request handler on the backend likely calls one or more services to retrieve the data it needs, and uses some kind of template engine to render the page. You could give 100ms to orchestration and rendering logic in your request handler (which is very generous, by the way), which leaves you with a performance goal of 900ms or less for individual services.

This forces you to think about performance issues at each level separately and brings performance bottlenecks to the surface. If you have a service that takes 2 seconds to execute, it will be immediately obvious that you won't be able to meet your objective of 900 milliseconds, and you will have to find a way to speed it up. Whether the solution is to cache intermediate results, parallelize execution of the service, invoke it asynchronously, or something else, more likely than not you will be able to solve the problem once you know that it exists, which brings us to the following topic.

Measure and monitor

Count what is countable, measure what is measurable, and what is not measurable, make measurable.

— Galileo

In order to know that the application is meeting its objectives, you need to measure. You need to measure how long each service takes to execute, page rendering time on the server, and page load time on the client.

You also need to measure the load a single server can handle, and how that number changes as you scale out. This will give you an idea of how well your application scales and will allow you to size the system properly. More importantly, it will allow you to predict the cost of scaling to support higher load levels.

During development, you can use a profiler such as YourKit (`www.yourkit.com`) to measure the performance of your server-side code and find hot spots that can be optimized. On the client, you can use FireBug (`getfirebug.com`), YSlow (`developer.yahoo.com/yslow`) and/or Page Speed (`code.google.com/p/page-speed`) to profile your web pages and determine opportunities for improvement.

For load testing, you can either use a commercial tool, such as HP LoadRunner, or an open source tool such as Apache JMeter (`jakarta.apache.org/jmeter`), The Grinder (`grinder.sourceforge.net`), or Pylot (`www.pylot.org`).

However, measuring performance and scalability should not be limited to development; you also need to monitor your application once it is deployed to the production environment. After all, the production system is the only one that will provide you with the realistic load and usage patterns.

In order to do that, you need to instrument your application and collect important performance metrics. You can do that using a standard management framework, such as JMX, or by using a tool such as ERMA (`erma.wikidot.com`), an open source instrumentation API developed at Orbitz.

When it comes to Coherence cluster monitoring, you can use JConsole to look at the statistics exposed through JMX, but more likely than not you will want to consider a commercial monitoring tool, such as Evident ClearStone Live (`www.evidentsoftware.com`) or SL RTView (`www.sl.com`).

In any case, the tools are many and you should choose the ones that best fit your needs. What is important is that you measure and monitor constantly and make course corrections if the measurements start to deviate.

Educate your team

It is important that everyone on the team understands performance and scalability goals, and the issues related to achieving them. While I tried to provide enough information in this chapter to set the stage for the remainder of the book, I barely scratched the surface.

If you want to learn more about the topics discussed in this chapter, I strongly recommend that you read Theo Schlossnagle's *Scalable Internet Architectures*, and Cal Henderson's *Building Scalable Websites*.

For client-side website optimization, *High Performance Websites: Essential Knowledge for Front-End Engineers* and *Even Faster Web Sites: Performance Best Practices for Web Developers* by Steve Souders provide some excellent advice.

Summary

In this chapter, we have discussed how to achieve performance, scalability, and availability, and how Coherence in particular can help.

In order to improve performance, you need to minimize both the latency and the amount of data that you move across the wire. Coherence features such as near caching and entry processors can help you achieve that.

Coherence really shines when it comes to improving the scalability of your application, as it allows you to scale the layer that is most difficult to scale—the data management layer. By adding Coherence to your architecture you can avoid the need to implement complex database scale-out strategies, such as database clustering or sharding.

To achieve high availability you need to remove single points of failure from the architecture. Although Coherence is highly available by design, you need to ensure that all other components are as well, by adding redundancy. Also, do not forget that you need to size the system properly and allow for failure. Otherwise, your "highly available" system might crash as soon as one of its components fails.

Finally, you have learned that performance, scalability, and availability cannot be added to the system as an afterthought, but need to be designed into the system from the very beginning, and measured and monitored both during development and in production.

Now, let's get our hands dirty and learn how to install and use Coherence.

2
Getting Started

When I first started evaluating Coherence, one of my biggest concerns was how easy it would be to set up and use, especially in a development environment. The whole idea of having to set up a cluster scared me quite a bit, as any other solution I had encountered up to that point that had the word "cluster" in it was extremely difficult and time consuming to configure.

My fear was completely unfounded—getting the Coherence cluster up and running is as easy as starting Tomcat. You can start multiple Coherence nodes on a single physical machine, and they will seamlessly form a cluster. Actually, it is easier than starting Tomcat.

In this chapter, you will learn how to install Coherence on your machine and how to configure your development environment to make working with Coherence as easy as possible. We will then cover the basics of the Coherence API as we develop a small utility that will allow us to import data into Coherence from CSV files. Finally, we will talk about testing, which due to the distributed nature of Coherence applications, can be a bit trickier than usual.

But first things first…

Installing Coherence

In order to install Coherence you need to download the latest release from the Oracle Technology Network (OTN) website. The easiest way to do so is by following the link from the main Coherence page on OTN. At the time of this writing, this page was located at `http://www.oracle.com/technology/products/coherence/index.html`, but that might change. If it does, you can find its new location by searching for 'Oracle Coherence' using your favorite search engine.

In order to download Coherence for evaluation, you will need to have an **Oracle Technology Network (OTN)** account. If you don't have one, registration is easy and completely free.

Once you are logged in, you will be able to access the Coherence download page, where you will find the download links for all available Coherence releases: one for Java, one for .NET, and one for each of the supported C++ platforms.

You can download any of the Coherence releases you are interested in while you are there, but for the remainder of this chapter and a large part of this book you will only need the first one. The latter two (.NET and C++) are client libraries that allow .NET and C++ applications to access the Coherence data grid, and will be covered towards the end of the book.

Coherence ships as a single ZIP archive. Once you unpack it you should see the README.txt file containing the full product name and version number, and a single directory named coherence. Copy the contents of the coherence directory to a location of your choice on your hard drive. The common location on Windows is c:\coherence and on Unix/Linux /opt/coherence, but you are free to put it wherever you want.

The last thing you need to do is to configure the environment variable COHERENCE_HOME to point to the top-level Coherence directory created in the previous step, and you are done.

Coherence is a Java application, so you also need to ensure that you have the Java SDK 1.4.2 or later installed and that JAVA_HOME environment variable is properly set to point to the Java SDK installation directory.

If you are using a JVM other than Sun's, you might need to edit the scripts used in the following section. For example, not all JVMs support the -server option that is used while starting the Coherence nodes, so you might need to remove it.

What's in the box?

The first thing you should do after installing Coherence is become familiar with the structure of the Coherence installation directory.

There are four subdirectories within the Coherence home directory:

- `bin`: This contains a number of useful batch files for Windows and shell scripts for Unix/Linux that can be used to start Coherence nodes or to perform various network tests
- `doc`: This contains the Coherence API documentation, as well as links to online copies of Release Notes, User Guide, and Frequently Asked Questions documents
- `examples`: This contains several basic examples of Coherence functionality
- `lib`: This contains JAR files that implement Coherence functionality

Shell scripts on Unix

If you are on a Unix-based system, you will need to add execute permission to the shell scripts in the `bin` directory by executing the following command:

```
$ chmod u+x *.sh
```

Starting up the Coherence cluster

In order to get the Coherence cluster up and running, you need to start one or more Coherence nodes. The Coherence nodes can run on a single physical machine, or on many physical machines that are on the same network. The latter will definitely be the case for a production deployment, but for development purposes you will likely want to limit the cluster to a single desktop or laptop.

The easiest way to start a Coherence node is to run `cache-server.cmd` batch file on Windows or `cache-server.sh` shell script on Unix. The end result in either case should be similar to the following screenshot:

```
Oracle Coherence Version 3.5.1/461
 Grid Edition: Development mode
Copyright (c) 2000, 2009, Oracle and/or its affiliates. All rights reserved.

2009-08-06 15:58:09.149/0.441 Oracle Coherence GE 3.5.1/461 <Info> (thread=main
2009-08-06 15:58:09.545/0.837 Oracle Coherence GE 3.5.1/461 <D5> (thread=Cluste
2009-08-06 15:58:12.747/4.039 Oracle Coherence GE 3.5.1/461 <Info> (thread=Clus
4, Role=CoherenceServer, Edition=Grid Edition, Mode=Development, CpuCount=8, Sc
2009-08-06 15:58:12.764/4.056 Oracle Coherence GE 3.5.1/461 <D5> (thread=Invoca
2009-08-06 15:58:12.943/4.235 Oracle Coherence GE 3.5.1/461 <D5> (thread=Distri
2009-08-06 15:58:12.986/4.278 Oracle Coherence GE 3.5.1/461 <D5> (thread=Replic
2009-08-06 15:58:12.990/4.282 Oracle Coherence GE 3.5.1/461 <D5> (thread=Optimi
2009-08-06 15:58:12.993/4.285 Oracle Coherence GE 3.5.1/461 <D5> (thread=Invoca
2009-08-06 15:58:12.994/4.286 Oracle Coherence GE 3.5.1/461 <Info> (thread=main

SafeCluster: Name=cluster:0xD1CB

Group{Address=224.3.5.1, Port=35461, TTL=4}

MasterMemberSet
  (
  ThisMember=Member(Id=1, Timestamp=2009-08-06 15:58:09.412, Address=192.168.1.
  OldestMember=Member(Id=1, Timestamp=2009-08-06 15:58:09.412, Address=192.168.
  ActualMemberSet=MemberSet(Size=1, BitSetCount=2
    Member(Id=1, Timestamp=2009-08-06 15:58:09.412, Address=192.168.1.7:8088, M
    )
  RecycleMillis=120000
  RecycleSet=MemberSet(Size=0, BitSetCount=0
    )
  )

Services
  (
  TcpRing{TcpSocketAccepter{State=STATE_OPEN, ServerSocket=192.168.1.7:8088}, C
  ClusterService{Name=Cluster, State=(SERVICE_STARTED, STATE_JOINED), Id=0, Ver
  InvocationService{Name=Management, State=(SERVICE_STARTED), Id=1, Version=3.1
  DistributedCache{Name=DistributedCache, State=(SERVICE_STARTED), LocalStorage
  ReplicatedCache{Name=ReplicatedCache, State=(SERVICE_STARTED), Id=3, Version
  Optimistic{Name=OptimisticCache, State=(SERVICE_STARTED), Id=4, Version=3.0,
  InvocationService{Name=InvocationService, State=(SERVICE_STARTED), Id=5, Vers
  )
```

There is quite a bit of information on this screen, and over time you will become familiar with each section. For now, notice two things:

- At the very top of the screen, you can see the information about the Coherence version that you are using, as well as the specific edition and the mode that the node is running in. Notice that by default you are using the most powerful, Grid Edition, in development mode.

- The `MasterMemberSet` section towards the bottom lists all members of the cluster and provides some useful information about the current and the oldest member of the cluster.

Now that we have a single Coherence node running, let's start another one by running the `cache-server` script in a different terminal window.

For the most part, the output should be very similar to the previous screen, but if everything has gone according to the plan, the `MasterMemberSet` section should reflect the fact that the second node has joined the cluster:

```
MasterMemberSet
  (
  ThisMember=Member(Id=2, ...)
  OldestMember=Member(Id=1, ...)
  ActualMemberSet=MemberSet(Size=2, BitSetCount=2
    Member(Id=1, ...)
    Member(Id=2, ...)
    )
  RecycleMillis=120000
  RecycleSet=MemberSet(Size=0, BitSetCount=0)
  )
```

You should also see several log messages on the first node's console, letting you know that another node has joined the cluster and that some of the distributed cache partitions were transferred to it.

If you can see these log messages on the first node, as well as two members within the `ActualMemberSet` on the second node, congratulations—you have a working Coherence cluster.

Troubleshooting cluster start-up

In some cases, a Coherence node will not be able to start or to join the cluster. In general, the reason for this could be all kinds of networking-related issues, but in practice a few issues are responsible for the vast majority of problems.

Multicast issues

By far the most common issue is that multicast is disabled on the machine. By default, Coherence uses multicast for its cluster join protocol, and it will not be able to form the cluster unless it is enabled. You can easily check if multicast is enabled and working properly by running the `multicast-test` shell script within the `bin` directory.

If you are unable to start the cluster on a single machine, you can execute the following command from your Coherence home directory:

```
$ . bin/multicast-test.sh -ttl 0
```

This will limit time-to-live of multicast packets to the local machine and allow you to test multicast in isolation. If everything is working properly, you should see a result similar to the following:

```
Starting test on ip=Aleks-Mac-Pro.home/192.168.1.7,
group=/237.0.0.1:9000, ttl=0
Configuring multicast socket...
Starting listener...
Fri Aug 07 13:44:44 EDT 2009: Sent packet 1.
Fri Aug 07 13:44:44 EDT 2009: Received test packet 1 from self
Fri Aug 07 13:44:46 EDT 2009: Sent packet 2.
Fri Aug 07 13:44:46 EDT 2009: Received test packet 2 from self
Fri Aug 07 13:44:48 EDT 2009: Sent packet 3.
Fri Aug 07 13:44:48 EDT 2009: Received test packet 3 from self
```

If the output is different from the above, it is likely that multicast is not working properly or is disabled on your machine.

This is frequently the result of a firewall or VPN software running, so the first troubleshooting step would be to disable such software and retry. If you determine that was indeed the cause of the problem you have two options. The first, and obvious one, is to turn the offending software off while using Coherence.

However, for various reasons that might not be an acceptable solution, in which case you will need to change the default Coherence behavior, and tell it to use the **Well-Known Addresses (WKA)** feature instead of multicast for the cluster join protocol.

Doing so on a development machine is very simple—all you need to do is add the following argument to the JAVA_OPTS variable within the cache-server shell script:

```
-Dtangosol.coherence.wka=localhost
```

With that in place, you should be able to start Coherence nodes even if multicast is disabled.

Localhost and loopback address

On some systems, `localhost` maps to a loopback address, 127.0.0.1.

If that's the case, you will have to specify the actual IP address or host name for the `tangosol.coherence.wka` configuration parameter. The host name should be preferred, as the IP address can change as you move from network to network, or if your machine leases an IP address from a DHCP server.

As a side note, you can tell whether the WKA or multicast is being used for the cluster join protocol by looking at the section above the `MasterMemberSet` section when the Coherence node starts.

If multicast is used, you will see something similar to the following:

```
Group{Address=224.3.5.1, Port=35461, TTL=4}
```

The actual multicast group address and port depend on the Coherence version being used. As a matter of fact, you can even tell the exact version and the build number from the preceding information. In this particular case, I am using Coherence 3.5.1 release, build 461.

This is done in order to prevent accidental joins of cluster members into an existing cluster. For example, you wouldn't want a node in the development environment using newer version of Coherence that you are evaluating to join the existing production cluster, which could easily happen if the multicast group address remained the same.

On the other hand, if you are using WKA, you should see output similar to the following instead:

```
WellKnownAddressList(Size=1,
  WKA{Address=192.168.1.7, Port=8088}
  )
```

Using the WKA feature completely disables multicast in a Coherence cluster, and is recommended for most production deployments, primarily due to the fact that many production environments prohibit multicast traffic altogether, and that some network switches do not route multicast traffic properly.

That said, configuring WKA for production clusters is out of the scope of this book, and you should refer to Coherence product manuals for details.

Binding issues

Another issue that sometimes comes up is that one of the ports that Coherence attempts to bind to is already in use and you see a bind exception when attempting to start the node.

By default, Coherence starts the first node on port `8088`, and increments port number by one for each subsequent node on the same machine. If for some reason that doesn't work for you, you need to identify a range of available ports for as many nodes as you are planning to start (both UDP and TCP ports with the same numbers must be available), and tell Coherence which port to use for the first node by specifying the `tangosol.coherence.localport` system property. For example, if you want Coherence to use port `9100` for the first node, you will need to add the following argument to the `JAVA_OPTS` variable in the `cache-server` shell script:

```
-Dtangosol.coherence.localport=9100
```

Accessing the data grid

Now that you have the Coherence data grid up and running, the next step is to put some data into the grid and check if we can retrieve it. After all, a data grid without any data is not a very useful thing.

You will shortly learn how to use the Coherence APIs to store and retrieve your application data from the grid, but for now let's keep things simple and use the Coherence command-line utility to perform basic grid operations.

Coherence console

Coherence ships with a command-line utility that allows you to manipulate caches within a data grid. Keep your grid nodes running and launch Coherence console by executing the `coherence.sh/cmd` script within the `bin` directory.

For the most part the resulting screen looks exactly the same as the screens for the previously started Coherence nodes. As a matter of fact, the Coherence console *is* a Coherence node, and you can see that it has joined the cluster as the third member.

The only significant difference is the prompt at the bottom of the screen:

```
Map (?):
```

This is where you can enter various commands to create caches, put values into them and get values from them, and perform many other operations. I will show you how to perform some of those tasks in this section, but keep in mind that the full description of the Coherence console functionality is out of the scope of this book. If you would like to learn more, feel free to consult the Coherence manuals for more details.

Warning: Use at your own risk

The Coherence console is a development tool and should not be used in production. Many things can go wrong, and you can easily loose data not only in the Coherence cache, but in the underlying data store as well if you are not careful.

Now that you can't say you haven't been warned, let's see what we can do with it ☺.

Creating caches

The first thing you need to do in order to store some data in the grid is to create a **named cache**. This can be easily accomplished from the console prompt, using the `cache` command:

```
Map (?): cache countries
```

This will create a cache with the name `countries`. You can later use that name to obtain a reference to the cache programmatically.

You will notice that the prompt changed to:

```
Map (countries):
```

This tells us that the currently active cache is the one we just created. What this means is that all the commands we execute next will be executed against that cache.

Working with the cache

Now that we have an active cache, let's put some data into it. This is also very simple—all we need to do is to execute the `put` command as many times as we want:

```
Map (countries): put USA "United States"
Map (countries): put GBR "United Kingdom"
Map (countries): put RUS Russia
Map (countries): put CHN China
Map (countries): put JPN Japan
Map (countries): put DEU Germany
```

```
Map (countries): put FRA France
Map (countries): put ITA Italy
Map (countries): put SRB Serbia
```

As you can see, the `put` command takes two arguments—key and value. If either of the two arguments contains a space, it has to be enclosed in quotes in order to be parsed properly.

You will also notice that each `put` command returns `null` (which was intentionally omitted earlier to reduce clutter). Actually, each cache `put` returns the old cache value for the specified key. In this case, we started with an empty cache, which is why `null` was returned for each command. If you modify an existing value, you will see that the original value is returned:

```
Map (countries): put USA "United States of America"
United States
```

We can now use the `list` command to see a list of all cache entries:

```
Map (countries): list
JPN = Japan
SRB = Serbia
CHN = China
GBR = United Kingdom
ITA = Italy
FRA = France
USA = United States of America
DEU = Germany
RUS = Russia
```

Notice that the Coherence cache behaves exactly like the standard `HashMap` and provides no order guarantees for cache items. This is typically not an issue, but it is good to know.

If you only want to find out how many items are in the cache, you can use the `size` command:

```
Map (countries): size
9
```

Now, that we have some data in the cache, we can retrieve a single item from it, using the `get` command:

```
Map (countries): get SRB
Serbia
```

Or we can delete an item using the `remove` command:

```
Map (countries): remove SRB
Serbia
```

Similar to a `put` command, `remove` returns the value that was just deleted from the cache.

You can verify that the item was indeed removed by issuing a `list` or `size` command again:

```
Map (countries): list
JPN = Japan
CHN = China
GBR = United Kingdom
ITA = Italy
FRA = France
USA = United States of America
DEU = Germany
RUS = Russia

Map (countries): size
8
```

Now, as much fun as all of this is, it won't take you long to realize that the Coherence console has some limitations. For one, the fact that you can only use primitive types, such as numbers and strings, for cache keys and values, will put fairly severe constraints on what you can accomplish.

In the next section, we will see how you can work with Coherence caches programmatically, and how you can store instances of your custom classes within the data grid. However, before we do that, let me show you why Coherence can have such a positive impact on your application's availability and reliability.

Switch to one of the Coherence nodes you started at the beginning of this chapter and stop it by pressing *Ctrl+C*. Now go back to the console window and issue a `list` command. You will notice that all the data is still there. To prove that I'm not playing any Jedi mind tricks on you, start a brand new Coherence node and after it comes up and joins the cluster, kill the other cache server node that you started earlier. Once again, list all the items in the cache from the console and you will see that no data was lost even though both of the original storage nodes have disappeared. Basically, as long as there are enough storage nodes in the grid to hold all the data, the data will be safe.

We will explore in detail why this is the case in the next chapter, but for now let's see how we can configure the development environment in order to do something slightly more useful.

Configuring the development environment

Before we can write our first Coherence application, we need to configure the development environment. This involves several steps, such as adding the necessary JAR files to the classpath, configuring the IDE to start Coherence nodes, and specifying configuration parameters that will ensure that each developer has a private Coherence cluster for development and testing.

Most of the examples in this section are specific to IntelliJ IDEA, which is the IDE that I am most familiar with. However, adapting them to Eclipse or any other IDE should be trivial—the principles are the same, even if the mechanics are slightly different.

Referencing necessary JAR files

In a day and age when every library seems to come with so many dependencies that we need build tools like Maven and Ivy to help us put everything together, you might be surprised to find out that Coherence has no external dependencies. For the most part, all you need is a reference to a single JAR file, `coherence.jar`, which can be found in the COHERENCE_HOME/lib directory.

You should also configure the API documentation by pointing your IDE to the COHERENCE_HOME/doc/api directory. This will allow you to access documentation for Coherence classes within your IDE.

For example, a fully configured project-level library referencing Coherence should look similar to the following in IntelliJ IDEA:

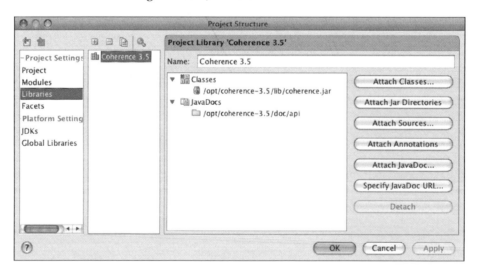

This configuration will be sufficient for the vast majority of examples in this book. That said, even though Coherence does not require any dependencies, it does provide a number of integrations with both Oracle and third-party libraries out of the box.

For example, Coherence provides a distributed implementation of CommonJ Work Manager specification. In order to use it you need to include both `commonj.jar` and `coherence-work.jar` into the classpath.

Similarly, if you want to use Hibernate, Oracle TopLink, or JPA integration for persistence, you will need to include `coherence-hibernate.jar`, `coherence-toplink.jar`, or `coherence-jpa.jar` respectively, as well as any JAR files required by the persistence provider of your choice.

Enabling IntelliSense for configuration files

Another thing you will likely want to configure in your IDE is the IntelliSense for Coherence configuration files.

Coherence uses a set of XML-based files for configuration. We will cover these files in more detail a bit later, but at the moment it should suffice to say that all of them have a corresponding DTD file within the `coherence.jar` file.

Most IDEs can take the advantage of that fact and provide assistance when editing XML documents, based on information in a DTD file. However, more likely than not, you will need to tell your IDE where to find the DTD files.

With IDEA, you need to create external resource definitions that point to the files within the `coherence.jar` file:

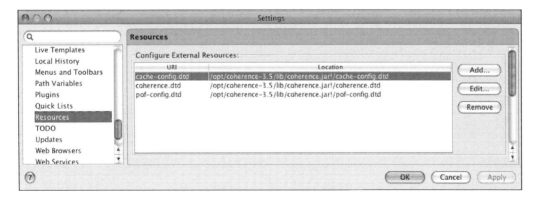

With other IDEs the process might be somewhat different, and you might need to extract these three DTD files from `coherence.jar` and place them in a location that will be accessible to everyone on the team.

Starting Coherence nodes within the IDE

So far we have used the `cache-server` shell script to start Coherence nodes, but that is not the most convenient way to do so during development.

For one, you will likely start and restart your development cluster many times a day, and switching between your IDE and a number of terminal windows all the time is not the most productive way to work.

Second, you will need to add your application's classes and any third-party libraries they depend on to the classpath of each Coherence node. While you could copy and edit the `cache-server` shell script to include necessary classes and JAR files into the classpath (and you will need to do so before deploying to production), this tends to be quite cumbersome during development.

Fortunately, as I mentioned earlier, Coherence is a regular Java application, which makes it quite simple to start within the IDE. If you look at the `cache-server` shell script, you will see that it really doesn't do much—it sets heap size and classpath, and launches `com.tangosol.net.DefaultCacheServer` using server JVM.

Doing the same within any IDE should be trivial. The following screenshot shows a sample configuration in IntelliJ IDEA:

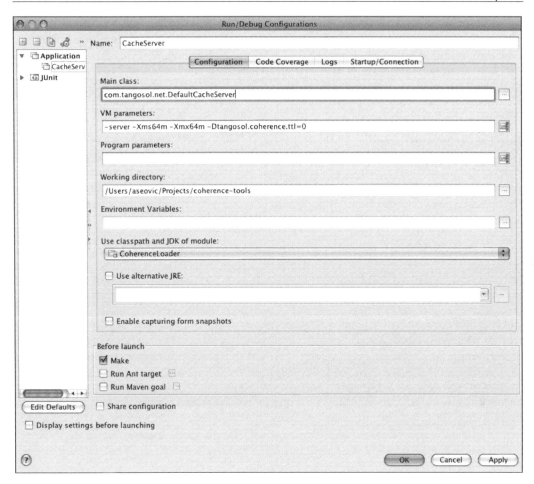

As you can see, I have configured the cache server to use server JVM and 64 MB of heap. This is significantly lower than the 512 MB allocated by the `cache-server` script, but it should be more than enough for development, as you will likely not use the complete data set. In any case, you can adjust heap size to fit your needs.

Now that we have `DefaultCacheServer` configured, we can launch as many nodes as we need within the IDE by simply clicking on a toolbar button. The following screenshot shows two Coherence nodes running within IntelliJ IDEA:

Creating a private cluster

One thing you will definitely want to do while working with Coherence is to ensure that each developer uses a private cluster on their own machine. The very fact that Coherence clusters so seamlessly can lead to some head scratching during development if this is not done.

Just recently a colleague of mine and I were working on two independent tasks, but we both had a few Coherence nodes running on our laptops. The initial implementation of the code he was working on had a trivial bug that loaded objects of a wrong type into one of the caches. He quickly fixed the bug, restarted the nodes on his machine, and was surprised to find out that the invalid objects were still in the cache, although now in addition to the objects of the correct type.

Fortunately, I was sitting right next to him and it didn't take us long to figure out what was going on and fix the problem. Basically, even though he restarted the nodes on his machine before rerunning the tests, the cluster as a whole, and the data within it survived because there were other nodes running on my laptop.

Even though the impact in this case was minimal, the situation might have been different if I was sitting in another office, so it is extremely important to create developer "sandboxes" when working with Coherence. It is also the reason why you need to pay close attention to the information within the `MasterMemberSet` section when starting Coherence nodes, and to investigate if the result does not match your expectations.

If you were wondering what that `tangosol.coherence.ttl` system property I specified when configuring `DefaultCacheServer` within the IDE meant, it is one of the ways to limit cluster reach. By setting it to zero, you can effectively limit multicast packets to a single machine and ensure that your cluster remains private.

If you are using Well-Known Addresses instead of multicast, you can achieve the same goal by setting the `tangosol.coherence.wka` system property to `localhost`.

That said, using system properties is only one way to configure Coherence, and in this case probably not the best. The issue is that you need to remember to specify the property in every run configuration you create, and to make sure that each developer does the same for configurations that are not shared. This creates a lot of opportunities for human error, and chances are that sooner or latter someone will forget to specify the necessary system property.

The good news is that you can achieve the same goal using configuration files, which can be committed into the source control repository and shared by the whole team. In addition, settings specified within the configuration files will apply automatically to all run/debug configurations that you create in your IDE.

Configuring Coherence

Coherence uses several configuration files, some of which will be covered in later chapters. In this section, we will cover one of the core configuration files, the **operational descriptor**.

Operational configuration

The operational descriptor is used to configure Coherence runtime parameters such as clustering, communication, services, logging, security, license information, and so on.

Coherence ships with a default operational descriptor, `tangosol-coherence.xml`, packaged within `coherence.jar`. If you look more carefully at the console printout of a Coherence node, you will see that the very first line printed is similar to the following:

```
2009-08-12 13:46:01.983/0.259 Oracle Coherence 3.5.1/461 <Info>
(thread=main, member=n/a): Loaded operational configuration from resource
"jar:file:/opt/coherence-3.5/lib/coherence.jar!/tangosol-coherence.xml"
```

While you are encouraged to review this file to see what the default configuration looks like, you will typically not modify it directly. Instead, you will use one or more **override files** to modify only those elements of the operational descriptor that need to be changed for your environment.

All you need to do is create an override file and place it in the Coherence node's classpath before `coherence.jar`.

There are several override files that you can use:

- If you want to change the settings globally, regardless of the mode Coherence is running in, you can create a file called `tangosol-coherence-override.xml` and use it to override any of the elements from a default deployment descriptor. The structure of the files is exactly the same, with the exception that all elements in the override file are optional.

- If you want your changes to apply only to the development environment, you can create an override file called `tangosol-coherence-override-dev.xml`. Any settings specified in this file will apply only when the Coherence is running in a development mode, which is the default.

- If you want your changes to apply only to the production environment, you can create a file called `tangosol-coherence-override-prod.xml`. In order to have settings from this file applied on your production servers, you should set the system property `tangosol.coherence.mode` to `prod` in the script that is used to start Coherence nodes.

You can also create all of these files, and they will be applied in order, from most specific to the default one. For example, if you define both `tangosol-coherence-override-dev.xml` and `tangosol-coherence-override.xml`, settings from the former will be used to override default settings, and settings from the latter will override both the default settings and the settings specified in the `tangosol-coherence-override-dev.xml`.

I will cover some of the most important operational parameters in the following sections but thorough coverage of all parameters is not in the scope of this book. If you would like to learn more, you should consult the Coherence product manuals, as well as `coherence.dtd` and `tangosol-coherence.xml` files within `coherence.jar` for detailed information on various configuration elements.

Configuring logging

By default, Coherence prints out log statements to `stderr` using its own logging subsystem. More likely than not, this is not the desired behavior—you will probably want to use the same logging framework for Coherence that you use for the rest of the application. Fortunately, Coherence supports both the JDK logging framework and Log4J.

In order to configure Coherence to use Log4J, you need to create an operational override file and define a `logging-config` section with a `destination` element set to `log4j`:

```
<coherence>
  <logging-config>
    <destination>log4j</destination>
  </logging-config>
</coherence>
```

You will likely want to use the same logging framework both in development and production, so you should place the code above into `tangosol-coherence-override.xml` file, and make sure that the file is in the classpath.

You will also need to configure Log4J by creating a `log4j.properties` file similar to the following, and placing it in the classpath as well:

```
log4j.logger.Coherence=DEBUG, CONSOLE, FILE

log4j.appender.CONSOLE=org.apache.log4j.ConsoleAppender
log4j.appender.CONSOLE.threshold=INFO
log4j.appender.CONSOLE.layout=org.apache.log4j.PatternLayout
log4j.appender.CONSOLE.layout.ConversionPattern=%m%n
```

```
log4j.appender.FILE=org.apache.log4j.RollingFileAppender
log4j.appender.FILE.File=logs/coherence.log
log4j.appender.FILE.MaxFileSize=10MB
log4j.appender.FILE.layout=org.apache.log4j.PatternLayout
log4j.appender.FILE.layout.ConversionPattern=%m%n
```

Obviously, you can set logging thresholds as you like, but my personal preference is to log errors, warnings, and informational messages to the console, and to write all messages into the log file. This allows me to immediately see on the console if anything is out of the ordinary, and to dig into the log file for details.

Writing log messages from all the nodes into a single log file also has tremendous benefits, as it allows you to see the events across the cluster in one place. This is very helpful when debugging Coherence applications.

In any case, while the exact logger configuration is up to you, there are two important things to notice in the previous sample:

- You need to configure a logger named **Coherence**, as that's the name that the internal logging subsystem looks for when delegating to Log4J.
- Also, because Coherence already formats log messages internally to include all necessary information, you should simply print out the message using the `%m%n` layout pattern in Log4J.

Of course, you could modify the standard Coherence message pattern and use Log4J for formatting, but using the default one will make the process much easier if you need to submit the log file to Coherence support team.

Configuring a private cluster

Now that you know how to use operational descriptors to configure Coherence, let's see how we can use configuration elements to ensure that each developer's cluster is private.

First off, because we want clusters to be private only in the development environment, you will need to create a `tangosol-coherence-override-dev.xml` file, and ensure that it is in the classpath at runtime. The next step will depend on whether you are using multicast or WKA for cluster join protocol.

In the former case, you will need to use the following configuration:

```
<coherence xml-override="/tangosol-coherence-override.xml">
  <cluster-config>
    <multicast-listener>
      <time-to-live>0</time-to-live>
```

```
            <join-timeout-milliseconds>1000</join-timeout-milliseconds>
        </multicast-listener>
    </cluster-config>
</coherence>
```

While you only need to specify the `time-to-live` element to ensure that cluster is private, it is recommended that you specify `join-timeout-milliseconds` as well, and to set it to a relatively small value (one to three seconds should be more than enough for a private cluster). This will override the default production setting of thirty seconds and ensure that your cluster nodes start quickly.

If you are using WKA, configuration will be slightly different:

```
<coherence xml-override="/tangosol-coherence-override.xml">
  <cluster-config>
    <unicast-listener>
      <well-known-addresses>
        <socket-address id="1">
          <address>localhost</address>
        </socket-address>
      </well-known-addresses>
    </unicast-listener>
    <multicast-listener>
        <join-timeout-milliseconds>1000</join-timeout-milliseconds>
    </multicast-listener>
  </cluster-config>
</coherence>
```

Notice that we still had to specify the `join-timeout-milliseconds` parameter. Even though multicast is not used, this setting still controls how long the member will wait for evidence of an existing cluster before starting a new cluster and electing itself as a senior member, so you need to specify it in order to avoid a 30-second delay when starting the first member.

Finally, you should notice `xml-override` attribute within the root configuration element and its value—this is what ensures that the `tangosol-coherence-override.xml` file we created in the previous section is loaded and used to override the settings in this file and the base operational descriptor, so make sure that you include it if you want the logging configuration we defined earlier to be used.

Now that we have both the development environment and Coherence configured properly, we are ready to write some code.

Using the Coherence API

One of the great things about Coherence is that it has a very simple and intuitive API that hides most of the complexity that is happening behind the scenes to distribute your objects. If you know how to use a standard `Map` interface in Java, you already know how to perform basic tasks with Coherence.

In this section, we will first cover the basics by looking at some of the foundational interfaces and classes in Coherence. We will then proceed to do something more interesting by implementing a simple tool that allows us to load data into Coherence from CSV files, which will become very useful during testing.

The basics: NamedCache and CacheFactory

As I have briefly mentioned earlier, Coherence revolves around the concept of **named caches**. Each named cache can be configured differently, and it will typically be used to store objects of a particular type. For example, if you need to store employees, trade orders, portfolio positions, or shopping carts in the grid, each of those types will likely map to a separate named cache.

The first thing you need to do in your code when working with Coherence is to obtain a reference to a named cache you want to work with. In order to do this, you need to use the `CacheFactory` class, which exposes the `getCache` method as one of its public members. For example, if you wanted to get a reference to the `countries` cache that we created and used in the console example, you would do the following:

```
NamedCache countries = CacheFactory.getCache("countries");
```

Once you have a reference to a named cache, you can use it to put data into that cache or to retrieve data from it. Doing so is as simple as doing gets and puts on a standard Java `Map`:

```
countries.put("SRB", "Serbia");
String countryName = (String) countries.get("SRB");
```

As a matter of fact, `NamedCache` is an interface that extends Java's `Map` interface, so you will be immediately familiar not only with `get` and `put` methods, but also with other methods from the `Map` interface, such as `clear`, `remove`, `putAll`, `size`, and so on.

The nicest thing about the Coherence API is that it works in exactly the same way, regardless of the cache topology you use. We will cover different cache topologies in much more detail in the next chapter, but for now let's just say that you can configure Coherence to replicate or partition your data across the grid. The difference between the two is that in the former case all of your data exists on each node in the grid, while in the latter only $1/n$ of the data exists on each individual node, where n is the number of nodes in the grid.

Regardless of how your data is stored physically within the grid, the NamedCache interface provides a standard API that allows you to access it. This makes it very simple to change cache topology during development if you realize that a different topology would be a better fit, without having to modify a single line in your code.

In addition to the Map interface, NamedCache extends a number of lower-level Coherence interfaces. The following table provides a quick overview of these interfaces and the functionality they provide:

Interface Name	Description
CacheMap	Provides a way to specify expiration for a map entry
ObservableMap	Adds the ability to register listeners for various cache events
QueryMap	Allows you to execute queries against the cache
InvocableMap	Enables execution of processing agents within the grid
ConcurrentMap	Adds support for distributed concurrency control

We will discuss these interfaces in more detail throughout the book, but for now let's stick with the basics and implement our first complete example using the Coherence API.

The "Hello World" example

In this section we will implement a complete example that achieves programmatically what we have done earlier using Coherence console — we'll put a few countries in the cache, list cache contents, remove items, and so on.

To make things more interesting, instead of using country names as cache values, we will use proper objects this time. That means that we need a class to represent a country, so let's start there:

```
public class Country implements Serializable, Comparable {

    private String code;
    private String name;
    private String capital;
    private String currencySymbol;
```

```java
    private String currencyName;

    public Country() {
    }

    public Country(String code, String name, String capital,
                   String currencySymbol, String currencyName) {
      this.code           = code;
      this.name           = name;
      this.capital        = capital;
      this.currencySymbol = currencySymbol;
      this.currencyName   = currencyName;
    }

    public String getCode() {
      return code;
    }

    public void setCode(String code) {
      this.code = code;
    }

    public String getName() {
      return name;
    }

    public void setName(String name) {
      this.name = name;
    }

    public String getCapital() {
      return capital;
    }

    public void setCapital(String capital) {
      this.capital = capital;
    }

    public String getCurrencySymbol() {
      return currencySymbol;
    }

    public void setCurrencySymbol(String currencySymbol) {
      this.currencySymbol = currencySymbol;
```

```
    }

    public String getCurrencyName() {
      return currencyName;
    }

    public void setCurrencyName(String currencyName) {
      this.currencyName = currencyName;
    }

    public String toString() {
      return "Country(" +
                      "Code = " + code + ", " +
                      "Name = " + name + ", " +
                      "Capital = " + capital + ", " +
                      "CurrencySymbol = " + currencySymbol + ", " +
                      "CurrencyName = " + currencyName + ")";
    }

    public int compareTo(Object o) {
      Country other = (Country) o;
      return name.compareTo(other.name);
    }
  }
}
```

There are several things to note about the Country class, which also apply to other classes that you want to store in Coherence:

1. Because the objects needs to be moved across the network, classes that are stored within the data grid need to be serializable. In this case we have opted for the simplest solution and made the class implement the java.io.Serializable interface. This is not optimal, both from performance and memory utilization perspective, and Coherence provides several more suitable approaches to serialization that we'll discuss in *Chapter 4, Implementing Domain Objects*.

2. We have implemented the toString method that prints out an object's state in a friendly format. While this is not a Coherence requirement, implementing toString properly for both keys and values that you put into the cache will help a lot when debugging, so you should get into a habit of implementing it for your own classes.

3. Finally, we have also implemented the Comparable interface. This is also not a requirement, but it will come in handy in a moment to allow us to print out a list of countries sorted by name.

Now that we have the class that represents the values we want to cache, it is time to write an example that uses it:

```java
import com.tangosol.net.NamedCache;
import com.tangosol.net.CacheFactory;

import ch02.Country;

import java.util.Set;
import java.util.Map;


public class CoherenceHelloWorld {
  public static void main(String[] args) {
    NamedCache countries = CacheFactory.getCache("countries");

    // first, we need to put some countries into the cache
    countries.put("USA", new Country("USA", "United States",
                "Washington", "USD", "Dollar"));
    countries.put("GBR", new Country("GBR", "United Kingdom",
                "London", "GBP", "Pound"));
    countries.put("RUS", new Country("RUS", "Russia", "Moscow",
                "RUB", "Ruble"));
    countries.put("CHN", new Country("CHN", "China", "Beijing",
                "CNY", "Yuan"));
    countries.put("JPN", new Country("JPN", "Japan", "Tokyo",
                "JPY", "Yen"));
    countries.put("DEU", new Country("DEU", "Germany", "Berlin",
                "EUR", "Euro"));
    countries.put("FRA", new Country("FRA", "France", "Paris",
                "EUR", "Euro"));
    countries.put("ITA", new Country("ITA", "Italy", "Rome",
                "EUR", "Euro"));
    countries.put("SRB", new Country("SRB", "Serbia", "Belgrade",
                "RSD", "Dinar"));
    assert countries.containsKey("JPN")
            : "Japan is not in the cache";

    // get and print a single country
    System.out.println("get(SRB) = " + countries.get("SRB"));

    // remove Italy from the cache
    int size = countries.size();
```

```
System.out.println("remove(ITA) = " + countries.remove("ITA"));
assert countries.size() == size - 1
        : "Italy was not removed";

// list all cache entries
Set<Map.Entry> entries = countries.entrySet(null, null);
for (Map.Entry entry : entries) {
   System.out.println(entry.getKey() + " = " + entry.getValue());
}
   }
}
```

Let's go through this code section by section.

At the very top, you can see import statements for `NamedCache` and `CacheFactory`, which are the only Coherence classes we need for this simple example. We have also imported our `Country` class, as well as Java's standard `Map` and `Set` interfaces.

The first thing we need to do within the `main` method is to obtain a reference to the `countries` cache using the `CacheFactory.getCache` method. Once we have the cache reference, we can add some countries to it using the same old `Map.put` method you are familiar with.

We then proceed to get a single object from the cache using the `Map.get` method, and to remove one using `Map.remove`. Notice that the `NamedCache` implementation fully complies with the `Map.remove` contract and returns the removed object.

Finally, we list all the countries by iterating over the set returned by the `entrySet` method. Notice that Coherence cache entries implement the standard `Map.Entry` interface.

Overall, if it wasn't for a few minor differences, it would be impossible to tell whether the preceding code uses Coherence or any of the standard `Map` implementations. The first telltale sign is the call to the `CacheFactory.getCache` at the very beginning, and the second one is the call to `entrySet` method with two `null` arguments. We have already discussed the former, but where did the latter come from?

The answer is that Coherence `QueryMap` interface extends Java `Map` by adding methods that allow you to filter and sort the entry set. The first argument in our example is an instance of Coherence `Filter` interface, which will be discussed in more detail in *Chapter 5, Querying the Data Grid*. In this case, we want all the entries, so we simply pass `null` as a filter.

The second argument, however, is more interesting in this particular example. It represents the `java.util.Comparator` that should be used to sort the results. If the values stored in the cache implement the `Comparable` interface, you can pass `null` instead of the actual `Comparator` instance as this argument, in which case the results will be sorted using their natural ordering (as defined by `Comparable.compareTo` implementation).

That means that when you run the previous example, you should see the following output:

```
get(SRB) = Country(Code = SRB, Name = Serbia, Capital = Belgrade,
CurrencySymbol = RSD, CurrencyName = Dinar)

remove(ITA) = Country(Code = ITA, Name = Italy, Capital = Rome,
CurrencySymbol = EUR, CurrencyName = Euro)

CHN = Country(Code = CHN, Name = China, Capital = Beijing, CurrencySymbol
= CNY, CurrencyName = Yuan)
FRA = Country(Code = FRA, Name = France, Capital = Paris, CurrencySymbol
= EUR, CurrencyName = Euro)
DEU = Country(Code = DEU, Name = Germany, Capital = Berlin,
CurrencySymbol = EUR, CurrencyName = Euro)
JPN = Country(Code = JPN, Name = Japan, Capital = Tokyo, CurrencySymbol =
JPY, CurrencyName = Yen)
RUS = Country(Code = RUS, Name = Russia, Capital = Moscow, CurrencySymbol
= RUB, CurrencyName = Ruble)
SRB = Country(Code = SRB, Name = Serbia, Capital = Belgrade,
CurrencySymbol = RSD, CurrencyName = Dinar)
GBR = Country(Code = GBR, Name = United Kingdom, Capital = London,
CurrencySymbol = GBP, CurrencyName = Pound)
USA = Country(Code = USA, Name = United States, Capital = Washington,
CurrencySymbol = USD, CurrencyName = Dollar)
```

As you can see, the countries in the list are sorted by name, as defined by our `Country.compareTo` implementation. Feel free to experiment by passing a custom `Comparator` as the second argument to the `entrySet` method, or by removing both arguments, and see how that affects result ordering.

If you are feeling really adventurous and can't wait for a few more chapters to learn about Coherence queries, take a sneak peek by changing the line that returns the entry set to:

```
Set<Map.Entry> entries = countries.entrySet(
                         new LikeFilter("getName", "United%"), null);
```

As a final note, you might have also noticed that I used Java assertions in the previous example to check that the reality matches my expectations (well, more to demonstrate a few other methods in the API, but that's beyond the point). Make sure that you specify the `-ea` JVM argument when running the example if you want the assertions to be enabled, or use the `run-helloworld` target in the included Ant build file, which configures everything properly for you.

That concludes the implementation of our first Coherence application. One thing you might notice is that the `CoherenceHelloWorld` application will run just fine even if you don't have any Coherence nodes started, and you might be wondering how that is possible.

The truth is that there *is* one Coherence node—the `CoherenceHelloWorld` application. As soon as the `CacheFactory.getCache` method gets invoked, Coherence services will start within the application's JVM and it will either join the existing cluster or create a new one, if there are no other nodes on the network. If you don't believe me, look at the log messages printed by the application and you will see that this is indeed the case.

Now that you know the basics, let's move on and build something slightly more exciting, and much more useful.

Coherence API in action: Implementing the cache loader

The need to load the data into the Coherence cache from an external data source is ever-present. Many Coherence applications warm up the caches by pre-loading data from a relational database or other external data sources.

In this section, we will focus on a somewhat simpler scenario and write a utility that allows us to load objects into the cache from a comma-separated (CSV) file. This type of utility is very useful during development and testing, as it allows us to easily load test data into Coherence.

Loader design

If we forget for a moment about the technologies we are using and think about moving data from one data store to another at a higher level of abstraction, the solution is quite simple, as the following pseudo-code demonstrates:

```
for each item in source
  add item to target
end
```

That's really all there is to it—we need to be able to iterate over the source data store, retrieve items from it, and import them into the target data store.

One thing we need to decide is how the individual items are going to be represented. While in a general case an item can be any object, in order to simplify things a bit for this particular example we will use a Java Map to represent an item. This map will contain property values for an item, keyed by property name.

Based on the given information, we can define the interfaces for source and target:

```
public interface Source extends Iterable<Map<String, ?>> {
    void beginExport();
    void endExport();
}
```

The Target interface is just as simple:

```
public interface Target {
    void beginImport();
    void endImport();
    void importItem(Map<String, ?> item);
}
```

One thing you will notice in the previous interfaces is that there are matching pairs of begin/end methods. These are lifecycle methods that are used to initialize source and target and to perform any necessary cleanup.

Now that we have Source and Target interfaces defined, we can use them in the implementation of our Loader class:

```
public class Loader {
    private Source source;
    private Target target;

    public Loader(Source source, Target target) {
        this.source = source;
        this.target = target;
    }

    public void load() {
        source.beginExport();
        target.beginImport();

        for (Map<String, ?> sourceItem : source) {
            target.importItem(sourceItem);
        }
```

```
      source.endExport();
      target.endImport();
  }
}
```

As you can see, the actual Java implementation is almost as simple as the pseudo-code on the previous page, which is a good thing.

However, that does imply that all the complexity and the actual heavy lifting are pushed down into our `Source` and `Target` implementations, so let's look at those.

Implementing CsvSource

On the surface, implementing a class that reads a text file line by line, splits each line into fields and creates a property map based on the header row and corresponding field values couldn't be any simpler. However, as with any other problem, there are subtle nuances that complicate the task.

For example, even though comma is used to separate the fields in each row, it could also appear within the content of individual fields, in which case the field as a whole needs to be enclosed in quotation marks.

This complicates the parsing quite a bit, as we cannot simply use `String.split` to convert a single row from a file into an array of individual fields. While writing a parser by hand wouldn't be too difficult, writing code that someone else has already written is not one of my favorite pastimes.

Super CSV (`http://supercsv.sourceforge.net`), written by Kasper B. Graversen, is an open source library licensed under the Apache 2.0 license that does everything we need and much more, and I strongly suggest that you take a look at it before writing any custom code that reads or writes CSV files.

Among other things, Super CSV provides the `CsvMapReader` class, which does exactly what we need—it returns a map of header names to field values for each line read from the CSV file. That makes the implementation of `CsvSource` quite simple:

```
public class CsvSource implements Source {
  private ICsvMapReader reader;
  private String[]      header;

  public CsvSource(String name) {
    this(new InputStreamReader(
        CsvSource.class.getClassLoader().getResourceAsStream(name)));
  }

  public CsvSource(Reader reader) {
```

```
        this.reader =
            new CsvMapReader(reader, CsvPreference.STANDARD_PREFERENCE);
    }

    public void beginExport() {
      try {
        this.header = reader.getCSVHeader(false);
      }
      catch (IOException e) {
        throw new RuntimeException(e);
      }
    }

    public void endExport() {
      try {
        reader.close();
      }
      catch (IOException e) {
        throw new RuntimeException(e);
      }
    }

    public Iterator<Map<String, ?>> iterator() {
      return new CsvIterator();
    }
}
```

As you can see `CsvSource` accepts a `java.io.Reader` instance as a constructor argument and wraps it with a `CsvMapReader`. There is also a convenience constructor that will create a `CsvSource` instance for any CSV file in a classpath, which is the most likely scenario for testing.

We use the `beginExport` lifecycle method to read the header row and initialize the `header` field, which will later be used by the `CsvMapReader` when reading individual data rows from the file and converting them to a map. In a similar fashion, we use the `endExport` method to close the reader properly and free the resources associated with it.

Finally, we implement the `Iterable` interface by returning an instance of the inner `CsvIterator` class from the `iterator` method. The `CsvIterator` inner class implements the necessary iteration logic for our source:

```
private class CsvIterator implements Iterator<Map<String, ?>> {
  private Map<String, String> item;

  public boolean hasNext() {
    try {
      item = reader.read(header);
    }
    catch (IOException e) {
      throw new RuntimeException(e);
    }
    return item != null;
  }

  public Map<String, ?> next() {
   return item;
  }

  public void remove() {
    throw new UnsupportedOperationException(
                "CsvIterator does not support remove operation");
  }
}
}
```

Thanks to the `CsvMapReader`, the implementation is quite simple. We read the next line from the file whenever the `hasNext` method is called, and store the result in the `item` field. The `next` method simply returns the item read by the previous call to `hasNext`.

That completes the implementation of `CsvSource`, and allows us to shift our focus back to Coherence.

Implementing CoherenceTarget

The last thing we need to do to complete the example is to create a `Target` interface implementation that will import items read from the CSV file into Coherence.

One of the things we will need to do is to convert the generic item representation from a `Map` into an instance of a class that represents the value we want to put into the cache. The naïve approach is to use Java reflection to create an instance of a class and set property values, but just as with the CSV parsing, the devil is in the details.

The property values read from the CSV files are all strings, but the properties of the target object might not be. That means that we need to perform type conversion as appropriate when setting property values on a target object.

Fortunately, we don't need to reinvent the wheel to do this. If you are familiar with the Spring Framework, you already know that property values, specified as strings within the XML configuration file, are automatically converted to appropriate type before they are injected into your objects. What you might not know is that this feature is easily accessible outside of Spring as well, in the form of the `BeanWrapper` interface and `BeanWrapperImpl` class.

Another problem we need to solve is key generation—when we put objects into a Coherence cache, we need to specify both the key and the value. The simplest option, and the one we will use for this example, is to extract the key from the target object itself. This will often be all we need, as most entities already have a field representing their identity, which is the ideal candidate for a cache key. In the case of our `Country` class, we will use the value of the `code` property as a cache key.

Finally, while we could insert every item into the cache using individual `put` calls, this is not the most efficient way to perform bulk loading of the data. As I mentioned in *Chapter 1, Achieving Performance, Scalability, and Availability Objectives*, each call to the `put` method is potentially a network call, and as such introduces some latency. A significantly better approach from a performance perspective is to batch multiple items and insert them into the cache all at once by calling the `putAll` method.

So, with the design considerations out of the way, let's look at the implementation of the `CoherenceTarget` class:

```
public class CoherenceTarget implements Target {
  public static final int DEFAULT_BATCH_SIZE = 1000;

  private NamedCache cache;
  private Class      itemClass;
  private String     idProperty;

  private Map batch;
  private int batchSize = DEFAULT_BATCH_SIZE;

  public CoherenceTarget(String cacheName, Class itemClass,
                         String idProperty) {
```

```
    this.cache      = CacheFactory.getCache(cacheName);
    this.itemClass  = itemClass;
    this.idProperty = idProperty;
  }

  public void setBatchSize(int batchSize) {
    this.batchSize = batchSize;
  }

  public void beginImport() {
    batch = new HashMap();
  }

  public void importItem(Map<String, ?> sourceItem) {
    BeanWrapper targetItem = new BeanWrapperImpl(itemClass);

    for (Map.Entry<String, ?> property : sourceItem.entrySet()) {
      targetItem.setPropertyValue(property.getKey(),
                                  property.getValue());
    }
    Object id = targetItem.getPropertyValue(idProperty);

    batch.put(id, targetItem.getWrappedInstance());
    if (batch.size() % batchSize == 0) {
      cache.putAll(batch);
      batch.clear();
    }
  }

  public void endImport() {
    if (!batch.isEmpty()) {
      cache.putAll(batch);
    }
  }
}
```

The constructor accepts three arguments: the name of the cache to import objects into, the class of cache items, and the name of the property of that class that should be used as a cache key. We initialize batch size to 1000 items by default, but the value can be easily overridden by calling the setBatchSize method.

The beginImport lifecycle method initializes the map representing a batch of items that need to be inserted, while the endImport method ensures that the last, potentially incomplete, batch is also inserted into the cache.

The real meat is in the `importItem` method, which creates a Spring `BeanWrapper` instance for the specified item class and sets its properties based on the entries in the `sourceItem` map. Once the target item is fully initialized, we use `BeanWrapper` again to extract the cache key from it and add the item to the batch.

Finally, whenever the batch size reaches the specified limit, we insert all items from the batch into the cache and clear the batch.

With this last piece in place, we are ready to test the loader.

Cache loader on steroids

The implementation of the cache loader presented in this chapter is a simplified version of the loader my colleague, Ivan Cikić, and I have implemented as part of the Coherence Tools project, which is available at `http://code.google.com/p/coherence-tools/`.

The full version has many additional features and removes some limitations of the implementation in this chapter. For example, it provides flexible mapping and transformation features, as well as multiple key generation strategies.

It also contains both `Source` and `Target` implementations for CSV files, XML files, and Coherence, allowing you to import data from the existing CSV and XML files into Coherence, and to export contents of a Coherence cache into one of these formats.

In any case, if you like the idea behind the Cache Loader but need more capabilities than presented in this chapter, check out the latest Coherence Tools release.

Testing the Cache loader

In order to test the loader, we will use a `countries.csv` file containing a list of most countries in the world (I'd say all, but being from Serbia I know firsthand that a list of countries in the world is anything but static ☺).

The file header matches exactly the property names in the `Country` class defined earlier, which is the requirement imposed by our loader implementation:

```
code,name,capital,currencySymbol,currencyName
AFG,Afghanistan,Kabul,AFN,Afghani
ALB,Albania,Tirana,ALL,Lek
DZA,Algeria,Algiers,DZD,Dinar
AND,Andorra,Andorra la Vella,EUR,Euro
AGO,Angola,Luanda,AOA,Kwanza
```

With the test data in place, let's write a JUnit test that will load all of the countries defined in the `countries.csv` file into the Coherence cache:

```java
public class LoaderTests {
    public static final NamedCache countries =
            CacheFactory.getCache("countries");

    @Before
    public void clearCache() {
        countries.clear();
    }

    @Test
    public void testCsvToCoherenceLoader() {
        Source source = new CsvSource("countries.csv");
        CoherenceTarget target =
                new CoherenceTarget("countries", Country.class, "code");
        target.setBatchSize(50);
        Loader loader = new Loader(source, target);
        loader.load();

        assertEquals(193, countries.size());

        Country srb = (Country) countries.get("SRB");
        assertEquals("Serbia",    srb.getName());
        assertEquals("Belgrade",  srb.getCapital());
        assertEquals("RSD",       srb.getCurrencySymbol());
        assertEquals("Dinar",     srb.getCurrencyName());
    }
}
```

As you can see, using the cache loader is quite simple—we initialize the source and target, create a `Loader` instance for them, and invoke the `load` method. We then assert that all the data from the test CSV file has been loaded, and that the properties of a single object retrieved from the cache are set correctly.

However, the real purpose of the previous test is neither to teach you how to use the loader (you could've easily figured that out yourself) nor to prove that the code in the preceding sections works (of course it does ☺). It is to lead us into the very interesting subject that follows.

Testing and debugging Coherence applications

From the application's perspective, Coherence is a data store. That means that you will need to use it while testing the data access code.

If you have ever had to test data access code that uses a relational database as a data store, you know that the whole process can be quite cumbersome. You need to set up test data, perform the test, and then clean up after each test, in order to ensure that the side effects of one test do not influence the outcome of another.

Tools such as DbUnit (`http://www.dbunit.org`) or Spring's transactional testing support can make the process somewhat easier, but unfortunately, nothing of that nature exists for Coherence.

The good news is that no such tools are necessary when working with Coherence. Setting up test data can be as simple as creating a bunch of CSV files and using the loader we implemented in the previous section to import them into the cache. Clearing data from the cache between the tests is even simpler—just call the `clear` method on the cache you are testing. In most cases, testing Coherence-related code will be very similar to the `LoaderTests` test case from the previous section and much simpler than testing database-related code.

However, Coherence is not only a data store, but a distributed processing engine as well, and that is where things can get interesting. When you execute a query or an aggregator, it executes across all the nodes in the cluster. When you execute an entry processor, it might execute on one or several, possibly even all nodes in parallel, depending on how it was invoked.

For the most part, you can test the code that executes within the cluster the same way you test more conventional data access code, by having each test case start a one-node cluster. This makes debugging quite simple, as it ensures that all the code, from test, to Coherence, to your custom processing code executing within Coherence runs in the same process.

However, you should bear in mind that by doing so you are not testing your code in the same environment it will eventually run in. All kinds of things change internally when you move from a one-node cluster to two-node cluster. For example, Coherence will not create backups in a single-node scenario, but it will as soon as the second node is added to the cluster.

In some cases you might have to test and debug your code in a true distributed environment, because it depends on things that are only true if you move beyond a single node.

Debugging in a distributed environment can get quite tricky. First of all, you will need to enable remote debugging on a cache server node by adding the following JVM arguments to `DefaultCacheServer` run configuration:

```
-Xdebug
-Xrunjdwp:transport=dt_socket,server=y,suspend=n,address=5005
```

Second, you will need to ensure that all the data is stored on a cache server node where remote debugging is enabled. That will ensure that the code you need to debug within the cluster, such as the entry processor mentioned earlier, is guaranteed to execute on that node.

Even though you will only be able to start one `DefaultCacheServer` now (because of the remote debug port it is bound to), as soon as your test invokes any `CacheFactory` method it will join the cluster as a second node. By default, the data is balanced automatically across all the nodes in the cluster, which will make it impossible to ensure that your processor executes where you want.

Fortunately, Coherence provides a feature that allows you to control which nodes are used to store cached data and which aren't. This feature is normally used to disable cache storage on application servers while allowing them to be full-blown members of the cluster in all other respects, but it can also be used to ensure that no data is cached on the test runner node when using remote debugging.

In order to activate it, you need to add the following JVM argument to your test runner configuration:

```
-Dtangosol.coherence.distributed.localstorage=false
```

Once everything is configured properly, you should be able to set a breakpoint, start the cache server, attach the debugger to it, and run the test. When the breakpoint is hit, the debugger will allow you to step through the code and inspect the variables in a remote process as you normally would, as shown in the following screenshot:

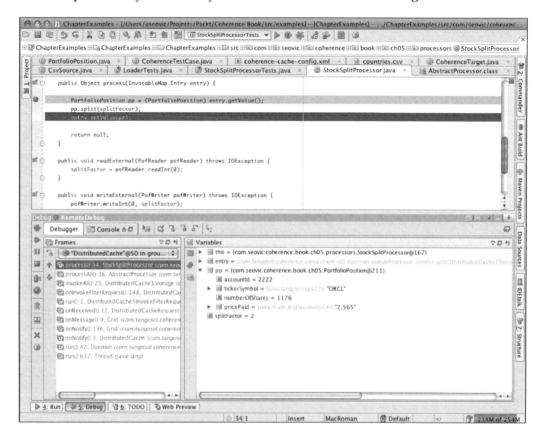

The bottom line is that even though debugging a distributed system poses some new challenges, you can overcome them using a combination of features found in Java, modern IDEs, and Coherence.

Also keep in mind that you won't have to do this very often—more likely than not you will be able to test and debug most of your code using a simple, single-node-in-a-single-process approach. However, it is good to know how to do it in a distributed environment as well, because sooner or later you will need to do it.

Summary

In this chapter, you have learned how to install Coherence and how to start one or more grid nodes. You experimented with the Coherence Console, and learned that it is a development and debugging tool that should *never* be used in production (just in case you forgot the earlier warning).

We also discussed how to configure the development environment while working with Coherence to make you most productive, and to ensure that each developer has their own, private cluster for development and testing.

We then discussed Coherence operational configuration, and you learned how to configure Coherence to use Log4J for logging and how to set up private developer clusters using the operational descriptor.

A large part of the chapter was devoted to the Coherence API. You learned how to perform basic cache operations programmatically, and along the way created a useful utility that allows you to import data from CSV files into Coherence.

Finally, I briefly talked about the testing and debugging of Coherence applications and provided some guidelines and suggestions on how to use remote debugging with Coherence.

In the next chapter, you will learn about the different ways to configure Coherence caches and how to choose the most appropriate cache topology based on your data and data access patterns.

3

Planning Your Caches

In the previous chapter, you learned how to create and use Coherence caches without ever having to configure them explicitly. However, if you had paid close attention during the Coherence node startup, you might have noticed the log message that appears immediately after the banner that prints out the Coherence version, edition, and mode:

```
Oracle Coherence Version 3.5.1/461
 Grid Edition: Development mode
Copyright (c) 2000, 2009, Oracle and/or its affiliates. All rights
reserved.

2009-08-19 10:59:32.778/0.730 Oracle Coherence GE 3.5.1/461 <Info>
(thread=main, member=n/a): Loaded cache configuration from "jar:file:/
opt/coherence-3.5/lib/coherence.jar!/coherence-cache-config.xml"
```

Just like the default deployment descriptor, the default cache configuration file is packaged within coherence.jar, which is the reason why everything we've done so far has worked.

While this is great for trying things out quickly, it is not the optimal way to run Coherence in either the development or production environment, as you will probably want to have more control over things such as cache topology, data storage within the cache and its persistence outside of it, cache expiration, and so on.

Fortunately, Coherence is fully configurable and allows you to control all these things in detail. However, in order to make good decisions, you need to know when each of the various alternatives should be used.

That is the subject we will cover in this chapter. We will first discuss the different cache topologies and their respective strengths and weaknesses. We will then talk about various data storage strategies, which should provide you enough information to choose the one that best fits your needs. Finally, we will cover the Coherence cache configuration file and provide a sample configuration you can use as a starting point for your own applications.

So let's start by looking under the hood and learning more about the inner workings of Coherence.

Anatomy of a clustered cache

You have already seen that using the Coherence cache is as simple as obtaining a reference to a `NamedCache` instance and using a `Map`-like API to get data from it (and put data into it). While the simplicity of the API is a great thing, it is important to understand what's going on under the hood so that you can configure Coherence in the most effective way, based on your application's data structures and data access patterns.

The simplicity of access to the Coherence named cache, from the API, might make you imagine the named cache as in the following diagram:

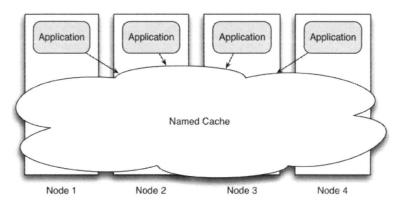

Basically, your application sees the Coherence named cache as a cloud-like structure that is spread across the cluster of nodes, but accessible locally using a very simple API. While this is a correct view from the client application's perspective, it does not fully reflect what goes on behind the scenes.

So let's clear the cloud and see what's hidden behind it.

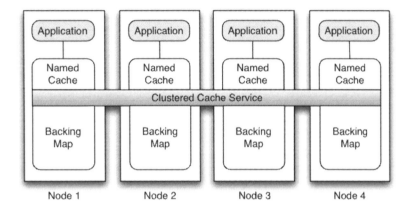

Whenever you invoke a method on a named cache instance, that method call gets delegated to the **clustered cache service** that the named cache belongs to. The preceding image depicts a single named cache managed by the single cache service, but the relationship between the named cache instances and the cache service is many to one—each named cache belongs to exactly one cache service, but a single cache service is typically responsible for more than one named cache.

The cache service is responsible for the distribution of cache data to appropriate members on cache writes, as well as for the retrieval of the data on cache reads.

However, the cache service is *not* responsible for the actual storage of the cached data. Instead, it delegates this responsibility to a **backing map**. There is one instance of the backing map 'per named cache per node', and this is where the cached data is actually stored.

There are many backing map implementations available out of the box, and we will discuss them shortly. For now, let's focus on the clustered cache services and the cache topologies they enable.

Clustered cache topologies

For each clustered cache you define in your application, you have to make an important choice—which cache topology to use.

There are two base cache topologies in Coherence: **replicated** and **partitioned**. They are implemented by two different clustered cache services, the Replicated Cache service and the Partitioned Cache service, respectively.

Distributed or partitioned?

You will notice that the partitioned cache is often referred to as a **distributed cache** as well, especially in the API documentation and configuration elements.

This is somewhat of a misnomer, as both replicated and partitioned caches are distributed across many nodes, but unfortunately the API and configuration element names have to remain the way they are for compatibility reasons.

I will refer to them as partitioned throughout the book as that name better describes their purpose and functionality, but please remember this caveat when looking at the sample code and Coherence documentation that refers to distributed caches.

When the Coherence node starts and joins the cluster using the default configuration, it automatically starts both of these services, among others:

```
Services
  (
  TcpRing{...}
  ClusterService{...}
  InvocationService{Name=Management, ...}
  DistributedCache{Name=DistributedCache, ...}
  ReplicatedCache{Name=ReplicatedCache, ...}
  Optimistic{Name=OptimisticCache, ...}
  InvocationService{Name=InvocationService, ...}
  )
```

While both replicated and partitioned caches look the same to the client code (remember, you use the same `Map`-based API to access both of them), they have very different performance, scalability, and throughput characteristics. These characteristics depend on many factors, such as the data set size, data access patterns, the number of cache nodes, and so on. It is important to take all of these factors into account when deciding the cache topology to use for a particular cache.

In the following sections, we will cover both cache topologies in more detail and provide some guidelines that will help you choose the appropriate one for your caches.

Optimistic Cache service

You might also notice the Optimistic Cache service in the previous output, which is another cache service type that Coherence supports.

The Optimistic Cache service is very similar to the Replicated Cache service, except that it doesn't provide any concurrency control. It is rarely used in practice, so we will not discuss it separately.

Replicated Cache service

The most important characteristic of the replicated cache is that each cache item is replicated to all the nodes in the grid. That means that every node in the grid that is running the Replicated Cache service has the full dataset within a backing map for that cache.

For example, if we configure a `Countries` cache to use the Replicated Cache service and insert several objects into it, the data within the grid would look like the following:

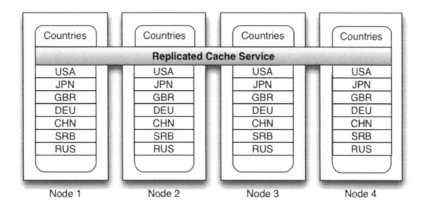

As you can see, the backing map for the `Countries` cache on each node has all the elements we have inserted.

This has significant implications on how and when you can use a replicated topology. In order to understand these implications better, we will analyze the replicated cache topology on four different criteria:

- Read performance
- Write performance
- Data set size
- Fault tolerance

Read performance

Replicated caches have excellent, zero-latency read performance because all the data is local to each node, which means that an application running on that node can get data from the cache at in-memory speed.

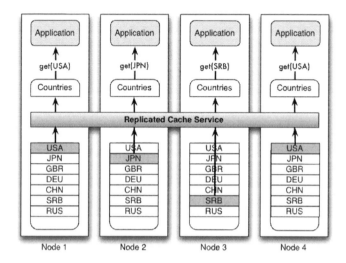

This makes replicated caches well suited for read-intensive applications, where minimal latency is required, and is the biggest reason you would consider using a replicated cache.

One important thing to note is that the locality of the data does not imply that the objects stored in a replicated cache are also in a ready-to-use, deserialized form. A replicated cache deserializes objects on demand. When you put the object into the cache, it will be serialized and sent to all the other nodes running the Replicated Cache service. The receiving nodes, however, will not deserialize the received object until it is requested, which means that you might incur a slight performance penalty when accessing an object in a replicated cache the first time. Once deserialized on any given node, the object will remain that way until an updated serialized version is received from another node.

Write performance

In order to perform write operations, such as put, against the cache, the Replicated Cache service needs to distribute the operation to all the nodes in the cluster and receive confirmation from them that the operation was completed successfully. This increases both the amount of network traffic and the latency of write operations against the replicated cache. The write operation can be imagined from the following diagram:

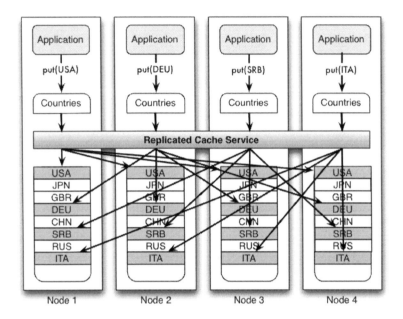

To make things even worse, the performance of write operations against a
replicated cache tends to degrade as the size of the cluster grows, as there
are more nodes to synchronize.

All this makes a replicated cache poorly suited for write-intensive applications.

Data set size

The fact that each node holds all the data implies that the total size of all replicated
caches is limited by the amount of memory available to a single node. Of course,
if the nodes within the cluster are not identical, this becomes even more restrictive
and the limit becomes the amount of memory available to the **smallest** node
in the cluster, which is why it is good practice to configure all the nodes in the
cluster identically.

There are ways to increase the capacity of the replicated cache by using one of the
backing map implementations that stores all or some of the cache data outside of the
Java heap, but there is very little to be gained by doing so. As as soon as you move
the replicated cache data out of RAM, you sacrifice one of the biggest advantages it
provides: zero-latency read access.

This might not seem like a significant limitation considering that today's commodity servers can be equipped with up to 256 GB of RAM, and the amount will continue to increase in the future. (Come to think of it, this is 26 thousand times more than the first hard drive I had, and an unbelievable 5.6 million times more than 48 KB of RAM my good old ZX Spectrum had back in the eighties. It is definitely possible to store a lot of data in memory these days.)

However, there is a caveat—just because you can have that much memory in a single physical box, doesn't mean that you can configure a single Coherence node to use all of it. There is obviously some space that will be occupied by the OS, but the biggest limitation comes from today's JVMs and more specifically the way memory is managed within the JVM.

Coherence node size on modern JVMs

At the time of writing (mid 2009), there are hard limitations on how big your Coherence nodes can be; these are imposed by the underlying **Java Virtual Machine (JVM)**.

The biggest problem is represented by the pauses that effectively freeze the JVM for a period of time during garbage collection. The length of this period is directly proportional to the size of the JVM heap, so, the bigger the heap, the longer it will take to reclaim the unused memory and the longer the node will seem frozen.

Once the heap grows over a certain size (2 GB at the moment for most JVMs), the garbage collection pause can become too long to be tolerated by users of an application, and possibly long enough that Coherence will assume the node is unavailable and kick it out of the cluster. There are ways to increase the amount of time Coherence waits for the node to respond before it kicks it out. However, it is usually not a good idea to do so as it might increase the actual cluster response time to the client application, even in the situations where the node really fails and should be removed from the cluster as soon as possible and its responsibilities transferred to another node.

Because of this, the recommended heap size for Coherence nodes is typically in the range of 1 to 2 GB, with 1 GB usually being the optimal size that ensures that garbage collection pauses are short enough to be unnoticeable. This severely limits the maximum size of the data set in a replicated cache.

Keeping the Coherence node size in a 1 to 2 GB range will also allow you to better utilize the processing power of your servers. As I mentioned earlier, Coherence can perform certain operations in parallel, across the nodes. In order to fully utilize modern servers, which typically have multiple CPUs, with two or four cores on each one, you will want to have multiple Coherence nodes on each physical server. There are no hard and fast rules here: you will have to test different configurations to determine which one works best for your application, but the bottom line is that in any scenario you will likely split your total available RAM across multiple nodes on a single physical box.

One of the new features introduced in Coherence 3.5 is the ability to manage data outside of the JVM heap, and I will cover it in more detail in the *Backing maps* section later in the chapter. Regardless, some information, such as indexes, is always stored on the JVM heap, so the heap size restriction applies to some extent to all configurations.

Fault tolerance

Replicated caches are very resilient to failure as there are essentially as many copies of the data as there are nodes in the cluster. When a single node fails, all that a Replicated Cache service needs to do in order to recover from the failure is to redirect read operations to other nodes and to simply ignore write operations sent to the failed node, as those same operations are simultaneously performed on the remaining cluster nodes.

When a failed node recovers or new node joins the cluster, failback is equally simple—the new node simply copies all the data from any other node in the cluster.

When to use it?

Replicated cache is a good choice only for small-to-medium size, read-only or read-mostly data sets. However, there are certain features of a partitioned cache that make most of the advantages of a replicated cache somewhat irrelevant, as you'll see shortly.

Partitioned Cache service

Unlike a replicated cache service, which simply replicates all the data to all cluster nodes, a partitioned cache service uses a **divide and conquer** approach—it partitions the data set across all the nodes in the cluster, as shown in the following diagram:

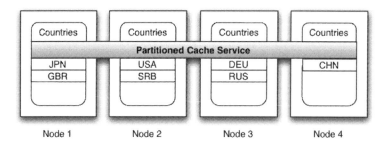

In this scenario, Coherence truly is reminiscent of a distributed hash map. Each node in the cluster becomes responsible for a subset of cache partitions (**buckets**), and the Partitioned Cache service uses an entry key to determine which partition (bucket) to store the cache entry in.

Let's evaluate the Partitioned Cache service using the same four criteria we used for the Replicated Cache service.

Read performance

Because the data set is partitioned across the nodes, it is very likely that the reads coming from any single node will require an additional network call. As a matter of fact, we can easily prove that in a general case, for a cluster of N nodes, (N-1)/N operations will require a network call to another node.

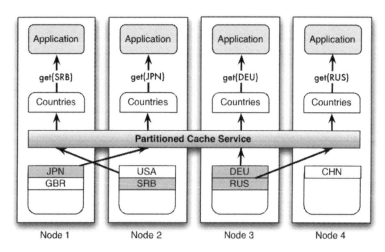

This is depicted in the preceding diagram, where three out of the four requests were processed by a node different from the one issuing the request.

However, it is important to note that if the requested piece of data is not managed locally, it will always take only one additional network call to get it, because the Partitioned Cache service is able to determine which node owns a piece of data based on the requested key. This allows Coherence to scale extremely well in a switched network environment, as it utilizes direct point-to-point communication between the nodes.

Another thing to consider is that the objects in a partitioned cache are always stored in a serialized binary form. This means that every read request will have to deserialize the object, introducing additional latency.

The fact that there is always at most one network call to retrieve the data ensures that reads from a partitioned cache execute in constant time. However, because of that additional network call and deserialization, this is still an order of magnitude slower than a read from a replicated cache.

Write performance

In the simplest case, partitioned cache write performance is pretty much the same as its read performance. Write operations will also require network access in the vast majority of cases, and they will use point-to-point communication to accomplish the goal in a single network call, as shown in the following screenshot

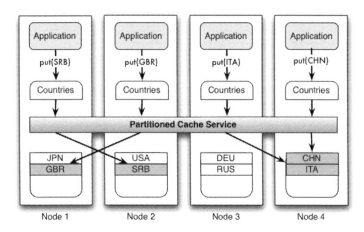

However, this is not the whole story, which is why I said "in the simplest case".

One thing you are probably asking yourself by now is "but what happens if a node fails?". Rest assured, partitioned caches can be fully fault tolerant, and we will get into the details of that in a section on fault tolerance. For now, let's fix the preceding diagram to show what partitioned cache writes usually look like.

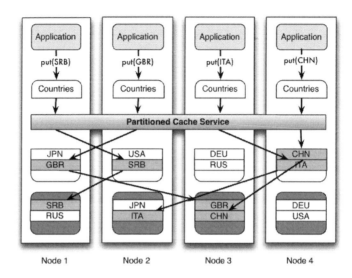

As you can see from the diagram, in addition to the backing map that holds the live cache data, the partitioned cache service also manages another map on each node—a **backup storage**.

Backup storage is used to store backup copies of cache entries, in order to ensure that no data is lost in the case of a node failure. Coherence ensures that backup copies of primary entries from a particular node are stored not only on a different node, but also on a different physical server if possible. This is necessary in order to ensure that data is safe even in the case of hardware failure, in which case all the nodes on that physical machine would fail simultaneously.

You can configure the number of backup copies Coherence should create. The default setting of one backup copy, as the preceding diagram shows, is the most frequently used configuration. However, if the objects can be easily restored from a persistent data store, you might choose to set the number of backup copies to zero, which will have a positive impact on the overall memory usage and the number of objects that can be stored in the cluster.

You can also increase the number of backup copies to more than one, but this is not recommended by Oracle and is rarely done in practice. The reason for this is that it guards against a very unlikely scenario—that two or more physical machines will fail at exactly the same time.

The chances are that you will either lose a single physical machine, in the case of hardware failure, or a whole cluster within a data center, in the case of catastrophic failure. A single backup copy, on a different physical box, is all you need in the former case, while in the latter no number of backup copies will be enough—you will need to implement much broader disaster recovery solution and guard against it by implementing cluster-to-cluster replication across multiple data centers.

If you use backups, that means that each partitioned cache write will actually require at least two network calls: one to write the object into the backing map of the primary storage node and one or more to write it into the backup storage of each backup node.

This makes partitioned cache writes somewhat slower than reads, but they still execute in constant time and are significantly faster than replicated cache writes.

Data set size

Because each node stores only a small (1/N) portion of the data set, the size of the data set is limited only by the total amount of space that is available to all the nodes in the cluster. This allows you to manage very large data sets in memory, and to scale the cluster to handle growing data sets by simply adding more nodes. Support for very large in-memory data sets (potentially terabytes in Coherence 3.5) is one of the biggest advantages of a partitioned over a replicated cache, and is often the main reason to choose it.

That said, it is important to realize that the actual amount of data you can store is significantly lower than the total amount of RAM in the cluster. Some of the reasons for this are obvious—if your data set is 1 GB and you have one backup copy for each object, you need at least 2 GB of RAM. However, there is more to it than that.

For one, your operating system and Java runtime will use some memory. How much exactly varies widely across operating systems and JVM implementations, but it won't be zero in any case. Second, the cache indexes you create will need some memory. Depending on the number of indexes and the size of the indexed properties and corresponding cache keys, this might amount to a significant quantity. Finally, you need to leave enough free space for execution of both Coherence code and your own code within each JVM, or a frequent full garbage collection will likely bring everything to a standstill, or worse yet, you will run out of memory and most likely bring the whole cluster down—when one node fails in a low-memory situation, it will likely have a domino effect on other nodes as they try to accommodate more data than they can handle.

Because of this, it is important that you size the cluster properly and use cache expiration and eviction policies to control the amount of data in the cache.

Fault tolerance

As we discussed in the section on write performance, a Partitioned Cache service allows you to keep one or more backups of cache data in order to prevent data loss in the case of a node failure.

When a node fails, the Partitioned Cache service will notify all other nodes to promote backup copies of the data that the failed node had primary responsibility for, and to create new backup copies on different nodes.

When the failed node recovers, or a new node joins the cluster, the Partitioned Cache service will fail back some of the data to it by repartitioning the cluster and asking all of the existing members to move some of their data to the new node.

When to use it?

It should be obvious by now that the partitioned cache should be your topology of choice for large, growing data sets, and write-intensive applications.

However, as I mentioned earlier, there are several Coherence features that are built on top of partitioned cache that make it preferable for many read-intensive applications as well. We will discuss one of these features in detail next and briefly touch upon the second one, which will be covered in a lot more detail later in the book.

Near cache

A **near cache** is a hybrid, two-tier caching topology that uses a combination of a local, size-limited cache in the front tier, and a partitioned cache in the back tier to achieve the best of both worlds: the zero-latency read access of a replicated cache and the linear scalability of a partitioned cache.

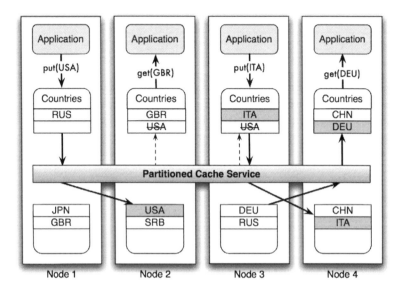

Basically, the near cache is a named cache implementation that caches a subset of the data locally and responds to read requests for the data within that subset directly, without asking the Partitioned Cache service to handle the request. This eliminates both network access and serialization overhead associated with the partitioned cache topology, and allows applications to obtain data objects at the same speed as with replicated caches.

On the other hand, the near cache simply delegates cache writes to the partitioned cache behind it, so the write performance is almost as good as with the partitioned cache (there is some extra overhead to invalidate entries in the front cache).

Near cache invalidation strategies

One problem typically associated with locally cached data is that it could become stale as the master data in the backend store changes. For example, if a near cache on a node A has object X cached locally, and node B updates object X in the cluster, the application running on node A (and other nodes that have object X cached locally) might end up holding a stale, and potentially incorrect, version of object X...

Fortunately, Coherence provides several invalidation strategies that allow the front tier of a near cache to evict stale objects based on the changes to the master copy of those objects, in a back-tier partitioned cache.

None

This strategy, as its name says, doesn't actually do anything to evict stale data.

The reason for that is that for some applications it doesn't really matter if the data is somewhat out of date. For example, you might have an e-commerce website that displays the current quantity in stock for each product in a catalog. It is usually not critical that this number is always completely correct—a certain degree of staleness is OK.

However, you probably don't want to keep using the stale data forever. So, you need to configure the front-tier cache to use time-based expiration with this strategy, based on how current your data needs to be.

The main benefit of the **None** strategy is that it scales extremely well, as there is no extra overhead that is necessary to keep the data in sync, so you should seriously consider it if your application can allow some degree of data staleness.

Present

The **Present** strategy uses event listeners to evict the front cache data automatically when the data in a back-tier cache changes.

It does that by registering a key-based listener for each entry that is *present* in its front cache (thus the name). As soon as one of those entries changes in a back cache or gets deleted, the near cache receives an event notification and evicts the entry from its front cache. This ensures that the next time an application requests that particular entry, the latest copy is retrieved from the back cache and cached locally until the next invalidation event is received.

This strategy has some overhead, as it registers as many event listeners with the partitioned cache as there are items in the front cache. This requires both processing cycles within the cluster to determine if an event should be sent, and network access for the listener registration and deregistration, as well as for the event notifications themselves.

One thing to keep in mind is that the invalidation events are sent asynchronously, which means that there is still a time window (albeit very small, typically in the low milliseconds range) during which the value in the front cache might be stale. This is usually acceptable, but if you need to ensure that the value read is absolutely current, you can achieve that by locking it explicitly before the read. That will require a network call to lock the entry in the back cache, but it will ensure that you read the latest version.

All

Just like the Present strategy, the **All** strategy uses Coherence events to keep the front cache from becoming stale. However, unlike the Present strategy, which registers one listener for each cache entry, the All strategy registers only a single listener with a back cache, but that single listener listens to all the events.

There is an obvious trade-off here: registering many listeners with the back cache, as the Present strategy does, will require more CPU cycles in the cluster to determine whether an event notification should be sent to a particular near cache, but every event received by the near cache will be useful. On the other hand, using a single listener to listen for all cache events, as the All strategy does, will require less cycles to determine if an event notification should be sent, but will result in a lot more notifications going to a near cache, usually over the network. Also, the near cache will then have to evaluate them and decide whether it should do anything about them or not, which requires more CPU cycles on a node running the near cache than the simple eviction as a result of an event notification for a Present strategy.

The choice of Present or All depends very much on the data access pattern. If the data is mostly read and typically updated by the node that has it cached locally (as is the case with session state data when sticky load balancing is used, for example), the Present strategy tends to work better. However, if the updates are frequent and there are many near caches with a high degree of overlap in their front caches, you will likely get better results using the All strategy, as many of the notifications will indeed be applicable to all of them.

That said, the best way to choose the strategy is to run some realistic performance tests using both and to see how they stack up.

Auto

The final invalidation strategy is the **Auto** strategy, which according to the documentation "switches between Present and All based on the cache statistics". Unfortunately, while that might have been the goal, the current implementation simply defaults to All, and there are indications that it might change in the future to default to Present instead.

This wouldn't be too bad on its own, but the problem is that Auto is also the default strategy for near cache invalidation. That means that if its implementation does indeed change in the future, all of the near caches using default invalidation strategy will be affected.

Because of this, you should always specify the invalidation strategy when configuring a near cache. You should choose between Present and All if event-based invalidation is required, or use None if it isn't.

When to use it?

The near cache allows you to achieve the read performance of a replicated cache as well as the write performance and scalability of a partitioned cache. This makes it the best topology choice for the read-mostly or balanced read-write caches that need to support data sets of any size.

This description will likely fit many of the most important caches within your application, so you should expect to use near cache topology quite a bit.

Continuous Query Cache

The **Continuous Query Cache** (CQC) is conceptually very similar to a near cache. For one, it also has a zero-latency front cache that holds a subset of the data, and a slower but larger back cache, typically a partitioned cache, that holds all the data. Second, just like the near cache, it registers a listener with a back cache and updates its front cache based on the event notifications it receives.

However, there are several major differences as well:

- CQC populates its front cache based on a query as soon as it is created, unlike the near cache, which only caches items after they have been requested by the application.

- CQC registers a query-based listener with a back cache, which means that its contents changes dynamically as the data in the back cache changes. For example, if you create a CQC based on a Coherence query that shows all open trade orders, as the trade orders are processed and their status changes they will automatically disappear from a CQC. Similarly, any new orders that are inserted into the back cache with a status set to Open will automatically appear in the CQC. Basically, CQC allows you to have a live dynamic view of the filtered subset of data in a partitioned cache.

- CQC can only be created programmatically, using the Coherence API. It cannot be configured within a cache configuration descriptor.

Because of the last point, we will postpone the detailed discussion on the CQC until we cover both cache events and queries in more detail, but keep in mind that it can be used to achieve a similar result to that which a near cache allows you to achieve via configuration: bringing a subset of the data closer to the application, in order to allow extremely fast, zero-latency read access to it without sacrificing write performance.

It is also an excellent replacement for a replicated cache—by simply specifying a query that returns all objects, you can bring the whole data set from a back cache into the application's process, which will allow you to access it at in-memory speed.

Backing maps

Now that we have covered various cache topologies, it is time to complete the puzzle by learning more about **backing maps**.

As you learned earlier, the backing map is where cache data within the cluster is actually stored, so it is a very important piece within the Coherence architecture. So far we have assumed that a backing map stores all the data in memory, which will be the case for many applications as it provides by far the best performance. However, there are situations where storing all the data in memory is either impossible, because the data set is simply too big, or impractical, because a large part of the data is rarely accessed and there is no need to have the fastest possible access to it at all times.

One of the nicest things about Coherence is that it is extremely flexible and configurable. You can combine different pieces that are available out of the box, such as caching services and backing maps, in many different ways to solve many difficult distributed data management problems. If nothing fits the bill, you can also write your own, custom implementations of various components, including backing maps.

However, there is rarely a need to do so, as Coherence ships with a number of useful backing map implementations that can be used to store data both on-heap as well as off-heap. We will discuss all of them in the following sections so you can make an informed decision when configuring backing maps for your caches.

Local cache

The **local cache** is commonly used both as the backing map for replicated and partitioned caches and as a front cache for near and continuous query caches. It stores all the data on the heap, which means that it provides by far the fastest access speed, both read and write, compared to other backing map implementations.

The local cache can be size-limited to a specific number of entries, and will automatically prune itself when the limit is reached, based on the specified eviction policy: **LRU (Least Recently Used)**, **LFU (Least Frequently Used)**, or **HYBRID**, which is the default and uses a combination of LRU and LFU to determine which items to evict. Of course, if none of these built-in eviction policies works for you, Coherence allows you to implement and use a custom one.

You can also configure the local cache to expire cache items based on their age, which is especially useful when it is used as a front cache for a near cache with invalidation strategy set to none.

Finally, the local cache implements full `Map`, `CacheMap`, and `ObservableMap` APIs, which means that you can use it within your application as a more powerful `HashMap`, which in addition to the standard `Map` operations supports item expiration and event notifications, while providing fully thread-safe, highly concurrent access to its contents.

External backing map

The **external backing map** allows you to store cache items off-heap, thus allowing far greater storage capacity, at the cost of somewhat-to-significantly worse performance.

There are several pluggable storage strategies that you can use with an external backing map, which allow you to configure where and how the data will be stored. These strategies are implemented as **storage managers**:

- **NIO Memory Manager**: This uses an off-heap NIO buffer for storage. This means that it is not affected by the garbage collection times, which makes it a good choice for situations where you want to have fast access to data, but don't want to increase the size or the number of Coherence JVMs on the server.

- **NIO File Manager**: This uses NIO memory-mapped files for data storage. This option is generally not recommended as its performance can vary widely depending on the OS and JVM used. If you plan to use it, make sure that you run some performance tests to make sure it will work well in your environment.

- **Berkeley DB Store Manager**: This uses Berkeley DB Java Edition embedded database to implement on-disk storage of cache items.

In addition to these concrete storage manager implementations, Coherence ships with a wrapper storage manager that allows you to make write operations asynchronous for any of the store managers listed earlier. You can also create and use your own custom storage manager by creating a class that implements the `com.tangosol.io.BinaryStoreManager` interface.

Just like the local cache, the external backing map can be size limited and can be configured to expire cache items based on their age. However, keep in mind that the eviction of cache items from disk-based caches can be very expensive. If you need to use it, you should seriously consider using the **paged external** backing map instead.

Paged external backing map

The **paged external backing map** is very similar to the external backing map described previously. They both support the same set of storage managers, so your storage options are exactly the same. The big difference between the two is that a paged external backing map uses paging to optimize LRU eviction.

Basically, instead of storing cache items in a single large file, a paged backing map breaks it up into a series of *pages*. Each page is a separate store, created by the specified store manager. The page that was last created is considered current and all write operations are performed against that page until a new one is created.

You can configure both how many pages of data should be stored and the amount of time between page creations. The combination of these two parameters determines how long the data is going to be kept in the cache. For example, if you wanted to cache data for an hour, you could configure the paged backing map to use six pages and to create a new page every ten minutes, or to use four pages with new one being created every fifteen minutes.

Once the page count limit is reached, the items in the oldest page are considered expired and are evicted from the cache, one page at a time. This is significantly more efficient than the individual delete operations against the disk-based cache, as in the case of a regular external backing map.

Overflow backing map

The **overflow backing map** is a composite backing map with two tiers: a fast, size-limited, in-memory front tier, and a slower, but potentially much larger back tier on a disk. At first sight, this seems to be a perfect way to improve read performance for the most recently used data while allowing you to store much larger data sets than could possibly fit in memory.

However, using an overflow backing map in such a way is not recommended. The problem is that the access to a disk-based back tier is much slower than the access to in-memory data. While this might not be significant when accessing individual items, it can have a huge negative impact on operations that work with large chunks of data, such as cluster repartitioning.

A Coherence cluster can be sized dynamically, by simply adding nodes or removing nodes from it. The whole process is completely transparent and it does not require any changes in configuration—you simply start new nodes or shut down existing ones. Coherence will automatically rebalance the cluster to ensure that each node handles approximately the same amount of data.

When that happens, whole partitions need to be moved from one node to another, which can be quite slow when disk-based caches are used, as is almost always the case with the overflow backing map. During the repartitioning requests targeted to partitions that are being moved are blocked, and the whole cluster might seem a bit sluggish, or in the worst case scenario completely stalled, so it is important to keep repartitioning as short as possible.

Because of this, it is recommended that you use an overflow map only when you are certain that most of the data will always fit in memory, but need to guard against occasional situations where some data might need to be moved to disk because of a temporary memory shortage. Basically, the overflow backing map can be used as a substitute for an eviction policy in these situations.

If, on the other hand, you need to support much larger data sets than could possibly fit in memory, you should use a **read-write backing map** instead.

Read-write backing map

The **read-write backing map** is another composite backing map implementation. However, unlike the overflow backing map, which has a two-tiered cache structure, the read-write backing map has a single internal cache (usually a local cache) and either a **cache loader**, which allows it to load data from the external data source on cache misses, or a **cache store**, which also provides the ability to update data in the external data store on cache puts.

As such, the read-write backing map is a key enabler of the read-through/ write-through architecture that places Coherence as an intermediate layer between the application and the data store, and allows for a complete decoupling between the two. It is also a great solution for situations where not all the data fits in memory, as it does not have the same limitations as overflow backing map does.

The key to making a read-write backing map work is to use it in front of a shared data store that can be accessed from all the nodes. The most obvious and commonly used data source that fits that description is a relational database, so Coherence provides several cache loader and cache **store** implementations for relational database access out of the box, such as JPA, Oracle TopLink, and Hibernate.

However, a read-write backing map is not limited to a relational database as a backend by any means. It can also be used in front of web services, mainframe applications, a clustered file system, or any other shared data source that can be accessed from Java.

Partitioned backing map

By default, a single backing map is used to store the entries from all cache partitions on a single node. This imposes certain restrictions on how much data each node can store.

For example, if you choose to use local cache as a backing map, the size of the backing map on a single node will be limited by the node's heap size. In most cases, this configuration will allow you to store up to 300-500 MB per node, because of the heap size limitations discussed earlier.

However, even if you decide to use NIO buffer for off-heap storage, you will be limited by the maximum direct buffer size Java can allocate, which is 2 GB (as a 32-bit integer is used to specify the size of the buffer). While you can still scale the size of the cache by adding more nodes, there is a practical limit to how far you can go. The number of CPUs on each physical machine will determine the upper limit for the number on nodes you can run, so you will likely need 100 or more physical boxes and 500 Coherence nodes in order to store 1 TB of data in a single cache.

In order to solve this problem and support in-memory caches in the terabytes range without increasing the node count unnecessarily, the **partitioned backing map** was introduced in Coherence 3.5.

The partitioned backing map contains one backing map instance for each cache partition, which allows you to scale the cache size by simply increasing the number of partitions for a given cache. Even though the theoretical limit is now 2 GB per partition, you have to keep in mind that a partition is a unit of transfer during cache rebalancing, so you will want to keep it significantly smaller (the officially recommended size for a single partition is 50 MB).

That means that you need to divide the expected cache size by 50 MB to determine the number of partitions. For example, if you need to store 1 TB of data in the cache, you will need at least 20,972 partitions. However, because the number of partitions should always be a prime number, you should set it to the next higher prime number, which in this case is 20,981 (you can find the list of first 10,000 prime numbers, from 1 to 104,729, at `http://primes.utm.edu/lists/small/10000.txt`).

The important thing to keep in mind is that the number of partitions has nothing to do with the number of nodes in the cluster—you can spread these 20 thousand plus partitions across 10 or 100 nodes, and 5 or 50 physical machines. You can even put them all on a single box, which will likely be the case during testing.

By making cache size dependent solely on the number of partitions, you can fully utilize the available RAM on each physical box and reach 1 TB cache size with a significantly smaller number of physical machines and Coherence nodes. For example, 50 nodes, running on 10 physical machines with 128 GB of RAM each, could easily provide you with 1 TB of in-memory storage.

Partitioned backing map and garbage collection

I mentioned earlier that you need to keep heap size for each Coherence JVM in the 1-2 GB range, in order to avoid long GC pauses.

However, this is typically not an issue with a partitioned backing map, because it is usually used in combination with off-heap, NIO buffer-based storage.

Cache configuration

Now that you understand the available cache topologies and data storage options, let's return to the subject we started this chapter with.

What you will realize when you start identifying entities within your application and planning caches for them is that many of those entities have similar data access patterns. Some will fall into the read-only or read-mostly category, such as reference, and you can decide to use either a replicated cache or a partitioned cache fronted by a near or continuous query cache for them.

Others will fall into a transactional data category, which will tend to grow in size over time and will have a mixture of reads and writes. These will typically be some of the most important entities that the application manages, such as invoices, orders, and customers. You will use partitioned caches to manage those entities, possibly fronted with a near cache depending on the ratio of reads to writes.

You might also have some write-mostly data, such as audit trail or log entries, but the point is that in the end, when you finish analyzing your application's data model, you will likely end up with a handful of entity categories, even though you might have many entity types.

If you had to configure a cache for each of these entity types separately, you would end up with a lot of repeated configuration, which would be very cumbersome to maintain if you needed to change something for each entity that belongs to a particular category.

This is why the Coherence cache configuration has two parts: **caching schemes** and **cache mappings**. The former allows you to define a single configuration template for all entities in a particular category, while the latter enables you to map specific named caches to a particular caching scheme.

Caching schemes

Caching schemes are used to define cache topology, as well as other cache configuration parameters, such as which backing map to use, how to limit cache size and expire cache items, where to store backup copies of the data, and in the case of a read-write backing map, even how to load data into the cache from the persistent store and how to write it back into the store.

While there are only a few top-level caching schemes you are likely to use, which pretty much map directly to the cache topologies we discussed in the first part of this chapter, there are many possible ways to configure them. Covering all possible configurations would easily fill a book on its own, so we will not go that far. In the remainder of this chapter we will look at configuration examples for the commonly used cache schemes, but even for those I will not describe every possible configuration option.

The Coherence *Developer's Guide* is your best resource on various options available for cache configuration using any of the available schemes, and you should now have enough background information to understand various configuration options available for each of them. I strongly encourage you to review the *Appendix D: Cache Configuration Elements* section in the *Developer's Guide* for more information about all configuration parameters for a particular cache topology and backing map you are interested in.

Distributed cache scheme

Let's look at an example of a caching scheme definition under a microscope, to get a better understanding of what it is made of.

```
<distributed-scheme>
  <scheme-name>example-distributed</scheme-name>
  <service-name>DistributedCache</service-name>

  <backing-map-scheme>
    <local-scheme>
      <scheme-ref>example-binary-backing-map</scheme-ref>
    </local-scheme>
  </backing-map-scheme>

  <autostart>true</autostart>
</distributed-scheme>
```

The preceding code is taken directly from the sample cache configuration file that is shiped with Coherence, and you have seen it before, when you issued the `cache countries` command in the Coherence Console in the previous chapter.

The top-level element, `distributed-scheme`, tells us that any cache that uses this scheme will use a **partitioned** topology (this is one of those unfortunate instances where **distributed** is used instead of partitioned for backwards compatibility reasons).

The `scheme-name` element allows us to specify a name for the caching scheme, which we can later use within cache mappings and when referencing a caching scheme from another caching scheme, as we'll do shortly.

The `service-name` element is used to specify the name of the cache service that all caches using this particular scheme will belong to. While the service type is determined by the root element of the scheme definition, the service name can be any name that is meaningful to you. However, there are two things you should keep in mind when choosing a service name for a scheme:

- Coherence provides a way to ensure that the related objects from different caches are stored on the same node, which can be very beneficial from a performance standpoint. For example, you might want to ensure that the account and all transactions for that account are collocated. You will learn how to do that in the next chapter, but for now you should remember that this feature requires that all related caches belong to the same cache service. This will automatically be the case for all caches that are mapped to the same cache scheme, but in the cases when you have different schemes defined for related caches, you will need to ensure that service name for both schemes is the same.

- All caches that belong to the same cache service share a pool of threads. In order to avoid deadlocks, Coherence prohibits re-entrant calls from the code executing on a cache service thread into the same cache service. One way to work around this is to use separate cache services. For example, you might want to use separate services for reference and transactional caches, which will allow you to access reference data without any restrictions from the code executing on a service thread of a transactional cache.

The next element, `backing-map-scheme`, defines the type of the backing map we want all caches mapped to this caching scheme to use. In this example, we are telling Coherence to use local cache as a backing map. Note that while many named caches can be mapped to this particular caching scheme, each of them will have its own instance of the local cache as a backing map. The configuration simply tells the associated cache service which scheme to use as a **template** when creating a backing map instance for the cache.

The `scheme-ref` element within the `local-scheme` tells us that the configuration for the backing map should be loaded from another caching scheme definition, `example-binary-backing-map`. This is a very useful feature, as it allows you to compose new schemes from the existing ones, without having to repeat yourself.

Finally, the `autostart` element determines if the cache service for the scheme will be started automatically when the node starts. If it is omitted or set to false, the service will start the first time any cache that belongs to it is accessed. Normally, you will want all the services on your cache servers to start automatically.

Local cache scheme

The scheme definition shown earlier references the local cache scheme named `example-binary-backing-scheme` as its backing map. Let's see what the referenced definition looks like:

```
<local-scheme>
  <scheme-name>example-binary-backing-map</scheme-name>

  <eviction-policy>HYBRID</eviction-policy>
  <high-units>{back-size-limit 0}</high-units>
  <unit-calculator>BINARY</unit-calculator>
  <expiry-delay>{back-expiry 1h}</expiry-delay>
  <flush-delay>1m</flush-delay>

  <cachestore-scheme></cachestore-scheme>
</local-scheme>
```

You can see that the `local-scheme` allows you to configure various options for the local cache, such as eviction policy, the maximum number of units to keep within the cache, as well as expiry and flush delay.

The `high-units` and `unit-calculator` elements are used together to limit the size of the cache, as the meaning of the former is defined by the value of the latter. Coherence uses **unit calculator** to determine the "size" of cache entries. There are two built-in unit calculators: **fixed** and **binary**.

The difference between the two is that the first one simply treats each cache entry as a single unit, allowing you to limit the number of objects in the cache, while the second one uses the size of a cache entry (in bytes) to represent the number of units it consumes. While the latter gives you much better control over the memory consumption of each cache, its use is constrained by the fact that the entries need to be in a serialized binary format, which means that it can only be used to limit the size of a partitioned cache.

In other cases you will either have to use the fixed calculator to limit the number of objects in the cache, or write your own implementation that can determine the appropriate unit count for your objects (if you decide to write a calculator that attempts to determine the size of deserialized objects on heap, you might want to consider using `com.tangosol.net.cache.SimpleMemoryCalculator` as a starting point).

One important thing to note in the example on the previous page is the use of *macro parameters* to define the size limit and expiration for the cache, such as {back-size-limit 0} and {back-expiry 1h}. The first value within the curly braces is the name of the macro parameter to use, while the second value is the default value that should be used if the parameter with the specified name is not defined. You will see how macro parameters and their values are defined shortly, when we discuss cache mappings.

Near cache scheme

Near cache is a composite cache, and requires us to define separate schemes for the front and back tier. We could reuse both scheme definitions we have seen so far to create a definition for a near cache:

```
<near-scheme>
  <scheme-name>example-near</scheme-name>

  <front-scheme>
    <local-scheme>
      <scheme-ref>example-binary-backing-map</scheme-ref>
    </local-scheme>
  </front-scheme>

  <back-scheme>
    <distributed-scheme>
      <scheme-ref>example-distributed</scheme-ref>
    </distributed-scheme>
  </back-scheme>

  <invalidation-strategy>present</invalidation-strategy>
  <autostart>true</autostart>
</near-scheme>
```

Unfortunately, the `example-binary-backing-map` won't quite work as a front cache in the preceding definition—it uses the binary unit calculator, which cannot be used in the front tier of a near cache. In order to solve the problem, we can override the settings from the referenced scheme:

```
<front-scheme>
  <local-scheme>
    <scheme-ref>example-binary-backing-map</scheme-ref>
    <high-units>{front-size-limit 0}</high-units>
    <unit-calculator>FIXED</unit-calculator>
  </local-scheme>
</front-scheme>
```

However, in this case it would probably make more sense not to use reference for the front scheme definition at all, or to create and reference a separate local scheme for the front cache.

Read-write backing map scheme

Using local cache as a backing map is very convenient during development and testing, but more likely than not you will want your data to be persisted as well. If that's the case, you can configure a read-write backing map as a backing map for your distributed cache:

```
<distributed-scheme>
  <scheme-name>example-distributed</scheme-name>
  <service-name>DistributedCache</service-name>

  <backing-map-scheme>
    <read-write-backing-map-scheme>
      <internal-cache-scheme>
        <local-scheme/>
      </internal-cache-scheme>
      <cachestore-scheme>
        <class-scheme>
          <class-name>
            com.tangosol.coherence.jpa.JpaCacheStore
          </class-name>
          <init-params>
            <init-param>
              <param-type>java.lang.String</param-type>
              <param-value>{cache-name}</param-value>
            </init-param>
            <init-param>
```

```
            <param-type>java.lang.String</param-type>
            <param-value>{class-name}</param-value>
          </init-param>
          <init-param>
            <param-type>java.lang.String</param-type>
            <param-value>PersistenceUnit</param-value>
          </init-param>
        </init-params>
      </class-scheme>
    </cachestore-scheme>
    </read-write-backing-map-scheme>
  </backing-map-scheme>

  <autostart>true</autostart>
</distributed-scheme>
```

The read-write backing map defined previously uses unlimited local cache to store the data, and a JPA-compliant cache store implementation that will be used to persist the data on cache puts, and to retrieve it from the database on cache misses.

We will discuss JPA cache store in much more detail in *Chapter 8, Implementing the Persistence Layer*, but from the preceding example it should be fairly obvious that its constructor accepts three arguments: entity name, which is in this example equivalent to a cache name, fully qualified name of entity class, and the name of the JPA persistence unit defined in the `persistence.xml` file.

Partitioned backing map

As we discussed earlier, the partitioned backing map is your best option for very large caches. The following example demonstrates how you could configure a partitioned backing map that will allow you to store 1 TB of data in a 50-node cluster, as we discussed earlier:

```
<distributed-scheme>
  <scheme-name>large-scheme</scheme-name>
  <service-name>LargeCacheService</service-name>

  <partition-count>20981</partition-count>

  <backing-map-scheme>
    <partitioned>true</partitioned>
    <external-scheme>
      <high-units>20</high-units>
      <unit-calculator>BINARY</unit-calculator>
      <unit-factor>1073741824</unit-factor>
```

```
    <nio-memory-manager>
      <initial-size>1MB</initial-size>
      <maximum-size>50MB</maximum-size>
    </nio-memory-manager>
  </external-scheme>
</backing-map-scheme>

<backup-storage>
  <type>off-heap</type>
  <initial-size>1MB</initial-size>
  <maximum-size>50MB</maximum-size>
</backup-storage>

<autostart>true</autostart>
</distributed-scheme>
```

We have configured `partition-count` to 20,981, which will allow us to store 1 TB of data in the cache while keeping the partition size down to 50 MB.

We have then used the `partitioned` element within the backing map scheme definition to let Coherence know that it should use the partitioned backing map implementation instead of the default one.

The `external-scheme` element is used to configure the maximum size of the backing map as a whole, as well as the storage for each partition. Each partition uses an NIO buffer with the initial size of 1 MB and a maximum size of 50 MB.

The backing map as a whole is limited to 20 GB using a combination of `high-units`, `unit-calculator`, and `unit-factor` values. Because we are storing serialized objects off-heap, we can use binary calculator to limit cache size in bytes. However, the `high-units` setting is internally represented by a 32-bit integer, so the highest value we could specify for it would be 2 GB.

In order allow for larger cache sizes while preserving backwards compatibility, Coherence engineers decided not to widen `high-units` to 64 bits. Instead, they introduced the `unit-factor` setting, which is nothing more than a multiplier for the `high-units` value. In the preceding example, the `unit-factor` is set to 1 GB, which in combination with the `high-units` setting of 20 limits cache size per node to 20 GB.

Finally, when using a partitioned backing map to support very large caches off-heap, we cannot use the default, on-heap backup storage. The backup storage is always managed per partition, so we had to configure it to use off-heap buffers of the same size as primary storage buffers.

Partitioned read-write backing map

Finally, we can use a partitioned read-write backing map to support automatic persistence for very large caches. The following example is really just a combination of the previous two examples, so I will not discuss the details. It is also a good illustration of the flexibility Coherence provides when it comes to cache configuration.

```
<distributed-scheme>
  <scheme-name>large-persistent-scheme</scheme-name>
  <service-name>LargePersistentCacheService</service-name>

  <partition-count>20981</partition-count>

  <backing-map-scheme>
    <partitioned>true</partitioned>
    <read-write-backing-map-scheme>
      <internal-cache-scheme>
        <external-scheme>
          <high-units>20</high-units>
          <unit-calculator>BINARY</unit-calculator>
          <unit-factor>1073741824</unit-factor>
          <nio-memory-manager>
            <initial-size>1MB</initial-size>
            <maximum-size>50MB</maximum-size>
          </nio-memory-manager>
        </external-scheme>
      </internal-cache-scheme>
      <cachestore-scheme>
        <class-scheme>
          <class-name>
            com.tangosol.coherence.jpa.JpaCacheStore
          </class-name>
          <init-params>
            <init-param>
              <param-type>java.lang.String</param-type>
              <param-value>{cache-name}</param-value>
            </init-param>
            <init-param>
              <param-type>java.lang.String</param-type>
              <param-value>{class-name}</param-value>
            </init-param>
            <init-param>
```

```
              <param-type>java.lang.String</param-type>
              <param-value>SigfePOC</param-value>
            </init-param>
          </init-params>
        </class-scheme>
      </cachestore-scheme>
    </read-write-backing-map-scheme>
  </backing-map-scheme>

  <backup-storage>
    <type>off-heap</type>
    <initial-size>1MB</initial-size>
    <maximum-size>50MB</maximum-size>
  </backup-storage>

  <autostart>true</autostart>
</distributed-scheme>
```

This concludes our discussion of caching schemes—it is now time to see how we can map our named caches to them.

Cache mappings

Cache mappings allow you to map cache names to the appropriate caching schemes:

```
<cache-mapping>
  <cache-name>repl-*</cache-name>
  <scheme-name>example-replicated</scheme-name>
</cache-mapping>
```

You can map either a full cache name, or a name pattern, as in the previous example. What this definition is basically saying is that whenever you call the CacheFactory. getCache method with a cache name that starts with repl-, a caching scheme with the name example-replicated will be used to configure the cache.

Coherence will evaluate cache mappings in order, and will map the cache name using the first pattern that matches. That means that you need to specify cache mappings from the most specific to the least specific.

Cache mappings can also be used to specify macro parameters used within a caching scheme definition:

```
<cache-mapping>
  <cache-name>near-accounts</cache-name>
  <scheme-name>example-near</scheme-name>
  <init-params>
    <init-param>
      <param-name>front-size-limit</param-name>
      <param-value>1000</param-value>
    </init-param>
  </init-params>
</cache-mapping>

<cache-mapping>
  <cache-name>dist-*</cache-name>
  <scheme-name>example-distributed</scheme-name>
  <init-params>
    <init-param>
      <param-name>back-size-limit</param-name>
      <param-value>8388608</param-value>
    </init-param>
  </init-params>
</cache-mapping>
```

In the preceding example, we are using macro parameter `front-size-limit` to ensure that we never cache more than thousand objects in the front tier of the `near-accounts` cache. In a similar fashion, we use `back-size-limit` to limit the size of the backing map of each partitioned cache whose name starts with `dist-` to 8 MB.

One thing to keep in mind when setting size limits is that all the numbers apply to a single node—if there are 10 nodes in the cluster, each partitioned cache would be able to store up to 80 MB. This makes it easy to scale the cache size by simply adding more nodes with the same configuration.

Sample cache configuration

As you can see in the previous sections, Coherence cache configuration is very flexible. It allows you both to reuse scheme definitions in order to avoid code duplication, and to override some of the parameters from the referenced definition when necessary.

Unfortunately, this flexibility also introduces a level of complexity into cache configuration that can overwhelm new Coherence users—there are so many options that you don't know where to start. My advice to everyone learning Coherence or starting a new project is to keep things simple in the beginning.

Whenever I start a new Coherence project, I use the following cache configuration file as a starting point:

```xml
<?xml version="1.0"?>

<!DOCTYPE cache-config SYSTEM "cache-config.dtd">

<cache-config>
  <caching-scheme-mapping>
    <cache-mapping>
      <cache-name>*</cache-name>
      <scheme-name>default-partitioned</scheme-name>
    </cache-mapping>
  </caching-scheme-mapping>
  <caching-schemes>

    <distributed-scheme>
      <scheme-name>default-partitioned</scheme-name>
      <service-name>DefaultPartitioned</service-name>

      <serializer>
        <class-name>
          com.tangosol.io.pof.ConfigurablePofContext
        </class-name>
        <init-params>
          <init-param>
            <param-type>java.lang.String</param-type>
            <param-value>pof-config.xml</param-value>
          </init-param>
        </init-params>
      </serializer>

      <backing-map-scheme>
        <local-scheme/>
      </backing-map-scheme>

      <autostart>true</autostart>
    </distributed-scheme>

  </caching-schemes>
</cache-config>
```

Everything but the serializer element, which will be discussed in the next chapter, should look familiar by now. We are mapping all caches to a default-partitioned cache scheme, which uses unlimited local cache as a backing map.

While this is far from what the cache configuration usually looks like by the end of the project, it is a good start and will allow you to focus on the business problem you are trying to solve. As the project progresses and you gain a better understanding of the requirements, you will refine the previous configuration to include listeners, persistence, additional cache schemes, and so on.

Summary

Coherence allows you to choose from several cache topologies. You can use replicated caches to provide fast access to read-only data, or partitioned caches to support large data sets and ensure that both reads and writes are performed in constant time, regardless of the cluster size, allowing for linear scalability. You can also use near and continuous query caches in front of a partitioned cache to get the best of both worlds.

There are also many options when it comes to data storage. You can use on-heap and off-heap storage, memory mapped files, or even disk-based storage. You can use a partitioned backing map to support very large data sets, and a read-write backing map to enable transparent loading and persistence of objects.

However, it is good to keep things simple in the beginning, so start by mapping all caches to a partitioned scheme that uses unlimited local cache as a backing map. You can refine cache configuration to better fit your needs (without having to modify the code) as your application starts to take form, so there is no reason to spend a lot of time up front on an elaborate cache scheme design.

Now that you know how to configure Coherence caches, it's time to learn how to design domain objects that will be stored in them.

4
Implementing
Domain Objects

In this chapter, you will learn how to implement classes from your domain model in order to make them work well with Coherence. While for the most part you can design and implement your objects the way you normally do, the fact that they will be stored within a distributed cache does impose some additional requirements and restrictions.

For one, your objects have to be serializable in order to be moved across the process and machine boundaries. The easiest way to accomplish this is by implementing the `java.io.Serializable` interface, but there are several alternative serialization mechanisms you can use with Coherence that perform better and result in a significantly smaller binary representation of your data. The latter is extremely important when you are working with an in-memory data grid, such as Coherence, as the more compact serialization format can save you quite a bit of money in terms of the hardware and software licenses you need.

Second, you need to plan ahead to allow for easy schema evolution of your data objects. While you don't have to worry about this too much when you use Coherence simply as a caching layer, many applications can benefit from using Coherence as a **system of record** and a database simply as a persistent data store. In those cases, it is typically undesirable, and sometimes even impossible, to bring the whole cluster down for an upgrade. Instead, you need to be able to upgrade the cluster node by node, while keeping the system as a whole fully operational and allowing multiple versions of the same classes to co-exist within the cluster. Coherence allows you to achieve this in a very effective way, but it does require a certain degree of assistance from you in order to make it happen.

Finally, you need to ensure that your application does not depend on sharing state (references to the same shared object) across multiple data objects. While dependence on the shared state is generally a bad idea and should be avoided, it will become your worst nightmare if your objects rely on it and you try to use them with Coherence (or any other distributed caching product, for that matter).

The reason for that is that your objects can share state only when they coexist within the same process. Once they get serialized and sent to another machine (which happens all the time in an application backed by a distributed cache), each one will have its own copy of the shared data, and will retain its own copy when deserialized.

We will discuss all of these topics shortly and you will learn how to make your objects good citizens of a Coherence cluster. But first, let's set the stage by defining the domain model for the sample application that will be used throughout the book.

Introducing the Coherent Bank sample application

If you are anything like me, you will agree that a good sample application is priceless. In this chapter, we will create the core domain model for Coherent Bank, a sample banking application that you can download from the book's website. We will continue to build it throughout the book, and I hope that you will find the end result as interesting to read as it was to write.

Oversimplification warning

I apologize in advance to the readers that write banking software for living—the requirements and the domain model that follow are severely constrained and oversimplified.

The goal is not to teach anyone how to write a banking application, but how to use Coherence. A banking application was chosen because most, if not all readers, are familiar with the problem domain, at least at the superficial level presented here.

Our sample application has three major components.

The first one is a customer-oriented online banking portal that allows customers to register, open accounts, pay bills, and view posted transactions. This is a typical Java web application that uses Spring MVC to implement REST services. We used Ext JS (www.extjs.com) to implement the UI, but you can easily replace it with the presentation technology of your choice.

The second component is a branch terminal application that is used by bank employees to check account balances and make cash deposits and withdrawals for the customers. This is a .NET desktop application written in C# that uses **Windows Presentation Foundation (WPF)** to implement the presentation layer.

Finally, no bank should be without ATMs, so we implemented a small command line application in C++ that emulates ATM deposits and withdrawals.

As you can see, the technical scope of the application is fairly broad, covering all three platforms that are supported by Coherence. While this does add some complexity to the sample application, please keep in mind that you don't have to read and understand the code for all three applications.

The bulk of the core logic for the application is implemented in Java, and that is what we'll focus on most. However, I do believe that it is important to show how that same logic can be invoked from .NET and C++ clients as well, and that the readers who need to build client applications using one of those two platforms will find the latter two examples very useful.

Coherent Bank requirements

In order to keep things simple despite the fact that we are creating a multi-platform application, we have decided to implement only a very small set of business requirements:

- A customer must be able to open one or more accounts.
- A customer must be able to deposit money into and withdraw money from the accounts either in the branch or using an ATM.
- A customer must be able to pay bills using an online banking portal.
- A customer must be able to view account transactions (deposits and withdrawals) for a given period.
- Withdrawal should only be allowed if there are sufficient funds in the account.
- Each account has a designated currency. All deposits and withdrawals in other currencies must be automatically converted to the account currency.

These requirements should be enough to make the implementation interesting without making it overly complex.

Coherent Bank domain model

Based on the previous requirements, we can define the following domain model to use as a starting point:

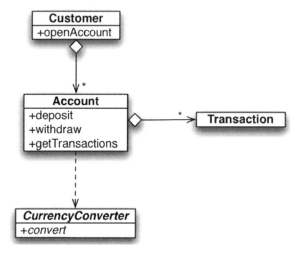

The preceding model is just a rough sketch containing the most important classes in the system. As we go along we will refine it and extend it, but for the time being this should be more than enough.

Domain model building blocks

If you have read *Domain Driven Design* by Eric Evans [DDD], much of the information in this section will simply refresh your knowledge of the domain model building blocks described by Eric, with a Coherence twist. If you haven't, this section will give you enough background information to allow you to identify various domain objects within the application, but I strongly suggest that you read Eric's book for a much more complete coverage of the topics presented here (and many others).

Rich versus Anemic domain models

The main argument Eric Evans makes in *Domain Driven Design* is that your domain objects should be used to implement business logic of your application, not just to hold data. While this logically makes perfect sense, it is not what most developers are used to, primarily because such architecture was discouraged by the J2EE spec, which pretty much required from you to turn your domain objects into property bags and implement all the logic in a higher-level service layer using session EJBs.

If you still develop the applications that way, you might be wondering if Coherence requires you to use rich domain objects. The short answer is: no, it does not. You can use any object with Coherence, as long as it is serializable, so you can easily use anemic domain objects as well.

The question, however, is why you would want to do that. If you are already creating custom classes for your objects, you might as well take the extra step and implement related behavior within them as well, instead of moving all the logic to a higher-level service layer. Otherwise, as Martin Fowler points out in his article **Anemic Domain Model** (`http://martinfowler.com/bliki/AnemicDomainModel.html`), you will be "robbing yourself blind and paying all the costs of a domain model without yielding any of the benefits".

After all, there isn't much you can achieve with an anemic domain object that you can't do using a more generic and readily available data structure, such as a map, so why even bother with custom objects if they are just dumb data holders?

In *Domain Driven Design*, Eric identifies a number of core building blocks of the domain model, such as **entities**, **aggregates**, **value objects**, **services**, **factories**, and **repositories**. The first three represent data objects in the model, and as such are the most important domain model artifacts from our perspective—they are what we will be storing in Coherence.

Entities and aggregates

An **entity** is an object that has an **identity**. The identity can be either a natural attribute of an object, such as the country code we used to identify `Country` objects in *Chapter 2, Getting Started*, or it can be a surrogate attribute that is generated by the system when the entity is first created. Regardless of the type of identity, what is important is that once an identity is assigned to an entity, it remains the same throughout its lifetime.

An **aggregate** is a special, composite entity type, which represents a containment relationship between an **aggregate root** and dependent **weak entities**. For example, an order contains one or more line items, and while both the order and each individual line item are entities in their own right, a single line item is only meaningful within the larger context of an order.

Entities and aggregates are the most important types of domain objects from the Coherence perspective, as they usually have one-to-one mapping to Coherence caches.

One of the most common mistakes that beginners make is to treat Coherence as an in-memory database and create caches that are too finely grained. For example, they might configure one cache for orders and a separate cache for line items.

While this makes perfect sense when using a relational database, it isn't the best approach when using Coherence. Aggregates represent units of consistency from a business perspective, and the easiest way to achieve atomicity and consistency when using Coherence is to limit the scope of mutating operations to a single cache entry. Because of this, you should almost always store whole aggregates as individual cache entries. In the previous example that we used, an order and all of its line items would be stored as a single cache entry in the `orders` cache.

One exception to this rule might be the case when the aggregate root contains an unbound, continuously growing collection of dependent entities, such as `Account` and `Transaction` items in our domain model. In this case, it makes sense to separate dependent entities into their own cache, in order to avoid infinite growth of the aggregate object and to allow different caching policies to be used (for example, we might decide to keep all the accounts in the cache at all times, but only the last 60 days of transactions for each account, in order to keep the amount of memory used by transactions relatively constant over time).

Implementing entities

The domain model for our banking application contains three entities so far: `Customer`, `Account`, and `Transaction`. The last two form an aggregate, with the `Account` as aggregate root.

Because an entity is such an important type of object within a Coherence application, we will define an interface that all our entities have to implement:

```
public interface Entity<T> {
    T getId();
}
```

The Entity interface is very simple, but it makes the fact that entities have an identity explicit. This is not strictly required, but it will come in handy on many occasions, such as when we implement repositories for our entities, as you'll see in a bit.

Entity implementation is quite simple for the most part: you define the attributes as you normally would and implement the necessary operations. In the case of the Account class, this might lead you to create something along these lines:

```java
public class Account
        implements Entity<Long>, Serializable {

    // data members
    private final Long m_id;
    private final Long m_customerId;
    private String m_description;
    private Money m_balance;
    private int m_lastTransactionId;

    // dependencies
    private transient CurrencyConverter m_currencyConverter;
    private transient TransactionRepository m_transactionRepository;

    // constructor, getters and setters omitted for brevity

    ...

    // core logic
    public Money withdraw(Money amount, String description)
            throws InsufficientFundsException {
        Money balance = m_balance;
        if (!balance.isSameCurrency(amount)) {
            CurrencyConversion conversion =
                getCurrencyConverter().convert(amount, getCurrency());
            amount = conversion.getConvertedAmount();
            description += " (" +
                conversion.getOriginalAmount() + " @ " +
                conversion.getExchangeRate() + ")";
        }

        if (amount.greaterThan(balance)) {
            throw new InsufficientFundsException(balance, amount);
        }
        m_balance = balance = balance.subtract(amount);
```

```
            postTransaction(TransactionType.WITHDRAWAL,
                                        description, amount, balance);


        return balance;
    }

    public Money deposit(Money amount, String description) {
        // omitted for brevity (similar to withdraw).
    }

    protected void postTransaction(TransactionType type,
                                    String description,
                                    Money amount, Money balance) {
        Transaction transaction =
                Transaction.create(m_id, ++m_lastTransactionId,
                                    type, description,
                                    amount, balance);
        getTransactionRepository().save(transaction);
    }
}
```

As you can see, except for the fact that we've implemented the Entity interface and made the class Serializable, there is nothing particularly interesting about this class. The logic within it is expressed using concepts from a domain and there is absolutely nothing that ties it to Coherence.

However, we are not done yet, as there are few more things to consider.

Identity management

If an entity has a natural attribute that can be used to uniquely identify an instance of an entity, it is usually best to use that attribute as an identity. Unfortunately, many entities do not have such an attribute, in which case a surrogate identity must be generated by the system and assigned to entity instance.

Most databases provide a built-in mechanism for this purpose. For example, SQL Server allows you to define a numeric field that is automatically incremented when a new record is inserted into the table, while Oracle has a sequence mechanism, which allows you to get the next number for the named sequence object and use it within your INSERT statement. Another option is to generate and use a **GUID** (**Globally Unique Identifier**) object as an identity, which might be the best (or even required) option for scenarios where replication and synchronization across multiple independent data stores is required.

When you use the identity generation features of your database, you essentially let it handle all the grunt work for you and your biggest problem becomes how to obtain the generated identifier from the database and update your in-memory object to reflect it.

Coherence, on the other hand, forces you to define an object's identity up front. Because identity is typically used as a cache key, it is impossible to put an object into the cache unless you have a valid identifier for it. Unfortunately, while Coherence allows you to use **UUIDs (Universally Unique Identifier**s) as object identifiers and even provides an excellent, platform independent implementation of UUID, it does not have an out-of-the-box mechanism for sequential identifier generation. However, it is not too difficult to implement one, and the Coherence Tools open source project I mentioned earlier provides one such implementation in the form of SequenceGenerator class.

The SequenceGenerator is very simple to use. All you need to do is create an instance of it, passing sequence name and the number of identifiers the client should allocate on each call to the server (a variation of a Hi/Lo algorithm). The generator uses Coherence cache internally to keep track of all the sequences, which allows it to be used from any cluster member. It is also thread-safe and intended to be shared by instances of an entity that it creates identifiers for, so you will typically create it as a static final field:

```
public class Account
    implements Entity<Long>, Serializable {

    private static IdentityGenerator<Long> s_idGen =
        SequenceGenerator.create("account.id", 20);

    ...
}
```

Creating entity instances

Now that we have identity generator, we should ensure that whenever a new object is created it is assigned a unique identity. While we could do this in a constructor, the idiom I like to use is to keep the constructor private and to provide a static factory method that is used to create new entity instances:

```
public class Account
    implements Entity<Long>, Serializable {

    ...

    private Account(Long id, Long customerId,
```

```
                        String description, Money balance) {
        m_id          = id;
        m_customerId  = customerId;
        m_description = description;
        m_balance     = balance;
    }

    static Account create(Customer customer,
                          String description,
                          Currency currency) {
        return new Account(s_idGen.generateIdentity(),
                           customer.getId(),
                           description,
                           new Money(0, currency));
    }

    ...
}
```

This way a single constructor can be used to properly initialize an object instance not only during the initial creation, but also when the object is loaded from a persistent store or deserialized, as we'll see shortly.

Managing entity relationships

One thing you might've noticed in the previous examples is that the Account does not have a direct reference to a Customer. Instead, we only store the Customer's identifier as part of the Account's state and use it to obtain the customer when necessary:

```
public class Account
    implements Entity<Long>, Serializable {

    private final Long m_customerId;

    ...

    public Customer getCustomer() {
        return getCustomerRepository()
                .getCustomer(m_customerId);
    }
}
```

This is a common pattern when using Coherence, as identity lookups from a cache are cheap operations, especially if we configure near caching for the customers cache in this example. By doing this, we ensure that a `Customer`, which can be shared by several `Account` classes, is always obtained from the authoritative source and avoid the issues that would be caused if the shared `Customer` instance was serialized as part of each `Account` object that references it.

On the other hand, this is only one side of the relationship. How would we model a one-to-many relationship, such as the relationship between a `Customer` and several `Account` classes, or an `Account` and several `Transaction` classes?

There are two possible approaches. The first one is to query the cache on the **many** side of the relationship. For example, we could query the `accounts` cache for all the accounts that have a specific customer ID. This is essentially the same approach you use with a relational database when you query a child table based on the foreign key that identifies the parent.

However, with Coherence you also have another option that will yield significantly better performance—you can store the identifiers of the child objects within the parent, and simply perform a `getAll` operation against the underlying Coherence cache when you need to retrieve them:

```
public class Customer
    implements Entity<Long>, Serializable {

    private Collection<Long> m_accountIds;

    ...

    public Collection<Account> getAccounts() {
        return getAccountRepository()
                .getAccounts(m_accountIds);
    }
}
```

This approach makes sense when the number of child objects is finite and you don't need to constrain the results in some other way. Neither of these is true for the `getTransactions` methods of the `Account` class—the transaction collection will likely grow indefinitely and the results of the `getTransactions` call need to be constrained by a time period. In this case, query against the `transactions` cache is a better approach.

Leaky abstractions

Notice that in the previous example, I passed a collection of account IDs directly to the `getAccounts` repository method, which leaks the fact that we are doing a bulk identity lookup from the underlying store.

This might make it difficult to implement a repository for the store that doesn't support such operation or might force us to implement it in a suboptimal manner. For example, if we had to implement the same repository for a relational database, our only option would be to use an `IN` clause when selecting from a child table. While this is not the end of the world, a more natural and better performing approach would be to query the child table on the foreign key.

We can make that possible by modifying the repository interface to expose the `getAccountsForCustomer` method that accepts a `Customer` instance instead of a collection of account IDs. That way the Coherence repository implementation would be able to perform identity lookup and the database repository implementation could execute the query on the foreign key.

The downside of such a change is that we would have to expose a getter for `m_accountIds` field to the outside world, which would break encapsulation. Considering that repositories tend to be leaky abstraction anyway and that they are rarely implemented for more than one specific persistence technology, the benefits of such change are questionable.

Dealing with dependencies

Both examples in the previous section had an external dependency on a repository, which begs the question on how these dependencies are provided to entities and by whom.

In a conventional application you could use Spring in combination with AspectJ or Dependency Injection features of your ORM to inject necessary dependencies into entities. However, implementing either of these approaches in a distributed system can be tricky, due to the fact that most repository implementations are not serializable.

The pattern I like to use is to lazily initialize dependencies by looking them up from a **Registry**:

```
private transient CustomerRepository m_customerRepository;

protected CustomerRepository getCustomerRepository() {
    if (m_customerRepository == null) {
        m_customerRepository =
                RepositoryRegistry.getCustomerRepository();
```

```
    }
    return m_customerRepository;
}

public void setCustomerRepository(CustomerRepository
customerRepository) {
    m_customerRepository = customerRepository;
}
```

In this example, the m_customerRepository field is lazily initialized by retrieving a CustomerRepository instance from a RepositoryRegistry. The registry itself is a singleton that simply wraps Spring application context, which enables easy configuration of concrete repository implementations to use.

Finally, the setter allows injection of fakes or mocks within unit tests, which significantly simplifies testing by not requiring the registry to be configured.

Specifying data affinity

In some cases you might want to tell Coherence to store related objects together. For example, if we had a way to ensure that all the transactions for any given account are stored within the same cache partition, we would be able to optimize the query that returns transactions for an account by telling Coherence to only search that one partition. That means that in a well-balanced cluster with a million transactions in a cache and thousand partitions, we would only need to search one thousandth of the data, or 1,000 transactions, to find the ones we need.

While it is not possible to tell Coherence explicitly where to put individual cache entries, there is a way to specify which objects should be collocated within the same partition.

Coherence uses the cache entry key (or entity identifier, depending how you look at it) to determine which node and cache partition an entry should be stored on. If you want to ensure that two entries are stored within the same partition, all you need to do is tell Coherence how to associate their keys.

You can achieve this in two different ways:

- By having your key classes implement the KeyAssociation interface
- By implementing and configuring an external KeyAssociator

Both approaches require that you implement custom classes for your related objects' keys, typically as value objects containing the identifier of the parent object you want to associate with in addition to the object's own identifier. For example, in order to associate `Transaction` instances with the `Account` they belong to, we can implement a custom identity class as follows:

```
public class Transaction
     implements Entity<Id>, Serializable {

     ...

     public static class Id
         implements Serializable, KeyAssociation {

         private Long m_accountId;
         private Long m_txNumber;

         public LineItemId(Long accountId, Long txNumber) {
             m_accountId = accountId;
             m_txNumber  = txNumber;
         }

         public Object getAssociatedKey() {
             return m_accountId;
         }

         public boolean equals(Object o) {
             ...
         }

         public int hashCode() {
             ...
         }
     }
}
```

The previous example uses the first of the two approaches, the `KeyAssociation` interface. The implementation of that interface is a single method, `getAssociatedKey`, which in this case returns the identifier of the parent `Account` instance.

The second approach requires you to implement key association logic in a separate class:

```java
public class TransactionAssociator implements KeyAssociator {

    public void init(PartitionedService partitionedService) {

    }

    public Object getAssociatedKey(Object key) {
        if (key instanceof Transaction.Id) {
            return ((Transaction.Id) key).getAccountId();
        }
        else {
            return key;
        }
    }
}
```

If you choose this approach, you will also need to configure the line items cache to use the `TransactionAssociator`:

```xml
<distributed-scheme>
    <!-- ... -->
    <key-associator>
        <class-name>TransactionAssociator</class-name>
    </key-associator>
</distributed-scheme>
```

Regardless of how you establish the association between your entities, Coherence will use the value returned by the `getAssociatedKey` method instead of the key itself to determine the storage partition for an object. This will ensure that all transactions for an account are stored within the same partition as the account itself.

Key association is not limited to aggregates and can be used to ensure that any related entities are collocated within the same partition. However, separately stored weak entities are usually very good candidates for key association, so you should keep that in mind when designing your domain model.

One potential issue with data affinity is that it might prevent Coherence from fully balancing the cluster. For example, if some accounts have many transactions and some only a few, you could run out of memory on one node even though there is plenty of room in the cluster as a whole. Because of this, you will only want to use data affinity if the associated objects are naturally well-balanced.

Value objects

Unlike entities, **value objects** are not uniquely identifiable within a system. They simply represent values from the domain, and are typically immutable (and if they are not, they probably should be). An example of a value object might be a Money object, representing monetary amount, or an Address object, representing a mailing address of a person or a company, and defined by attributes such as street, street number, city, state, postal code, and country.

The value objects are typically used as attributes of entities. That means that they won't have their own cache, but will be stored as part of an entity's serialized state, within the cache for an entity they belong to. For example, our Account entity has a balance attribute represented by the Money value object, which will be serialized and stored with the rest of the account's state.

Implementing the Money value object

It is amazing that there is no built-in Money class in standard class libraries in either Java or .NET, especially considering the fact that most applications deal with monetary values one way or another.

However, that might work to our advantage in this case, as it gives us the opportunity to create a portable implementation of Money in Java, .NET, and C++. In this section, we will look at the Java implementation, but the other two are available within the sample application if you would like to see the details.

The Money class is an immutable class that simply encapsulates the amount and currency attributes:

```
public class Money implements Serializable {
    private final BigDecimal m_amount;
    private final Currency m_currency;

    public Money(BigDecimal amount, Currency currency) {
        m_amount = amount.setScale(
                        currency.getDefaultFractionDigits(),
                        RoundingMode.HALF_EVEN);
        m_currency = currency;
    }

    public BigDecimal getAmount() {
        return m_amount;
    }

    public Currency getCurrency() {
```

```
            return m_currency;
    }
}
```

In addition to the constructor shown earlier, the class also provides a number of convenience constructors that allow you to specify the amount as a string, integer, or floating-point value, and currency either as a currency code or an actual `java.util.Currency` instance.

However, the main reason for creating the Money class is not to capture its attributes, but to define the behavior applicable to monetary values:

```
public class Money implements Serializable {

    ...

    public boolean isSameCurrency(Money money) {
        return m_currency.equals(money.m_currency);
    }

    public Money add(Money money) {
        checkCurrency(money);
        return new Money(m_amount.add(money.m_amount), m_currency);
    }

    public Money subtract(Money money) {
        checkCurrency(money);
        return new Money(m_amount.subtract(money.m_amount), m_currency);
    }

    public boolean greaterThan(Money money) {
        checkCurrency(money);
        return m_amount.compareTo(money.m_amount) > 0;
    }

    public boolean lessThan(Money money) {
        checkCurrency(money);
        return m_amount.compareTo(money.m_amount) < 0;
    }
}
```

This gives us everything we need to work with monetary values within our application, and ensures that currency is taken into account when performing arithmetic operations or comparisons on two monetary values.

Value objects as identifiers

Value objects can also be used as identifiers for an entity; while they don't have an identity themselves, they are often used to represent composite identifiers containing two or more entity attributes. An example of such a value object is the `Transaction.Id` class we created earlier.

While in most cases all that Coherence cares about is that value objects are serializable, when they are used as identifiers you also need to ensure that they implement the `equals` and `hashCode` methods properly, and that the serialized binary form of equivalent value objects is identical.

This is very important, because key-based lookups against the Coherence cache depend on either standard object equality, or the binary equality of serialized keys. The exact requirement varies based on how objects are stored internally within the cache, but as a best practice, you should ensure that your identity object's serialized form is always consistent with `equals`. That way you won't have to worry about the details regarding the internal behavior of the cache type you are using.

Broken keys

I cannot stress the importance of this enough, as I have seen time and time again broken implementations of key classes, which have caused a lot of headache and wasted time.

By far the most common reason for broken keys is the omission of non-transient fields in the implementation of the `equals` method, so make sure that doesn't happen to you — if the field is serialized, it should be used for comparison within the `equals` implementation as well.

Services

In a rich domain model, the best places to put business logic are the domain objects that the behavior naturally belongs to, such as entities and aggregates. However, in most applications there is some behavior that doesn't clearly belong to any of the data objects. In such cases, you can define **services** within the domain itself that implement the necessary logic.

These domain-layer services are not the same as the course-grained services most of us got accustomed to while building applications using session EJBs. They are much lighter and much more focused, usually encapsulating only a handful of business methods, and very often only one or two.

You will typically still have a set of coarse-grained services within the orchestration layer, that are used to coordinate multiple activities within the domain layer and transform output into the most appropriate format for the presentation layer. They can also come in handy as a boundary for some of the infrastructure-level services, such as transactions and security.

However, the big difference between these orchestration-layer services and the services most of us used to implement using session beans is that session beans tended to contain most, if not all of the business logic, making domain objects dumb data holders in the process. The orchestration-layer services, on the other hand, are there purely for coordination and boundary definition purposes, while the business logic is implemented within the domain model.

Implementing the CurrencyConverter service

A good example of a domain service is the CurrencyConverter we defined within our domain model. The conversion logic clearly doesn't belong to the Account, so introducing a service whose only responsibility is to perform currency conversions makes perfect sense.

The best way to implement services in general is to hide the implementation behind an interface. That way the implementation can be easily replaced without any impact on the service clients.

We will follow that approach and define a CurrencyConverter interface:

```
public interface CurrencyConverter {

    CurrencyConversion convert(Money amount,
                               Currency targetCurrency);

}
```

As you can see, the interface is quite simple—it defines a single method that accepts the amount to convert and target currency as arguments and returns a `CurrencyConversion` value object:

```
public class CurrencyConversion {

    private final Money m_originalAmount;
    private final Money m_convertedAmount;

    public CurrencyConversion(Money originalAmount,
                                Money convertedAmount) {
        m_originalAmount  = originalAmount;
        m_convertedAmount = convertedAmount;
    }


    public Money getOriginalAmount() {
        return m_originalAmount;
    }

    public Money getConvertedAmount() {
        return m_convertedAmount;
    }

    public BigDecimal getExchangeRate() {
        BigDecimal exchangeRate =
            m_convertedAmount.getAmount()
                .divide(m_originalAmount.getAmount());
        return exchangeRate.setScale(4, RoundingMode.HALF_EVEN);
    }
}
```

Finally, we have a service implementation that looks up the exchange rate for the requested conversion and performs the conversion. The actual implementation is not that important for the further discussion and is available in the sample code download, so I will omit the code in order to save some trees.

Factories

When we discussed creation of entity instances I mentioned that I prefer a static factory method to a direct use of a constructor. In most cases, either of those two options will be all you need. However, in some cases the creational logic for an entity might be complex, in which case implementing a factory as a separate class might be the best approach.

In most cases, implementing a factory as a separate class is not very different from the static factory method approach. For example, the following factory class is functionally equivalent to the static factory method we created earlier:

```
public class AccountFactory {

    private static IdentityGenerator<Long> s_idGen =
        SequenceGenerator.create("account.id", 20);

    public Account createAccount(Customer customer,
                                 String description,
                                 Currency currency) {
        return new Account(s_idGen.generateIdentity(),
                           customer.getId(),
                           description,
                           new Money(0, currency));
    }
}
```

However, the fact that the factory is now a separate class opens up some interesting possibilities. For example, we could get rid of the hardcoded SequenceGenerator dependency and use Spring to configure the factory instance:

```
public class AccountFactory {

    private IdentityGenerator<Long> m_idGen;

    public AccountFactory(IdentityGenerator<Long> idGen) {
        m_idGen = idGen;
    }

    public Account createAccount(Customer customer,
                                 String description,
                                 Currency currency) {
        return new Account(m_idGen.generateIdentity(),
                           customer.getId(),
                           description,
                           new Money(0, currency));
    }
}
```

The following Spring configuration could then be used to wire the
AccountFactory instance:

```
<bean id="accountFactory" class="domain.AccountFactory">
    <constructor-arg>
        <bean class="c.s.c.identity.sequence.SequenceGenerator">
            <constructor-arg value="account.id"/>
            <constructor-arg value="20"/>
        </bean>
    </constructor-arg>
</bean>
```

That way you can let Spring manage dependencies and will be able to provide a fake
or mock for the identity generator within unit tests, which alone might be a good
enough reason to take this extra step.

Repositories

The factories are useful when we need to create new instances of domain objects,
but in many cases we simply need to retrieve the existing instances. In order to
accomplish that, we can use a **repository**.

According to *Domain Driven Design*, a repository can be thought of as an unlimited,
memory-backed object store containing all objects of a specific type. If that definition
reminds you of a Coherence cache, you are not alone—a Coherence cache is a great
object repository indeed.

Ideally, the repository interface should be completely independent of the underlying
infrastructure and should be expressed in terms of domain objects and their
attributes only. For example, we could define AccountRepository like this:

```
public interface AccountRepository {
    Account getAccount(Long id);
    Collection<Account> getAccounts(Collection<Long> accountIds);
    void save(Account account);
}
```

As you can see, the interface is completely Coherence agnostic, and can be
implemented for pretty much any data source. A Coherence implementation
might look like this:

```
public class CoherenceAccountRepository
    implements AccountRepository {

    private static final NamedCache s_accounts =
                        CacheFactory.getCache("accounts");
```

```
    public Account getAccount(Long id) {
        return (Account) s_accounts.get(id);
    }

    public Collection<Account> getAccounts(
                                    Collection<Long> accountIds) {
        return (Collection<Account>)
                s_accounts.getAll(accountIds).values();
    }

    public void save(Account account) {
        s_accounts.put(account.getId(), account);
    }
}
```

What you will quickly notice if you start implementing repositories this way is
that basic CRUD operations tend to repeat within every repository implementation,
so it makes sense to pull them up into an **abstract base** class in order to avoid
implementing them over and over again:

```
public abstract class AbstractCoherenceRepository<K, V extends
                                                    Entity<K>> {
    public abstract NamedCache getCache();

    public V get(K key) {
        return (V) getCache().get(key);
    }

    public Collection<V> getAll(Collection<K> keys) {
        return getCache().getAll(keys).values();
    }

    public void save(V value) {
        getCache().putAll(
            Collections.singletonMap(value.getId(), value));
    }

    public void saveAll(Collection<V> values) {
        Map batch = new HashMap(values.size());
        for (V value : values) {
            batch.put(value.getId(), value);
        }

        getCache().putAll(batch);
    }
}
```

This abstract base class for our repository implementations uses generics to specify the key and value type for the cache that the repository is used to access, and constrains value type to the types that implement the Entity interface we defined earlier. This allows us to implement the save and saveAll methods as mentioned earlier, because we can obtain the cache key for any entity by calling its getId method.

NamedCache.put versus NamedCache.putAll

One thing to note is the implementation of the save method. While I could've just made a simple call to a NamedCache.put method, I have chosen to use putAll instead, in order to improve performance by eliminating one network call.

The reason for this is that the NamedCache.put method strictly follows the contract defined by the Map interface and returns the old value from the cache. This is fine when you are accessing a map in-process or need the old value, but in this case neither is true and using put would simply increase the latency.

Our CoherenceAccountRepository implementation now simply becomes:

```
public class CoherenceOrderRepository
        extends AbstractCoherenceRepository<Long, Account>
        implements AccountRepository {

    private static final NamedCache m_accounts =
                            CacheFactory.getCache("accounts");

    public NamedCache getCache() {
        return m_accounts;
    }

    public Account getAccount(Long id) {
        return super.get(id);
    }

    public Collection<Account> getAccounts(
                                        Collection<Long> accountIds) {
        return super.getAll(accountIds);
    }
}
```

This concludes our coverage of different types of data objects within a domain model and how to map them to Coherence caches. For the most part, you should now know enough to be able to implement your data objects and put them into the cache.

One thing you might've noticed is that, aside from the repository implementation, none of the domain classes we implemented thus far have any dependency on or knowledge of Coherence, despite the somewhat leaky repository abstraction. This is an example of what DDD calls **persistence ignorance** (**PI**) and is extremely important as it allows us to unit test our domain model objects in isolation.

For the most part, you can use the domain objects we implemented in this section without any modifications. However, there are several important considerations that we haven't discussed yet that you need to understand in order to implement your data objects (entities and aggregates) in an optimal way.

Implementing object serialization

One of the most important choices you need to make for your domain objects (from the Coherence perspective) is how they will be serialized. Coherence works just fine with objects that simply implement `java.io.Serializable` interface, so that is typically the easiest way to try things out. However, that is also the slowest way to serialize your objects, as it heavily depends on reflection. It also introduces a lot of overhead into the object's serialized binary form, as it embeds into it things such as full class name, field names, and field types.

Serialization performance will impact most operations against a distributed cache, while the size of the serialized binary form will not only have an impact on network throughput, but more importantly, it will ultimately determine how much data you can store within a cluster of a certain size. Or, looking at it from a different angle, it will determine how many servers, how much RAM and how many Coherence licenses you will need in order to manage your data.

Coherence provides several serialization mechanisms that are significantly faster than the standard Java serialization and typically also result in a much smaller serialized binary form. The reason why there are several of them is that they were introduced one by one, in an effort to improve performance. The latest one, called **Portable Object Format** or **POF**, was introduced in Coherence 3.2 in order to allow .NET clients to access data within a Coherence cluster, but has since then become the recommended serialization format for pure Java applications as well.

POF basics

POF is an extremely compact, platform-independent binary serialization format. It can be used to serialize almost any Java, .NET, or C++ object into a **POF value**.

A **POF value** is a binary structure containing **type identifier** and **value**. The **type identifier** is an integer number, where numbers less than zero are used for the **intrinsic types**, while the numbers greater than zero can be used for custom **user types**.

User types are what we are interested in most, as all the domain objects we will create within an application are considered user types. The value of a user type is encoded within the POF stream as a list of **indexed attributes**, where each data member of a user type is encoded by specifying its index within the type. The attribute value is then encoded as a POF value, defined previously.

The fact that attribute indexes are used instead of attribute names makes POF very compact and fast, but it puts burden on the serializer implementation to ensure that attributes are written to and read from the POF stream in the same order, using the same indexes.

This decision, as well as the decision to use an integer type identifier instead of class name to represent the type of the value was made consciously, in order to make POF platform independent—Java class name is meaningless to a .NET client and vice-versa, and attribute names might be as well. The consequence is that unlike many other serialization formats, POF is not a self-describing serialization format by design, and it requires an external means of correlating platform independent user type identifiers with platform-specific classes.

A brief history of POF

Back in December of 2005, during the first The Spring Experience conference in Miami, I was working with Rob Harrop on the interoperability solution that would allow Spring.NET clients to communicate with Spring-managed Java services on the server. We had several working implementations, including SOAP web services and a custom IIOP implementation for .NET, but we weren't really happy with any of them, as they either had significant limitations, required too much configuration, were just plain slow, or all of the above, as was the case with SOAP web services.

What we wanted was something that was easy to configure, didn't impose inheritance requirements on our services and was as fast as it could be. The only option we saw was to implement a custom binary serialization mechanism that would be platform independent, but neither of us was brave enough to start working on it.

The very next week I was at JavaPolis in Antwerp, Belgium, listening to Cameron Purdy's talk on Coherence. One of the things he mentioned was how Java serialization is extremely slow and how Tangosol's proprietary `ExternalizableLite` serialization mechanism is some ten to twelve times faster. With Spring interop still fresh in mind, I approached Cameron after the talk and asked him if it would be possible to port `ExternalizableLite` to .NET. He just looked at me and said: "We need to talk.".

Well, we did talk, and what I learned was that Tangosol wanted to implement the .NET client for Coherence, as many customers were asking for it, and that in order to do that they needed a platform-independent serialization format and serializer implementations in both Java and .NET. A few months later, I received an e-mail with a serialization format specification, complete Java POF implementation and a question "Can you implement this in .NET for us?"

Over the next six months or so we implemented both POF and the full-blown .NET client for Coherence. All I can say is that the experience for me was very intense, and was definitely one of those humbling projects where you realize how little you really know. Working with Cameron and Jason Howes on POF and Coherence for .NET was a lot of fun and a great learning experience.

Although, I knew it would be that way as soon as I saw the following sentence in the POF specification:

In other words, PIF-POF is explicitly not intended to be able to answer all questions, nor to be all things to all people. If there is an 80/20 rule and a 90/10 rule, PIF-POF is designed for the equivalent of a 98/2 rule: it should suffice for all but the designs of an esoteric and/or convoluted mind.

POF context

A **POF context** provides a way to assign POF type identifiers to your custom types. There are two implementations that ship with Coherence, and you are free to implement your own if neither fits the bill, which is highly unlikely.

The first implementation is a `SimplePofContext`, which allows you to register user types programmatically, by calling the `registerUserType` method. This method takes three arguments: POF type identifier, a class of a user type, and a **POF serializer** to use.

The last argument, POF serializer, can be an instance of any class that implements the
com.tangosol.io.pof.PofSerializer interface. You can implement the serializer
yourself, or you can implement the com.tangosol.io.pof.PortableObject
interface within your data objects and use the built-in PortableObjectSerializer,
as in the following example:

```
SimplePofContext ctx = new SimplePofContext();

ctx.registerUserType(1000,
                     Account.class,
                     new PortableObjectSerializer(1000));
ctx.registerUserType(1001,
                     Transaction.class,
                     new PortableObjectSerializer(1001));
ctx.registerUserType(1002,
                     Customer.class,
                     new Customer.Serializer());
```

Regardless of the option chosen, you will also have to implement the actual
serialization code that reads and writes object's attributes from/to a POF stream.
We will get to that shortly, but now let's take a look at the other implementation
of a PofContext interface, a ConfigurablePofContext class.

ConfigurablePofContext

The ConfigurablePofContext allows you to define mappings of user types to POF
type identifiers in an external configuration file and is most likely what you will be
using within your applications.

The POF configuration file is an XML file that has the following format:

```
<!DOCTYPE pof-config SYSTEM "pof-config.dtd">

<pof-config>

    <user-type-list>

        <include>otherPofConfig</include>

        <user-type>
            <type-id>typeId</type-id>
            <class-name>userTypeClass</class-name>
            <serializer>
                <class-name>serializerClass</class-name>
                <init-params>...</init-params>
```

```
            </serializer>
        </user-type>


        ...


    </user-type-list>

</pof-config>
```

The `include` element allows us to import user type definitions from another file. This enables us to separate POF configuration into multiple files in order to keep those files close to the actual types they are configuring, and to import all of them into the main POF configuration file that the application will use.

The serializer definition within the `user-type` element is optional, and if it is not specified `PortableObjectSerializer` will be used. For example, if we were to create a configuration file for the same user types we registered manually with the `SimplePofContext` in the previous example, it would look like this:

```
<!DOCTYPE pof-config SYSTEM "pof-config.dtd">

<pof-config>

    <user-type-list>

        <user-type>
            <type-id>1000</type-id>
            <class-name>
                sample.domain.Account
            </class-name>
        </user-type>

        <user-type>
            <type-id>1001</type-id>
            <class-name>
                sample.domain.Transaction
            </class-name>
        </user-type>

        <user-type>
            <type-id>1002</type-id>
            <class-name>
                sample.domain.Customer
            </class-name>
```

```
        <serializer>
            <class-name>
                sample.domain.Customer$Serializer
            </class-name>
        </serializer>
    </user-type>

</user-type-list>

</pof-config>
```

There is another thing worth pointing out regarding user type registration within a POF context.

You have probably noticed that I used type identifiers of 1000 and greater, even though any positive integer can be used. The reason for this is that the numbers below 1000 are reserved for various user types within Coherence itself, such as filter and entry processor implementations.

All internal user types are configured in the `coherence-pof-config.xml` file within `coherence.jar`, and you should import their definitions into your main POF configuration file using an `include` element:

```
<include>coherence-pof-config.xml</include>
```

Finally, it is worth noting that even though POF is the recommended serialization format from Coherence 3.4, it is not enabled within the cluster by default, for backwards compatibility reasons. In order to enable it you need to either configure it on a per service basis within the cache configuration file, or enable it globally by specifying the following system properties:

```
-Dtangosol.pof.enabled=true
-Dtangosol.pof.config=my-pof-config.xml
```

Implementing serialization code

The easiest way to implement POF serialization is to make your objects implement the `PortableObject` interface.

```
public interface PortableObject extends Serializable {

    void readExternal(PofReader pofReader)
                                throws IOException;

    void writeExternal(PofWriter pofWriter)
                                throws IOException;
}
```

The methods defined by the `PortableObject` interface return no value and accept a single argument that allows us to read the indexed attributes from the POF stream, in the case of `readExternal`, or to write attributes into the POF stream in `writeExternal`. To learn how to implement these methods, let's look at the implementation of a POF-enabled `Customer` class:

```
public class Customer
    implements Entity<Long>, PortableObject {

    // data members
    private final Long m_id;
    private String m_name;
    private String m_email;
    private Address m_address;
    private Collection<Long> m_accountIds;

    public Customer() {
    }

    public void readExternal(PofReader pofReader)
                            throws IOException {
        m_id        = pofReader.readLong(0);
        m_name      = pofReader.readString(1);
        m_email     = pofReader.readString(2);
        m_address   = (Address) pofReader.readObject(3);
        m_accountIds = pofReader.readCollection(
                                    4, new ArrayList<Long>());
    }

    public void writeExternal(PofWriter pofWriter)
                            throws IOException {
        pofWriter.writeLong(0, m_d);
        pofWriter.writeString(1, m_name);
        pofWriter.writeString(2, m_email);
        pofWriter.writeObject(3, m_address);
        pofWriter.writeCollection(4, m_accountIds);
    }

}
```

As you can see, while it probably isn't the most exciting code to write, serialization code is fairly straightforward and simply uses the appropriate `PofReader` and `PofWriter` methods to read and write attribute values.

Once you implement the `PortableObject` interface, all you need to do is register your user type within the POF context by adding a `user-type` element for it into the POF configuration file, as we've done in the previous section. You can omit the `serializer` element, and `PortableObjectSerializer` will be used by default.

The second way to implement serialization logic is to create a separate serializer class that implements the `PofSerializer` interface:

```
public interface PofSerializer {

    void serialize(PofWriter pofWriter, Object o)
                            throws IOException;

    Object deserialize(PofReader pofReader)
                            throws IOException;
}
```

As you can see, the methods that need to be implemented are very similar to the ones defined by the `PortableObject` interface, so the logic within them will also look familiar:

```
public class CustomerSerializer implements PofSerializer {

    public void serialize(PofWriter writer, Object obj)
                                        throws IOException {
        Customer c = (Customer) obj;

        writer.writeLong(0, c.getId());
        writer.writeString(1, c.getName());
        writer.writeString (2, c.getEmail());
        writer.writeObject(3, c.getAddress());
        writer.writeCollection(4, c.getAccountIds());

        writer.writeRemainder(null);
    }

    public Object deserialize(PofReader reader)
                                        throws IOException {

        Long    id    = reader.readLong(0);
        String  name  = reader.readString(1);
        String  email = reader.readString (2);
        Address address = (Address) reader.readObject(3);
        Collection<Long> accountIds =
                reader.readCollection(4, new ArrayList<Long>());
```

```
            pofReader.readRemainder();

            return new Customer(id, name, email, address, accountIds);
        }
    }
```

Apart from the fact that we now have to use getters to retrieve attribute values, there are only two things that are different: calls to `writeReminder` and `readReminder` methods, and the `Customer` creation in the deserialization method.

The `read/writeReminder` methods are part of the schema evolution support, which we will discuss in more detail shortly. For now, all you need to know is that you have to call them in order to properly terminate reading or writing of a user type instance from or into a POF stream. The `PortableObjectSerializer` does that for us, so we didn't have to worry about it when we implemented serialization within `PortableObject` methods, but you do need to do it in your custom implementations of `PofSerializer`.

The way the `Customer` instance is created within the `deserialize` method points out one of the major differences between the two possible serialization implementations: if you write a custom serializer you have complete control over the object creation. You can use a parameterized constructor, as in the previous example, or a factory that encapsulates possibly complex creational logic.

On the other hand, in order for the `PortableObjectSerializer` to work, your class needs to provide a public default constructor. While in many cases this isn't a problem as there are other application components that require default constructors, such as ORM tools, in some situations this might be an issue and you might want to implement external serializers in order to have complete control over the instantiations of your objects. This brings us to our next topic: How to decide on which option to use.

PortableObject or PofSerializer?

One of the reasons you should choose custom `PofSerializer` implementation is what we discussed previously—when you have complex creational logic for your objects and need to have complete control over their instantiation.

A second, very obvious reason is that you may not be able to add the necessary POF serialization code to a class. While it is usually possible to add such code to your own classes, being able to have the code in a separate `PofSerializer` implementation means that you can serialize other peoples' non-POF-compliant classes using POF, including classes that come with the JDK, various frameworks, application servers, and even packaged applications.

For example, we have used the `java.util.Currency` class within the `Money` implementation. In order to make `Money` as a whole portable, we need to ensure that `Currency` is portable as well. The only way to do that is by creating an external serializer:

```
public class CurrencySerializer implements PofSerializer {

    public void serialize(PofWriter writer, Object obj)
                                            throws IOException {
        Currency currency = (Currency) obj;

        writer.writeString(0, currency.getCurrencyCode());
        writer.writeRemainder(null);
    }

    public Object deserialize(PofReader reader)
                                            throws IOException {
        String currencyCode = reader.readString(0);
        pofReader.readRemainder();

        return Currency.getInstance(currencyCode);
    }
}
```

Another good reason to choose an external serializer is when you can write a single serializer that is able to handle many different types. For example, let's take a look at serialization of enum values.

In order to serialize enums in a platform-independent way, the best option is to write the name of the enum value into a POF stream. On the surface, this seems easy enough to do directly within the serialization code:

```
public enum TransactionType {
    DEPOSIT,
    WITHDRAWAL
}

public class Transaction implements PortableObject {

    // data members
    private TransactionType m_type;

    public Transaction() {
    }
```

```
    public void readExternal(PofReader pofReader)
                                    throws IOException {
        m_type = Enum.valueOf(TransactionType.class,
                                pofReader.readString(0));
    }

    public void writeExternal(PofWriter pofWriter)
                                    throws IOException {
        pofWriter.writeString(0, m_type.name());
    }
}
```

Unfortunately, there are several issues with the approach.

For one, you will have to repeat a somewhat cumbersome piece of code that is used to deserialize enums for each serializable enum field within your application. Second, if you need to serialize an instance of a collection that contains one or more enum values, you will not have a sufficient degree of control that will allow you to inject the custom deserialization logic used previously.

Because of this, it is much better solution to implement a custom PofSerializer that can be used to serialize all enum types:

```
public class EnumPofSerializer implements PofSerializer {{

    public void serialize(PofWriter writer, Object o)
                                        throws IOException {
        if (!o.getClass().isEnum()) {
            throw new IOException(
                    "EnumPofSerializer can only be used to " +
                    "serialize enum types.");
        }

        writer.writeString(0, ((Enum) o).name());
        writer.writeRemainder(null);
    }

    public Object deserialize(PofReader reader)
                                        throws IOException {

        PofContext pofContext = reader.getPofContext();
        Class enumType = pofContext.getClass(reader.getUserTypeId());
        if (!enumType.isEnum()) {
            throw new IOException(
                    "EnumPofSerializer can only be used to " +
```

```
                        "deserialize enum types.");
     }

        Enum enumValue = Enum.valueOf(enumType, reader.readString(0));
        reader.readRemainder();

        return enumValue;
     }
}
```

Now all we have to do is register our enum types within the POF configuration, specifying `EnumPofSerializer` as their serializer, and use `read/writeObject` methods to serialize them:

```
public void readExternal(PofReader pofReader)
                              throws IOException {
    m_type = (TransactionType) pofReader.readObject(0);
}

public void writeExternal(PofWriter pofWriter)
                              throws IOException {
    pofWriter.writeObject(0, m_type);
}
```

This greatly simplifies enum serialization and ensures that they are serialized consistently throughout the application. Better yet, it will allow for a completely transparent serialization of enum values within various collections.

The previous examples demonstrate some great uses for external serializers, but we still haven't answered the question we started this section with—which approach to use when serializing our domain objects.

Implementing the `PortableObject` interface is quick and easy, and it doesn't require you to configure a serializer for each class. However, it forces you to define a public default constructor, which can be used by anyone to create instances of your domain objects that are in an invalid state.

An external serializer gives you full control over object creation, but is more cumbersome to write and configure. It also might force you to break the encapsulation, as we did earlier, by providing a `getAccountIds` method on the `Customer` class in order to allow serialization of account identifiers.

The last problem can be easily solved by implementing the external serializer as a static inner class of the class it serializes. That way, it will be able to access its private members directly, which is really what you want to do within the serializer.

In addition to that, the Coherence Tools project provides `AbstractPofSerializer`, an abstract base class that makes the implementation of external serializers significantly simpler by removing the need to read and write the remainder. We will actually discuss the implementation of this class shortly, but for now let's see how the customer serializer would look like if implemented as a static inner class that extends `AbstractPofSerializer`:

```
public class Customer
    implements Entity<Long> {
    ...

    public static class Serializer
            extends AbstractPofSerializer<Customer> {

        protected void serializeAttributes(Customer c,
                                               PofWriter writer)
            throws IOException {
            writer.writeLong       (0, c.m_id);
            writer.writeString     (1, c.m_name);
            writer.writeString     (2, c.m_email);
            writer.writeObject     (3, c.m_address);
            writer.writeCollection(4, c.m_accountIds);
        }

        protected Customer createInstance(PofReader reader)
            throws IOException {
            return new Customer(
                    reader.readLong(0),
                    reader.readString(1),
                    reader.readString(2),
                    (Address) reader.readObject(3),
                    reader.readCollection(4, new ArrayList<Long>()));
        }
    }
}
```

I believe you will agree that implementing the external serializer this way is almost as simple as implementing the `PortableObject` interface directly (we still need to configure the serializer explicitly), but without its downsides.

Because of this, my recommendation is to implement external serializers in the manner presented for all domain classes, and to implement the `PortableObject` interface directly only within the classes that are closely related to Coherence infrastructure, such as entry processors, filters, and value extractors, which will be discussed in the following chapters.

Collection serialization with POF

While implementation of the POF serialization code is straightforward, one subject that deserves a more detailed discussion is collection serialization.

POF does not encode collection type into the POF stream. If it did, it wouldn't be portable, as collection types are platform dependent. For example, if it encoded the type of a `java.util.LinkedList` into the stream, there would be no way for a .NET client to deserialize the collection as there is no built-in linked list type in .NET.

Instead, POF leaves it to the serialization code to decide which collection type to return by providing a **collection template** to the `PofReader.readCollection` method:

```
List myList = pofReader.readCollection(0, new LinkedList());
```

The situation with maps is similar:

```
Map myMap = pofReader.readMap(1, new TreeMap());
```

You can specify `null` in both cases, but you should never do that if you care about the type of the returned object and not just about the fact that it implements the `Collection` or `Map` interface. If you do, Coherence will return an instance of a default type, which is probably not what you want.

For example, you might've noticed that I specified a new `ArrayList` as a collection template whenever I was reading account IDs from the POF stream in the `Customer` serialization examples. The reason for that is that I need the collection of account IDs to be mutable after deserialization (so the customer can open a new account). If I didn't provide a template, account IDs would be returned as `ImmutableArrayList`, one of the internal `List` implementations within Coherence.

To make things even worse, there is no guarantee that the default implementation will even remain the same across Coherence versions, and you might get surprised if you move from one supported platform to another (for example, the .NET Coherence client returns an object array as a default implementation). The bottom line is that you should always specify a template when reading collections and maps.

The situation with object arrays is similar: if you want the serializer to return an array of a specific type, you should provide a template for it.

```
myProductArray = pofReader.readObjectArray(2, new Product[0]);
```

If you know the number of elements ahead of time you should size the array accordingly, but more likely than not you will not have that information. In that case, you can simply create an empty array as in the previous example, and let the POF serializer resize it for you.

The only exception to this rule is if you have written the array into the stream using the `PofWriter.writeObjectArray` overload that writes out a uniform array, in which case the serializer will have enough information to create an array of a correct type even if you don't specify a template for it.

This brings us to the discussion about uniform versus non-uniform collection and array write methods.

If you browse the API documentation for `PofWriter`, you will notice that there are multiple overloaded versions of the `writeCollection`, `writeMap`, and `writeObjectArray` methods.

The basic ones simply take the attribute index and value as arguments and they will write the value out using a non-uniform format, which means that the element type will be encoded for each element in a collection. Obviously, this is wasteful if all elements are of the same type, so `PofWriter` provides methods that allow you to specify element type as well, or in the case of the `writeMap` method, both the key type and the value type of map entries.

If your collection, array or a map is uniform, and most are, you should always use the uniform versions of write methods and specify the element type explicitly. This can significantly reduce the size of the serialized data by allowing the POF serializer to write type information only once instead of for each element.

Adding support for schema evolution

Now that you know everything you need to know about serialization and POF, let's discuss the closely related subject of schema evolution support in Coherence.

The fact of life is that things change, and this applies to domain objects as well. New releases of an application usually bring new features, and new features typically require new attributes within domain objects.

In a typical non-Coherence application, you can introduce new columns into database tables, add attributes to your classes, modify ORM configuration files, or custom database access logic and be on your way. However, when your objects are stored within a Coherence cluster, things are not that simple.

The main reason for that is that Coherence stores objects, not raw data, and objects have a specific serialization format, be it POF or something else. You can modify the database schema, your classes, and O-R mapping code just as you used to, but you will also have to decide what to do with the objects stored within Coherence caches that were serialized in a format that is likely incompatible with the serialization format of your modified classes.

There are really only a two possible choices you can make:

- Shut down the whole cluster, perform an upgrade, and reload the data into the cache using the latest classes
- Make your classes evolvable

It is important to note that there is nothing wrong with the first option and if your application can be shut down temporarily for an upgrade, by all means, go for it. However, many Coherence-powered solutions are mission-critical applications that cannot be shut down for any period of time, and many of them depend on Coherence being the system of record.

In those cases, you need to be able to upgrade the Coherence cluster node by node, while keeping the system as a whole fully operational, so your only option is to add support for schema evolution to your objects.

Implementing Evolvable objects

The first step you need to take when adding support for schema evolution to your application is to make your data objects implement the com.tangosol. io.Evolvable interface:

```
public interface Evolvable extends java.io.Serializable {
    int getImplVersion();
    int getDataVersion();
    void setDataVersion(int i);

    com.tangosol.util.Binary getFutureData();
    void setFutureData(com.tangosol.util.Binary binary);
}
```

The Evolvable interface defines the attributes each object instance needs to have in order to support the schema evolution. This includes the following:

- **Implementation Version** is the version number of the **class implementation**. This is typically defined as a constant within the class, which is then returned by the getImplVersion method. You need to increment the implementation version for a new release if you have added any attributes to the class.
- **Data Version** is the version number of the **class data**. You can also think of it as the version number of the serialized form of a class. The Data Version attribute is set by the serializer during deserialization, based on the version number found in the POF stream.

- **Future Data** is used to store attributes that exist within the POF stream but are not read explicitly by the deserializer of an older version of a class. They are simply stored within an object as a binary blob so they can be written out into the POF stream during serialization, thus preventing data loss during round tripping.

To illustrate all of this, let's return to our earlier example and see how we could add evolution support to the Customer class:

```
public class Customer
    implements Entity<Long>, Evolvable {

    // evolvable support
    public static final int IMPL_VERSION = 1;

    private int dataVersion;
    private Binary futureData;

    // data members
    private Long m_id;
    private String m_name;
    private String m_email;

    // constructors, getters and setters omitted for brevity
    ...

    public int getImplVersion() {
        return IMPL_VERSION;
    }

    public int getDataVersion() {
        return dataVersion;
    }

    public void setDataVersion(int dataVersion) {
        this.dataVersion = dataVersion;
    }

    public Binary getFutureData() {
```

```
        return futureData;
    }

    public void setFutureData(Binary futureData) {
        this.futureData = futureData;
    }
}
```

It is immediately obvious that the implementation of this interface will be the same for all evolvable classes, so it makes sense to pull the dataVersion and futureData attributes into a base class and define the getImplVersion method as abstract. As a matter of fact, such a class already exists within coherence.jar, and is called AbstractEvolvable.

Using AbstractEvolvable as a base class greatly simplifies implementation of evolvable objects, as you only need to implement the getImplVersion method:

```
public class Customer
    extends AbstractEvolvable
    implements Entity<Long> {

    // evolvable support
    public static final int IMPL_VERSION = 1;

    // data members
    private Long m_id;
    private String m_name;
    private String m_email;

    // constructors, getters and setters omitted for brevity
    ...

    public int getImplVersion() {
        return IMPL_VERSION;
    }
}
```

Implementing serialization for Evolvable objects

The `Evolvable` interface simply defines which information class instances need to be able to provide in order for the class to support schema evolution. The rest of the work is performed by a serializer that knows how to use that information to support serialization across multiple versions of a class.

The easiest way to add schema evolution support to your application is to use an out-of-the-box serializer that implements the necessary logic. One such serializer is the `PortableObjectSerializer` we discussed earlier, and it makes schema evolution a breeze. You simply implement both `PortableObject` and `Evolvable` interfaces within your class (or even simpler, a convenience `EvolvablePortableObject` interface), and the serializer takes care of the rest.

However, if you follow my earlier advice and implement external serializers for your domain objects, you need to handle object evolution yourself.

The algorithm to implement is fairly simple. When deserializing an object, we need to:

- Read the data version from the POF stream and set the `dataVersion` attribute
- Read object attributes as usual
- Read the remaining attributes, if any, from the POF stream and set the `futureData` attribute

The last item is only meaningful when we are deserializing a newer object version. In all other cases `futureData` will be `null`.

When serializing an object, we need to do the exact opposite for steps 2 and 3, but the first step is slightly different:

- Set the data version of the POF stream to the *greater of implementation version or data version*
- Write object attributes as usual
- Write future data into the POF stream

The reason why we need to write the **greater of implementation** or **data version** in the first step, is that we always want to have the latest possible version in the POF stream. If we deserialize a newer version of an object, we need to ensure that its version is written into the POF stream when we serialize the object again, as we'll be including its original data into the POF stream as well. On the other hand, if we deserialized an older version, we should write a new version, containing new attributes while serializing the object again.

This is actually the key element of the schema evolution strategy in Coherence that allows us to upgrade the cluster node by node, upgrading the data stored within the cluster in the process as well.

Imagine that you have a ten-node Coherence cluster that you need to upgrade. You can shut a single node down, upgrade it with new JAR files and restart it. Because the data is partitioned across the cluster and there are backup copies available, the loss of a single node is irrelevant—the cluster will repartition itself, backup copies of the data will be promoted to primary copies, and the application or applications using the cluster will be oblivious to the loss of a node.

When an upgraded node rejoins the cluster, it will become responsible for some of the data partitions. As the data it manages is deserialized, instances of new classes will be created and the new attributes will be either calculated or defaulted to their initial values. When those instances are subsequently serialized and stored in the cluster, their version is set to the latest implementation version and any node or client application using one of the older versions of the class will use the futureData attribute to preserve new attributes.

As you go through the same process with the remaining nodes, more and more data will be incrementally upgraded to the latest class version, until eventually all the data in the cluster uses the current version.

What is important to note is that client applications do not need to be simultaneously upgraded to use the new classes. They can continue to use the older versions of the classes and will simply store future data as a binary blob on reads, and include it into the POF stream on writes. As a matter of fact, you can have ten different applications, each using different versions of the data classes, and they will all continue to work just fine, as long as all classes are evolvable.

Now that we have the theory covered, let's see how we would actually implement a serializer for our Customer class to support evolution.

```
public class CustomerSerializer implements PofSerializer {

    public void serialize(PofWriter writer, Object o)
                                      throws IOException {
        Customer c = (Customer) o;

        int dataVersion = Math.max(c.getImplVersion(),
                                   c.getDataVersion());
        writer.setVersionId(dataVersion);

        writer.writeLong(0, c.getId());
        writer.writeString(1, c.getName());
        writer.writeString (2, c.getEmail());
        writer.writeObject(3, c.getAddress());
        writer.writeCollection(4, c.getAccountIds());

        writer.writeRemainder(c.getFutureData());
    }

    public Object deserialize(PofReader reader)
                                      throws IOException {

        Long    id    = reader.readLong(0);
        String  name  = reader.readString(1);
        String  email = reader.readString (2);
        Address address = (Address) reader.readObject(3);
        Collection<Long> accountIds =
              reader.readCollection(4, new ArrayList<Long>());

        Customer c = new Customer(id, name, email, address,
                                                  accountIds);
        c.setDataVersion(pofReader.getVersionId());
        c.setFutureData(pofReader.readRemainder());

        return c;
    }
}
```

The highlighted code is simple, but it is immediately obvious that it has nothing to do with the Customer class per se, as it only depends on the methods defined by the Evolvable interface. As such, it simply begs for refactoring into an abstract base class that we can reuse for all of our serializers:

```
public abstract class AbstractPofSerializer<T>
        implements PofSerializer {

    protected abstract void
        serializeAttributes(T obj, PofWriter writer)
            throws IOException;

    protected abstract void
        deserializeAttributes(T obj, PofReader reader)
            throws IOException;

    protected abstract T createInstance(PofReader reader)
            throws IOException;

    public void serialize(PofWriter writer, Object obj)
                                    throws IOException {
        T instance = (T) obj;
        boolean isEvolvable = obj instanceof Evolvable;
        Evolvable evolvable = null;

        if (isEvolvable) {
            evolvable = (Evolvable) obj;
            int dataVersion = Math.max(
                            evolvable.getImplVersion(),
                            evolvable.getDataVersion());
            writer.setVersionId(dataVersion);
        }

        serializeAttributes(instance, writer);

        Binary futureData = isEvolvable
                        ? evolvable.getFutureData()
                        : null;
        writer.writeRemainder(futureData);
    }
```

```
    public Object deserialize(PofReader reader)
                                    throws IOException {
        T instance = createInstance(reader);

        Evolvable evolvable     = null;
        boolean   isEvolvable = instance instanceof Evolvable;
        if (isEvolvable) {
            evolvable = (Evolvable) instance;
            evolvable.setDataVersion(
                        reader.getVersionId());
        }

        deserializeAttributes(instance, reader);

        Binary futureData = reader.readRemainder();
        if (isEvolvable) {
            evolvable.setFutureData(futureData);
        }

        return instance;
    }
}
```

The only thing worth pointing out is the fact that both the `createInstance` method and `deserializeAttributes` method read attributes from the POF stream. The difference between the two is that `createInstance` should only read the attributes that are necessary for instance creation, such as constructor or factory method arguments. All other object attributes should be read from the stream and set within the `deserializeAttributes` method.

Summary

In this chapter, we have covered some very important topics.

We discussed how various types of domain objects map to Coherence caches, how to model object relationships, and how you can use key association to ensure that related objects are stored within the same Coherence partition. We also talked about identity management and you learned how to use the identity generator provided by Coherence Tools project.

Then we moved on to discuss access to Coherence caches from your domain objects through repository interfaces and implemented a reusable base class for repository implementations that need to access data within Coherence caches.

Finally, we talked about serialization and schema evolution of domain objects and learned how to implement both in a way that optimizes serialization performance and size of the serialized objects, while allowing for rolling upgrades of an application that do not require us to shut the whole cluster down.

The material in this and the previous chapter provides you with enough information to place Coherence into the overall application architecture, create domain objects that work well with Coherence, and map them to Coherence caches.

In the next chapter, you will learn how to query and aggregate data in the Coherence cluster.

5
Querying the Data Grid

So far, you have learned how to access data in the Coherence cache using identity-based operations, such as `get` and `put`. In many cases this will be exactly what you need, but there will also be many other situations where you either won't know an object's identity or you will simply need to look up one or more objects based on attributes other than the identity.

Coherence allows you to do that by specifying a **filter** for set-based operations defined by the `QueryMap` interface, which we mentioned briefly in *Chapter 3, Planning Your Caches*.

```
public interface QueryMap extends Map {
   Set keySet(Filter filter);
   Set entrySet(Filter filter);
   Set entrySet(Filter filter, Comparator comparator);
   ...
}
```

As you can see from the previous interface definition, all three methods accept a filter as the first argument, which is an instance of a class implementing a very simple `com.tangosol.util.Filter` interface:

```
public interface Filter {
    boolean evaluate(Object o);
}
```

Basically, the `Filter` interface defines a single method, `evaluate`, which takes an object to evaluate as an argument and returns true if the specified object satisfies the criteria defined by the filter, or false if it doesn't.

This mechanism is very flexible, as it allows you to filter your cached objects any way you want. For example, it would be quite simple to implement a filter that can be used to retrieve all the account transactions in a specific period:

```java
public class TransactionFilter implements Filter {

  private Long m_accountId;
  private Date m_from;
  private Date m_to;

  public TransactionFilter(Long accountId, Date from, Date to) {
    m_accountId = accountId;
    m_from      = from;
    m_to        = to;
  }

  public boolean evaluate(Object o) {
    Transaction tx = (Transaction) o;
    return tx.getId().getAccountId().equals(m_accountId)
           && tx.getTime().compareTo(from) >= 0
           && tx.getTime().compareTo(to) <= 0;
  }
}
```

While the previous sample filter implementation is perfectly valid and will return correct results if executed against the `transactions` cache, it would be very cumbersome if you had to define every single query criterion in the application by implementing a custom filter class as we did previously.

Fortunately, Coherence provides a number of built-in filters that make custom filter implementation unnecessary in the vast majority of cases.

Built-in filters

Most queries can be expressed in terms of object attributes and standard logical and relational operators, such as AND, OR, equals, less than, greater than, and so on. For example, if we wanted to find all the transactions for an account, it would be much easier if we could just execute the query analogous to the `select * from Transactions where account_id = 123` SQL statement than to write a custom filter that checks if the `accountId` attribute is equal to `123`.

The good news is that Coherence has a number of built-in filters that allow us to do exactly that. The following table lists all the filters from the `com.tangosol.util.filter` package that you can use to construct custom queries:

Filter Class	Description
EqualsFilter	Compares two values for equality.
NotEqualsFilter	Compares two values for inequality.
IsNullFilter	Checks if the value is null.
IsNotNullFilter	Checks if the value is not null.
LessFilter	Checks if the first value is smaller than the second value.
LessEqualsFilter	Checks if the first value is smaller than or equal to the second value.
GreaterFilter	Checks if the first value is greater than the second value.
GreaterEqualsFilter	Checks if the first value is greater than or equal to the second value.
BetweenFilter	Checks if the value is within certain range.
LikeFilter	Checks if the value matches specified pattern, similar to the SQL LIKE operator.
InFilter	Checks if the value is within a specified collection.
InKeySetFilter	Checks if the entry key is within a specified collection.
ContainsFilter	Checks if the collection contains a specified element.
ContainsAllFilter	Checks if the collection contains all of the elements from another collection.
ContainsAnyFilter	Checks if the collection contains any of the elements from another collection.
AndFilter	Returns the logical and of two other filters.
OrFilter	Returns the logical or of two other filters.
XorFilter	Returns the logical exclusive or of two other filters.
NotFilter	Negates the results of another filter.
LimitFilter	Allows paging through the results of another filter.
AlwaysFilter	Returns true.
NeverFilter	Returns false.
AllFilter	Returns logical and of all filters in a filter array.
AnyFilter	Returns logical or of all filters in a filter array.

As you can see, pretty much all of the standard Java logical operators and SQL predicates are covered. This will allow us to construct query expressions as complex as the ones we can define in Java code or the SQL where clause.

The bad news is that there is no query language in Coherence that allows you to specify a query as a string. Instead, you need to create the expression tree for the query programmatically, which can make things a bit tedious.

For example, the `where` clause of the SQL statement we specified earlier, `select * from Transactions where account_id = 123`, can be represented by the following Coherence filter definition:

```
Filter filter = new EqualsFilter("getId.getAccountId", 123);
```

In this case it is not too bad: we simply create an instance of an `EqualsFilter` that will extract the value of an `accountId` attribute from a `Transaction.Id` instance and compare it with 123. However, if we modify the query to filter transactions by date as well, the filter expression that we need to create becomes slightly more complex:

```
Filter filter = new AndFilter(
                new EqualsFilter("getId.getAccountId", accountId),
                new BetweenFilter("getTime", from, to));
```

If you need to combine several logical expressions, this can quickly get out of hand, so we will look for a way to simplify filter creation shortly. But first, let's talk about something we used in the examples without paying much attention to it—**value extractors**.

Value extractors

As you can see from the previous examples, a query is typically expressed in terms of object attributes, such as `accountId` or `time`, while the `evaluate` method defined by the `Filter` interface accepts a whole object that the attributes belong to, such as a `Transaction` instance.

That implies that we need a generic way to extract attribute values from an object instance—otherwise, there would be no way to define reusable filters, such as the ones in the table earlier that ship with Coherence, and we would be forced to implement a custom filter for each query we need to execute. In order to solve this problem and enable extraction of attribute values from an object, Coherence introduces **value extractors**.

A **value extractor** is an object that implements a `com.tangosol.util.ValueExtractor` interface:

```
public interface ValueExtractor {
  Object extract(Object target);
}
```

The sole purpose of a value extractor is to extract a derived value from the target object that is passed as an argument to the `extract` method. The result could be a single attribute value, a combination of multiple attributes (concatenation of first and last name, for example), or in general, a result of some transformation of a target object.

Reflection extractor

In the vast majority of cases, you will want to extract a value of the single attribute of a target object, in which case you can use the built-in `ReflectionExtractor` class. The `ReflectionExtractor` accepts a method name as a constructor argument, invokes the specified method on a target object via reflection, and returns the result of that method invocation.

As a matter of fact, the `ReflectionExtractor` is used so often that you can simply specify a method name as a string in most places where a value extractor is expected and an instance of a `ReflectionExtractor` will be created automatically for you, which is what we took advantage of in the previous filter definitions. For example, the filter definition:

```
Filter filter = new BetweenFilter("getTime", from, to);
```

Is really just a shorter form of:

```
Filter filter = new BetweenFilter(
                 new ReflectionExtractor("getTime"),
                 from, to);
```

I will have to admit that as useful as `ReflectionExtractor` is, I have never liked it much. The main reason for this is that it forces you to spell out a full method name for an attribute, when a property name, as defined by the Java Bean specification should've been enough and would've made the code more readable. This is especially bothersome when accessing a Coherence cluster from a .NET client, in which case the `'get'` prefix in front of the property name truly feels unnatural.

Fortunately, it is easy to fix the problem by implementing a similar value extractor that uses introspection to obtain an attribute value:

```
public class PropertyExtractor
            implements ValueExtractor, Serializable {

  private final String m_propertyName;
  private transient volatile Method m_readMethod;

  public PropertyExtractor(String propertyName) {
    m_propertyName = propertyName;
```

```
    }

    public Object extract(Object o) {
      if (o == null) {
        return null;
      }

      Class targetClass = o.getClass();
      try {
        if (readMethod ==
                null || readMethod.getDeclaringClass() != targetClass) {
          PropertyDescriptor pd =
                    new PropertyDescriptor(propertyName, o.getClass());
          readMethod = pd.getReadMethod();
        }
        return readMethod.invoke(o);
      }
      catch (Exception e) {
        throw new RuntimeException(e);
      }
    }
  }
}
```

Now we can use `PropertyExtractor` instead of `ReflectionExtractor` in our
filter definitions:

```
Filter filter = new BetweenFilter(
                    new PropertyExtractor("time"),
                    from, to);
```

In this example the difference is not significant and it could even be argued that
the `PropertyExtractor` makes the code harder to read as we have to specify it
explicitly, instead of using a filter constructor that takes string as an argument
and creates `ReflectionExtractor` for us. However, in the next section we
will implement a helper class that makes filter creation much simpler, and the
`PropertyExtractor` will allow us to make things as simple as they can be.

Expression languages and value extractors

If you are familiar with any of the popular expression languages, such as MVEL, OGNL, or SpEL, you will notice that I could've easily implemented the previous value extractor using one of them. Not only would that allow me to do a simple property extraction, but I would be able to use much more sophisticated expressions for extraction.

Considering that I created SpEL (Spring Expression Language) while working on Spring.NET a few years back, you can imagine that I am a big proponent of their usage. To prove that, I have implemented value extractors for MVEL, OGNL, SpEL, Groovy, and even Java 6 Scripting in Coherence Tools, so you can easily use your favorite EL with Coherence.

Other built-in value extractors

While the `ReflectionExtractor` is definitely the one that is used most often, there are several other value extractors that ship with Coherence.

IdentityExtractor

The simplest extractor is the `IdentityExtractor`, which doesn't really extract anything from the target object, but returns the target object itself. This extractor can come in handy when you actually want filters to operate on the cache value itself instead of on one of its attributes, which is typically the case only if the value is of a simple type, such as one of the intrinsic numeric types or a string.

ChainedExtractor and MultiExtractor

There are also two composite value extractors, `ChainedExtractor` and `MultiExtractor`. Both of them accept an array of value extractors as a constructor argument, but they use them differently.

The `ChainedExtractor` executes extractors one by one, using the result of the previous extractor as the target object to evaluate the next extractor against. For example, you can use the `ChainedExtractor` to extract the `accountId` attribute from a `Transaction` instance:

```
ValueExtractor ex =
    new ChainedExtractor(new ValueExtractor[] {
                new ReflectionExtractor("getId"),
                new ReflectionExtractor("getAccountId") });
```

This is necessary because the `Transaction` class does not expose the `accountId` attribute directly—we need to extract the `id` attribute from a transaction first, and then extract `accountId` from a `Transaction.Id` instance.

Avoiding the need for chaining

Of course, we could've easily avoided the need for chaining if we simply exposed the `accountId` attribute directly on the `Transaction` class. Doing that is trivial and makes perfect sense in this case.

However, if I had done that, I'd have to come up with an example of `ChainedExtractor` usage that is outside of our domain.

When creating a `ChainedExtractor` you can also use a convenience constructor that will parse a dot-separated string and create an array of `ReflectionExtractor` instances automatically:

```
ValueExtractor ex =
    new ChainedExtractor("getId.getAccountId");
```

As a matter of fact, you don't even need to go that far—all built-in filters will automatically create a `ChainedExtractor` containing an array of `ReflectionExtractors` from a dot-separated string, which is the feature we relied on earlier when we defined a query that returns transactions for a specific account.

On the other hand, `MultiExtractor` will execute all extractors against the same target object and return the list of extracted values. While you will rarely use this extractor when querying the cache, it can be very convenient when you want to extract only a subset of an object's attributes during aggregation (which we'll discuss shortly), in order to minimize the amount of data that needs to be transferred across the wire.

PofExtractor

One of the features introduced in Coherence 3.5 is `PofExtractor`—an extractor that can be used to extract values from the POF-serialized binaries without deserialization. This can provide a huge performance boost and reduced memory footprint for queries that would otherwise have to deserialize every single object in the cache in order to evaluate the filter.

However, you will only see those benefits when working with caches containing large objects. For small objects, the overhead of initializing a structure that is used to keep track of the location of serialized attributes within a binary POF value will likely be higher (both from memory and performance perspective) than the full deserialization of an object.

Implementing a custom value extractor

While the built-in value extractors should be sufficient for most usage scenarios, there might be some situations where implementing a custom one makes sense. We have already implemented one custom value extractor, `PropertyExtractor`, in order to improve on the built-in `ReflectionExtractor` and allow ourselves to specify JavaBean property names instead of the full method names, but there are other scenarios when this might be appropriate.

One reason why you might want to implement a custom value extractor is to enable transformation of cache values from their native type to some other type. For example, most applications use UI controls such as drop-downs or list boxes to present a list of possible choices to the user. Let's assume that we need to display a list of countries in a drop-down on the registration screen for new customers.

We already have a cache containing all the countries, so we could easily get all the values from it and send them to the client, which would use them to populate the drop-down. However, the `Country` class we defined in *Chapter 2* has a number of attributes we don't need in order to populate the drop-down list, such as capital, currency symbol, and currency name—the only attributes we do need are the country code and country name, so by sending any other information to the client we would only be wasting network bandwidth.

As a matter of fact, for most, if not all, drop-downs and list boxes in an application we will need only an identifier that will be returned as a selected value, and a description that should be used for display purposes. That means that we can define a class containing only those two attributes:

```java
public class LookupValue implements Serializable {
  private Object m_id;
  private String m_description;

  public LookupValue(Object id, String description) {
    m_id = id;
    m_description = description;
  }

  public Object getId() {
    return m_id;
  }

  public String getDescription() {
    return m_description;
  }
}
```

Now that we have a holder class that can be used to represent any lookup value, the remaining question is how we can transform instances of the Country class into the instances of the LookupValue class. The answer is simple—we can write a custom value extractor that will do it for us:

```
public class LookupValueExtractor
        extends    AbstractExtractor
        implements PortableObject, Serializable {

  private ValueExtractor m_idExtractor;
  private ValueExtractor m_descriptionExtractor;

  public LookupValueExtractor(ValueExtractor idExtractor,
                              ValueExtractor descriptionExtractor) {
    m_idExtractor          = idExtractor;
    m_descriptionExtractor = descriptionExtractor;
  }

  public Object extractFromEntry(Map.Entry entry) {
    Object id = InvocableMapHelper.extractFromEntry(m_idExtractor,
                                                    entry);
    String description = (String)
    InvocableMapHelper.extractFromEntry(m_descriptionExtractor, entry);

    return new LookupValue(id, description);
  }

  // equals and hashCode omitted for brevity
}
```

The implementation is actually very simple: we allow users to specify two value extractors, an idExtractor and a descriptionExtractor, that we use to extract the values that are used to create a LookupValue instance. However, one thing deserves clarification.

Instead of simply implementing the ValueExtractor interface, we are extending the AbstractExtractor class and implementing the extractFromEntry method. The reason for this is that we want to be able to extract id and description not only from the entry value, but from the entry key as well.

In order to achieve that, we rely on the InvocableMapHelper class, which provides a utility method that can be used to extract a value from any object that implements Map.Entry interface.

Of course, the `LookupValueExtractor` is only part of the story—we still need a way to execute this extractor against all the objects in the `countries` cache and get the collection of extracted lookup values back. We will see what the best way to do that is shortly, but for now let's return to Coherence filters and see how we can make complex queries easier to create.

Simplifying Coherence queries

As you have probably realized by now, Coherence queries can become quite cumbersome to create as the number of attributes used within the query grows, especially if non-default value extractors need to be used.

One, and possibly the best, approach would be to implement a real query language. We could define a grammar for Coherence queries that would be used to parse a SQL-like query string into a parse tree representing a Coherence filter. This would actually be fairly straightforward, as grammar elements would map pretty much directly to the built-in filters provided by Coherence.

However, this would distract us from the main topic of the book and lead us into the discussion of topics such as language grammars and parsers, so implementation of a full-blown Coherence query language is out of the scope of this book.

What we will do instead is implement a `FilterBuilder` class that will allow us to define the queries in a simpler way. While this approach won't allow us to express all possible queries, it will cover a large number of the most common use cases.

Filter builder

The idea behind the `FilterBuilder` implementation is that many queries are based on simple attribute comparisons, where multiple attribute comparisons are concatenated using the logical AND, or less often OR operator.

If you review the table of the built-in filter types at the beginning of this chapter, you will see that Coherence already provides all the core facilities we need to implement this: we have all the common comparison operators, as well as some of the less common ones, and there are `AllFilter` and `AnyFilter`, which allow us to create logical AND and OR filters for an array of filters respectively. What we don't have is an easy way to create an array of filters, and that's exactly what the `FilterBuilder` will help us do.

The goal is to be able to create a filter using code similar to this:

```
Filter filter = new FilterBuilder()
                        .equals("id.accountId", 123)
                        .between("time", from, to)
                        .build();
```

This will allow us to define complex queries in a much shorter and significantly more readable way. In order to support the previous syntax, we can implement the FilterBuilder class as follows:

```
public class FilterBuilder {
  private Class defaultExtractorType;
  private List<Filter> filters = new ArrayList<Filter>();

  // constructors
  public FilterBuilder() {
    this(PropertyExtractor.class);
  }

  public FilterBuilder(Class defaultExtractorType) {
    this.defaultExtractorType = defaultExtractorType;
  }

  // public members

  public FilterBuilder equals(String propertyName,
                              Object value) {
    return equals(createExtractor(propertyName), value);
  }

  public FilterBuilder equals(ValueExtractor extractor,
                              Object value) {
    filters.add(new EqualsFilter(extractor, value));
    return this;
  }

  public FilterBuilder notEquals(String propertyName,
                                 Object value) {
    return notEquals(createExtractor(propertyName), value);
  }

  public FilterBuilder notEquals(ValueExtractor extractor,
                                 Object value) {
    filters.add(new NotEqualsFilter(extractor, value));
```

```
      return this;
   }

   public FilterBuilder greater(String propertyName,
                               Comparable value) {
     return greater(createExtractor(propertyName), value);
   }

   public FilterBuilder greater(ValueExtractor extractor,
                                Comparable value) {
     filters.add(new GreaterFilter(extractor, value));
     return this;
   }

   // and so on...
}
```

Basically, we are implementing two overloaded methods for each built-in filter: one that accepts a value extractor as the first argument, and one that accepts a string and creates a value extractor for it.

However, unlike the built-in filters, we do not create an instance of a `ReflectionExtractor` automatically, but delegate the actual creation of an extractor to the `createExtractor` factory method:

```
protected ValueExtractor createExtractor(String propertyName) {
   if (propertyName.indexOf('.') >= 0) {
     return new ChainedExtractor(
                   createExtractorArray(propertyName.split(".")));
   }
   if (propertyName.indexOf(',') >= 0) {
     return new MultiExtractor(
                   createExtractorArray(propertyName.split(",")));
   }
   return createDefaultExtractor(propertyName);
}
```

As you can see, if the specified property name is a dot-separated string, we will create an instance of a `ChainedExtractor`. Similarly, we will create an instance of a `MultiExtractor` for a comma-separated list of property names.

For all other properties, we will delegate extractor creation to the
createDefaultExtractor method:

```
protected ValueExtractor createDefaultExtractor(String propertyName) {
    Constructor ctor = getConstructor(defaultExtractorType);
    return (ValueExtractor) ctor.newInstance(propertyName);
}
```

This allows us to control on a case-by-case basis which value extractor should be
used within our filter. In most cases, the default PropertyExtractor should work
just fine, but you can easily change the behavior by specifying a different extractor
class as a constructor argument:

```
Filter filter = new FilterBuilder(ReflectionExtractor.class)
                    .equals("getCustomerId", 123)
                    .greater("getTotal", 1000.0)
                    .build();
```

You can even specify your own custom extractor class—the only requirement is that
it implements a constructor that accepts a single string argument.

Obtaining query results

The easiest way to obtain query results is to invoke one of the
QueryMap.entrySet methods:

```
Filter filter = ...;
Set<Map.Entry> results = cache.entrySet(filter);
```

This will return a set of Map.Entry instances representing both the key and the value
of a cache entry, which is likely not what you want. More often than not you need
only values, so you will need to iterate over the results and extract the value from
each Map.Entry instance:

```
List values = new ArrayList(results.size());
for (Map.Entry entry : entries) {
    values.add(entry.getValue());
}
```

After doing this a couple times you will probably want to create a utility method for this task. Because all the queries should be encapsulated within various repository implementations, we can simply add the following utility methods to our AbstractCoherenceRepository class:

```
public abstract class AbstractCoherenceRepository<K, V extends
                                                   Entity<K>> {

    . . .

    protected Collection<V> queryForValues(Filter filter) {
      Set<Map.Entry<K, V>> entries = getCache().entrySet(filter);
      return extractValues(entries);
    }

    protected Collection<V> queryForValues(Filter filter,
                                            Comparator comparator) {
      Set<Map.Entry<K, V>> entries =
              getCache().entrySet(filter, comparator);
      return extractValues(entries);
    }

    private Collection<V> extractValues(Set<Map.Entry<K, V>> entries) {
      List<V> values = new ArrayList<V>(entries.size());
      for (Map.Entry<K, V> entry : entries) {
        values.add(entry.getValue());
      }
      return values;
    }
```

What happened to the QueryMap.values() method?

Obviously, things would be a bit simpler if the QueryMap interface also had an overloaded version of the values method that accepts a filter and optionally comparator as arguments.

I'm not sure why this functionality is missing from the API, but I hope it will be added in one of the future releases. In the meantime, a simple utility method is all it takes to provide the missing functionality, so I am not going to complain too much.

Controlling query scope using data affinity

As we discussed in the previous chapter, data affinity can provide a significant performance boost because it allows Coherence to optimize the query for related objects. Instead of executing the query in parallel across all the nodes and aggregating the results, Coherence can simply execute it on a single node, because data affinity guarantees that all the results will be on that particular node. This effectively reduces the number of objects searched to approximately **C/N**, where **C** is the total number of objects in the cache query is executed against, and **N** is the number of partitions in the cluster.

However, this optimization is not automatic—you have to target the partition to search explicitly, using `KeyAssociatedFilter`:

```
Filter query  = ...;
Filter filter = new KeyAssociatedFilter(query, key);
```

In the previous example, we create a `KeyAssociatedFilter` that wraps the query we want to execute. The second argument to its constructor is the cache key that determines the partition to search.

To make all of this more concrete, let's look at the final implementation of the code for our sample application that returns account transactions for a specific period. First, we need to add the `getTransactions` method to our `Account` class:

```
public Collection<Transaction> getTransactions(Date from, Date to) {
   return getTransactionRepository().findTransactions(m_id, from, to);
}
```

Finally, we need to implement the `findTransactions` method within the `CoherenceTransactionRepository`:

```
public Collection<Transaction> findTransactions(
                   Long accountId, Date from, Date to) {

   Filter filter = new FilterBuilder()
           .equals("id.accountId", accountId)
           .between("time", from, to)
           .build();

   return queryForValues(
           new KeyAssociatedFilter(filter, accountId),
           new DefaultTransactionComparator());
}
```

As you can see, we target the query using the account identifier and ensure that the results are sorted by transaction number by passing `DefaultTransactionComparator` to the `queryForValues` helper method we implemented earlier. This ensures that Coherence looks for transactions only within the partition that the account with the specified `id` belongs to.

Querying near cache

One situation where a direct query using the `entrySet` method might not be appropriate is when you need to query a near cache.

Because there is no way for Coherence to determine if all the results are already in the front cache, it will always execute the query against the back cache and return all the results over the network, even if some or all of them are already present in the front cache. Obviously, this is a waste of network bandwidth.

What you can do in order to optimize the query is to obtain the keys first and then retrieve the entries by calling the `CacheMap.getAll` method:

```
Filter filter = ...;

Set keys    = cache.keySet(filter);
Map results = cache.getAll(keys);
```

The `getAll` method will try to satisfy as many results as possible from the front cache and delegate to the back cache to retrieve only the missing ones. This will ensure that we move the bare minimum of data across the wire when executing queries, which will improve the throughput.

However, keep in mind that this approach might increase latency, as you are making two network roundtrips instead of one, unless all results are already in the front cache. In general, if the expected result set is relatively small, it might make more sense to move all the results over the network using a single `entrySet` call.

Another potential problem with the idiom used for near cache queries is that it could return invalid results. There is a possibility that some of the entries might change between the calls to `keySet` and `getAll`. If that happens, `getAll` might return entries that do not satisfy the filter anymore, so you should only use this approach if you know that this cannot happen (for example, if objects in the cache you are querying, or at least the attributes that the query is based on, are immutable).

Sorting the results

We have already seen that the `entrySet` method allows you to pass a `Comparator` as a second argument, which will be used to sort the results. If your objects implement the `Comparable` interface you can also specify `null` as a second argument and the results will be sorted based on their natural ordering. For example, if we defined the natural sort order for transactions by implementing `Comparable` within our `Transaction` class, we could've simply passed `null` instead of a `DefaultTransactionComparator` instance within the `findTransactions` implementation shown earlier.

On the other hand, if you use near cache query idiom, you will have to sort the results yourself. This is again an opportunity to add utility methods that allow you to query near cache and to optionally sort the results to our base repository class. However, there is a lot more to cover in this chapter, so I will leave this as an exercise for the reader.

Paging over query results

The `LimitFilter` is somewhat special and deserves a separate discussion. Unlike other filters, which are used to compose query criteria, the `LimitFilter` is used to control how many result items are returned at a time. Basically, it allows you to page through query results **n** items at a time.

This also implies that unlike other filters, which are constructed, executed, and discarded, an instance of a `LimitFilter` is something you might need to hold on to for an extended period of time, as it is a mutable object that keeps track of the current page number, top and bottom anchor objects, and other state that is necessary to support paging.

Let's look at a simple example to better demonstrate the proper usage of a `LimitFilter`:

```
NamedCache countries = CacheFactory.getCache("countries");

LimitFilter filter = new LimitFilter(
                        new LikeFilter("getName", "B%"), 5);

Set<Map.Entry> entries = countries.entrySet(filter, null);
// contains countries 1-5 whose name starts with a letter 'B'

filter.nextPage();
entries = countries.entrySet(filter, null);
// contains countries 6-10 whose name starts with a letter 'B'
```

```
filter.setPage(4);
entries = countries.entrySet(filter, null);
// contains countries 21-25 whose name starts with 'B'
```

As you can see, you can page through the result by executing the same query over and over again and modifying the current page of the `LimitFilter` between the query executions by calling the `nextPage`, `previousPage`, or `setPage` method.

The `LimitFilter` is extremely powerful as it allows you to execute the main query only once and then obtain the results in chunks of the size you specify. It maps very nicely to a common requirement for results paging within a web application, allowing you to bring the web server only the data it needs to generate the current page, thus reducing network traffic and improving application performance and scalability. You can safely store an instance of a `LimitFilter` within a user's HTTP session and reuse it later when the user navigates to another page of the results.

One thing to note in the preceding example is that we are using the `entrySet` method to retrieve the results, contrary to what we have discussed in the previous section. The reason for that is that we want to return countries sorted by name (natural order), and as I mentioned earlier, if we need to support paging over the sorted results we have no other option but to sort them within the cluster using an overload of the `entrySet` method that accepts a comparator.

However, this is really not an issue, as the amount of data sent over the wire will be naturally limited by the `LimitFilter` itself and will typically be very small, so we don't need to optimize the query for the near caching scenario.

Using indexes to improve query performance

Just as you can use indexes to improve query performance against a relational database, you can use them to improve the performance of a Coherence query. That is not to say that Coherence indexes are the same as database indexes—in fact, they are very different, and we'll discuss how indexes are implemented in Coherence shortly.

However, they are similar in the way they work, as they allow query processor to optimize queries by:

1. Limiting the number of entries that have to be evaluated by the filter
2. Avoiding the need for object deserialization by providing the necessary information within the index itself

Both of these features are very important and can have a significant impact on query performance. For that reason, it is recommended that you always create indexes for the attributes that you query on.

Anatomy of an Index

A Coherence index is an instance of a class that implements the com.tangosol.util.MapIndex interface:

```
public interface MapIndex {
  ValueExtractor getValueExtractor();
  boolean isOrdered();
  Map getIndexContents();
  Object get(Object key);
}
```

The getValueExtractor method returns the value extractor used to extract the attribute that should be indexed from an object, while the isOrdered method returns whether the index is sorted or not.

The get method allows us to obtain a value of the indexed attribute for the specified key directly from an index, which avoids object deserialization and repeat value extraction.

Finally, the getIndexContents method returns the actual index contents. This is a map that uses the value extracted from the indexed attribute as a key, while the value for each index entry is a set of cache keys corresponding to that attribute value.

Looking at an example should make the previous paragraph much easier to understand.

Let's assume that we have the following entries in the cache:

Key	Value
1	Person(firstName = 'Aleksandar', lastName = 'Seovic')
2	Person(firstName = 'Marija', lastName = 'Seovic')
3	Person(firstName = 'Ana Maria', lastName = 'Seovic')
4	Person(firstName = 'Novak', lastName = 'Seovic')
5	Person(firstName = 'Aleksandar', lastName = 'Jevic')

If we create an index on the lastName attribute, our index contents will look like this:

Key	Value
Jevic	{ 5 }
Seovic	{ 1, 2, 3, 4 }

On the other hand, an index on the `firstName` attribute will look like this:

Key	Value
Aleksandar	{ 1, 5 }
Ana Maria	{ 3 }
Marija	{ 2 }
Novak	{ 4 }

Index internals

Keep in mind that while I'm showing the actual values in the previous examples, the Coherence index actually stores both keys and values in their internal binary format.

For the most part you shouldn't care about this fact, but it is good to know if you end up accessing index contents directly.

The previous example should also make it obvious why indexes have such a profound effect on query performance.

If we wanted to obtain a list of keys for all people in the cache that have last name 'Seovic', without an index Coherence would have to deserialize each cache entry, extract the `lastName` attribute and perform a comparison, and if the comparison matches then it would add the cache entry key to the resulting list of keys.

With an index, Coherence doesn't need to do any of this—it will simply look up an index entry with the key **Seovic** and return the set of keys from that index entry.

Creating indexes

Now that we know how Coherence indexes are structured and why we should use them, let's look at how we can create them.

At the beginning of this chapter, we showed an incomplete definition of a `QueryMap` interface. What we omitted from it are the two methods that allow us to create and remove cache indexes:

```
public interface QueryMap extends Map {
   Set keySet(Filter filter);
   Set entrySet(Filter filter);
   Set entrySet(Filter filter, Comparator comparator);

   void addIndex(ValueExtractor extractor,
```

```
                  boolean isOrdered,
                  Comparator comparator);

    void removeIndex(ValueExtractor extractor);
}
```

As you can see, in order to create an index you need to specify three things:

- The value extractor that should be used to retrieve attribute value to use as an index key
- The flag specifying whether the index should be ordered or not
- Finally, the comparator to use for ordering

The first argument is by far the most important, as it determines index contents. It is also used as the index identifier, which is why you need to ensure that all value extractors you create implement the `equals` and `hashCode` methods properly.

If you decide to create an ordered index, index entries will be stored within a `SortedMap` instance, which introduces some overhead on index updates. Because of that, you should only order indexes for attributes that are likely to be used for sorting query results or in range queries, such as greater, less, between, and so on.

The last argument allows you to specify a comparator to use for index ordering, but you can specify `null` if the attribute you are indexing implements the `Comparable` interface and you want the index to use natural ordering. Of course, if an index is not ordered, you should always specify `null` for this argument.

Now that we know all of this, let's see what the code to define indexes on `firstName` and `lastName` attributes from the previous example should look like:

```
NamedCache people = CacheFactory.getCache("people");

people.addIndex(new PropertyExtractor("firstName"), false, null);
people.addIndex(new PropertyExtractor("lastName"), true, null);
```

As you can see, adding indexes to a cache is very simple. In this case we have created an unordered index on the `firstName` attribute and an ordered index using natural string ordering on the `lastName` attribute.

The last thing you should know is that the call to the `addIndex` method is treated by Coherence as a hint that an index should be created. What this means in practice is that you can safely create the same set of indexes on each Coherence node, even if another node has already created those same indexes. If an index for the specified extractor already exists, Coherence will simply ignore all subsequent requests for its creation.

Coherence query limitations

You have probably noticed by now that all the filters we have used as examples are evaluated against a single cache. This is one of the limitations of the Coherence query mechanism—it is not possible to perform an equivalent of a table join and execute the query against it.

However, while the ability to execute queries across multiple caches would come in handy occasionally, this is not too big a problem in practice. In most cases, you can perform any necessary table joins before loading the data into the cache, so you end up with all the information you need to query on in a single cache. Remember, the purpose of Coherence is to bring data closer to the application in a format that is easily consumable by the application, so transforming data from multiple tables into instances of a single aggregate is definitely something that you will be doing often.

That said, there will still be cases when you don't have all the data you need in a single cache, and you really, really need that join. In those cases the solution is to execute the query directly against the backend database and obtain a list of identifiers that you can use to retrieve objects from a cache.

Another important limitation you should be aware of is that Coherence queries only take into account objects that are already in the cache— they will not load any data from the database into the cache automatically. Because partial results are typically not what you want, this implies that you need to preload all the data into the cache before you start executing queries against it.

Alternatively, you can choose not to use Coherence queries at all and adopt the same approach as in the previous case by querying the database directly in order to obtain identifiers for the objects in the result, and using those identifiers to look up objects in the cache. Of course, this assumes that your cache is configured to automatically load the missing objects from the database on gets, which is something you will learn how to do in *Chapter 8, Implementing the Persistence Layer*.

Aggregators

Coherence filters are great when you need to retrieve a subset of objects from the cache based on a certain criteria, but there are cases when you want to process these objects as well in order to return a single result.

For example, you might want to retrieve the total amount of all orders for a particular customer. One possible solution is to retrieve all the orders for the customer using a filter and to iterate over them on the client in order to calculate the total. While this will work, you need to consider the implications:

1. You might end up moving a lot of data across the network in order to calculate a result that is only few bytes long

2. You will be calculating the result in a single-threaded fashion, which might introduce a performance bottleneck into your application

The better approach would be to calculate partial results on each cache node for the data it manages, and to aggregate those partial results into a single answer before returning it to the client. Fortunately, we can use Coherence **aggregators** to achieve exactly that.

By using an aggregator, we limit the amount of data that needs to be moved across the wire to the aggregator instance itself, the partial results returned by each Coherence node the aggregator is evaluated on, and the final result. This reduces the network traffic significantly and ensures that we use the network as efficiently as possible. It also allows us to perform the aggregation in parallel, using full processing power of the Coherence cluster.

At the very basic, an **aggregator** is an instance of a class that implements the com.tangosol.util.InvocableMap.EntryAggregator interface:

```
interface EntryAggregator extends Serializable {
    Object aggregate(Set set);
}
```

However, you will rarely have the need to implement this interface directly. Instead, you should extend the com.tangosol.util.aggregator.AbstractAggregator class that also implements the com.tangosol.util.InvocableMap.ParallelAwareAggregator interface, which is required to ensure that the aggregation is performed in parallel across the cluster.

The AbstractAggregator class has a constructor that accepts a value extractor to use and defines the three abstract methods you need to override:

```
public abstract class AbstractAggregator
        implements InvocableMap.ParallelAwareAggregator {

    public AbstractAggregator(ValueExtractor valueExtractor) {
        ...
    }
```

```
   protected abstract void init(boolean isFinal);
   protected abstract void process(Object value, boolean isFinal);
   protected abstract Object finalizeResult(boolean isFinal);
}
```

The `init` method is used to initialize the result of aggregation, the `process` method is used to process a single aggregation value and include it in the result, and the `finalizeResult` method is used to create the final result of the aggregation.

Because aggregators can be executed in parallel, the `init` and `finalizeResult` methods accept a flag specifying whether the result to initialize or finalize is the final result that should be returned by the aggregator or a partial result, returned by one of the parallel aggregators.

The `process` method also accepts an `isFinal` flag, but in its case the semantics are somewhat different—if the `isFinal` flag is `true`, that means that the object to process is the result of a single parallel aggregator execution that needs to be incorporated into the final result. Otherwise, it is the value extracted from a target object using the value extractor that was specified as a constructor argument.

This will all be much clearer when we look at an example. Let's write a simple aggregator that returns an average value of a numeric attribute:

```
public class AverageAggregator
        extends AbstractAggregator {

  private transient double sum;
  private transient int    count;

  public AverageAggregator() {
    // deserialization constructor
  }

  public AverageAggregator(ValueExtractor valueExtractor) {
    super(valueExtractor);
  }

  public AverageAggregator(String propertyName) {
    super(propertyName);
  }

  protected void init(boolean isFinal) {
    sum   = 0;
    count = 0;
  }
```

```
protected void process(Object value, boolean isFinal) {
    if (value != null) {
        if (isFinal) {
            PartialResult pr = (PartialResult) o;
            sum    += pr.getSum();
            count += pr.getCount();
        }
        else {
            sum += ((Number) o).doubleValue();
            count++;
        }
    }
}

protected Object finalizeResult(boolean isFinal) {
    if (isFinal) {
        return count == 0 ? null : sum / count;
    }
    else {
        return new PartialResult(sum, count);
    }
}

static class PartialResult implements Serializable {
    private double sum;
    private int    count;

    PartialResult(double sum, int count) {
        this.sum = sum;
        this.count = count;
    }

    public double getSum() {
        return sum;
    }

    public int getCount() {
        return count;
    }
}
```

As you can see, the `init` method simply sets both the `sum` and the `count` fields to zero, completely ignoring the value of the `isFinal` flag. This is OK, as we want those values to start from zero whether we are initializing our main aggregator or one of the parallel aggregators.

The `finalizeResult` method, on the other hand, depends on the `isFinal` flag to decide which value to return. If it is `true`, it divides the `sum` by the `count` in order to calculate the average and returns it. The only exception is if the `count` is zero, in which case the result is undefined and the `null` value is returned.

However, if the `isFinal` flag is false, the `finalizeResult` simply returns an instance of a `PartialResult` inner class, which is nothing more than a holder for the partial sum and related count on a single node.

Finally, the `process` method also uses the `isFinal` flag to determine its correct behavior. If it's `true`, that means that the value to be processed is a `PartialResult` instance, so it reads partial sum and count from it and adds them to the main aggregator's `sum` and `count` fields. Otherwise, it simply adds the value to the `sum` field and increments the `count` field by one.

We have implemented `AverageAggregator` in order to demonstrate with a simple example how the `isFinal` flag should be used to control the aggregation, as well as to show that the partial and the final result do not have to be of the same type. However, this particular aggregator is pretty much a throw-away piece of code, as we'll see in the next section.

Built-in aggregators

Just as with filters, Coherence ships with a number of useful built-in aggregators, and an equivalent of the `AverageAggregator` is one of them. Actually, there are two `average` aggregators built-in, as you can see in the following table:

Filter Class	Description
BigDecimalAverage	Calculates the average for a set of numeric values extracted from the cache entries and returns the result as a `BigDecimal`.
BigDecimalMax	Returns the maximum value, as a `BigDecimal`, for a set of numeric values extracted from the cache entries.
BigDecimalMin	Returns the minimum value, as a `BigDecimal`, for a set of numeric values extracted from the cache entries.
BigDecimalSum	Calculates the sum for a set of numeric values extracted from the cache entries and returns the result as a `BigDecimal`.
DoubleAverage	Calculates the average for a set of numeric values extracted from the cache entries and returns the result as a `Double`.

Filter Class	Description
DoubleMax	Returns the maximum value, as a Double, for a set of numeric values extracted from the cache entries.
DoubleMin	Returns the minimum value, as a Double, for a set of numeric values extracted from the cache entries.
DoubleSum	Calculates the sum for a set of numeric values extracted from the cache entries and returns the result as a Double.
LongMax	Returns the maximum value, as a Long, for a set of numeric values extracted from the cache entries.
LongMin	Returns the minimum value, as a Long, for a set of numeric values extracted from the cache entries.
LongSum	Calculates the sum for a set of numeric values extracted from the cache entries and returns the result as a Long.
ComparableMax	Returns the maximum value for a set of Comparable values extracted from the cache entries.
ComparableMin	Returns the minimum value for a set of Comparable values extracted from the cache entries.
Count	Returns the number of values in an entry set; equivalent to SQL's "select count(*)".
DistinctValues	Returns a set of unique values extracted from the cache entries; equivalent to SQL's "select distinct".
CompositeAggregator	Executes a collection of aggregators against the same entry set and returns the list of results, one for each aggregator in the collection.
GroupAggregator	A wrapper aggregator that allows you to split entries in a set based on some criteria and to aggregate each subset separately and independently.

The important thing to note about the various average, max, min, and sum aggregators is that they differ from each other in how they treat the numeric values they are aggregating, as well as by the type of the return value.

For example, while you can use the DoubleAverage aggregator to calculate the average for any set of java.lang.Number-derived values, you should be aware that each individual value will be converted to Double first using the Number.doubleValue method, which might lead to rounding errors. What you will typically want to do is use the most appropriate aggregator based on the actual type of the values you are aggregating, and convert the final result to the desired type if necessary.

Using aggregators

So far we have learned how to implement an aggregator and which aggregators are shipped with Coherence, but we haven't learned how to use them yet.

In order to execute an aggregator, you need to use one of the methods defined by the `com.tangosol.util.InvocableMap` interface:

```
public interface InvocableMap extends Map {
  Object aggregate(Collection keys,
                   InvocableMap.EntryAggregator aggregator);

  Object aggregate(Filter filter,
                   InvocableMap.EntryAggregator aggregator);
}
```

There are few more methods in the `InvocableMap` interface that we will cover in more detail in the next chapter, but these two are all we need to execute aggregators against cache entries.

The first overload of the `aggregate` method accepts an explicit collection of keys for a set of entries to aggregate, while the second one uses a filter to determine the set of entries aggregation should be performed on. Both methods accept an aggregator instance as a second argument, which can be either one of the built-in aggregators or a custom aggregator you have implemented.

Implementing LookupValuesAggregator

Earlier in the chapter, we started the implementation of a generic solution that will allow us to extract lookup values that are suitable for data binding to UI controls such as drop-downs and list boxes. So far, we have implemented a `LookupValueExtractor`, which allows us to extract a `LookupValue` instance from any object, in any cache.

In this section we will complete the exercise by implementing a `LookupValuesAggregator`—a simple aggregator that can be used to aggregate extracted lookup values into a list.

```
public class LookupValuesAggregator
            extends AbstractAggregator {

  private transient List<LookupValue> results;

  public LookupValuesAggregator(ValueExtractor idExtractor,
                                ValueExtractor descriptionExtractor){
```

```
        super(new LookupValueExtractor(idExtractor,
                                    descriptionExtractor));
    }

    protected void init(boolean isFinal) {
        results = new ArrayList<LookupValue>();
    }

    protected void process(Object value, boolean isFinal) {
        if (isFinal) {
            results.addAll((Collection<LookupValue>) value);
        }
        else {
            results.add((LookupValue) value);
        }
    }

    protected Object finalizeResult(boolean isFinal) {
        return results;
    }
}
```

As you can see, both `init` and `finalizeResult` methods are trivial—the first one simply initializes the `results` list, while the second one returns it. This works both for the main and parallel aggregators, so we can ignore the `isFinal` flag.

The `process` method, however, uses the `isFinal` flag to determine if it should add a single `LookupValue` instance or the list of `LookupValue`s returned by the parallel aggregator to the `results` collection.

Summary

In this chapter, you have learned how to query Coherence caches and how to perform aggregations on the data within the cache. We have covered built-in filters and aggregators and learned how to build custom ones.

We also talked about indexes and the impact they have on query performance. I cannot stress enough how important indexes are—make sure that you always use them and you will avoid a lot of potential performance problems.

In the next chapter, we will look at the remaining methods defined by the `InvocableMap` and learn one of the most important Coherence features from the scalability and performance perspective—a feature that allows us to process data in place and in parallel across the cluster.

6
Parallel and In-Place Processing

The scalability of a system is determined by the number of operations that have to be performed sequentially. Consequently, one of the best ways to ensure that a system scales well is to design it in such a way that as many operations as possible are performed in parallel.

For example, imagine what would happen if web server software such as Apache or IIS processed incoming HTTP requests sequentially, using a single thread. How many simultaneous requests could it process per second? Not very many. Would it be able to fully utilize a number of multicore CPUs on the modern hardware it runs on? Probably not.

Instead, in order to support many simultaneous users and to scale up to the limits of the hardware it runs, a web server uses a pool of worker threads (or, in the case of Apache, multiple processes) that perform most of the request processing and send the response. The main server thread simply accepts the requests and dispatches them to worker threads. That way, multiple requests can be processed in parallel, removing the bottleneck from the system.

Performing processing in multiple threads is a great way to parallelize execution on a single machine and ensure that the application scales up with the hardware. However, in order to take full advantage of the scale-out architecture, you need to ensure that processing can be performed in parallel across all the machines in the cluster. As I mentioned in the *Chapter 1, Achieving Performance, Scalability, and Availability Objectives*, a web farm with a load balancer in front achieves that, but only at the expense of making the application layer stateless and storing both the persistent and transient state in a database.

Coherence provides a number of features that allow you to perform work in parallel across the cluster, effectively removing a potential bottleneck from the system by enabling you to significantly reduce the load on the database server. In addition to that, it gives you the ability to harness the power of the whole cluster to perform computationally intensive work. Considering how important parallelization of work is for the system scalability, you should always look for ways to leverage some of these features within your application.

In the previous chapter we discussed the aggregators, which are one of the ways to perform data processing in parallel across the Coherence cluster. In this chapter we will look at three additional ways to leverage the computing power of the cluster to perform one or more tasks in parallel: the **entry processors**, the **invocation service**, and a clustered implementation of the **CommonJ Work Manager** specification.

Entry processors

An **entry processor** is an object that allows you to process one or more cache entries locally on the storage node, eliminating the need to move them across the network.

For example, let's say that you have a cache containing portfolio positions. If you are a large broker, you will likely have millions of positions in the cache. An oversimplified, but for our purposes sufficient implementation of a `PortfolioPosition` class might look like this:

```
public class PortfolioPosition implements PortableObject {

  private int        accountId;
  private String     tickerSymbol;
  private int        numberOfShares;
  private BigDecimal pricePaid;

  // constructors and accessors omitted for brevity

  public BigDecimal getPurchaseValue() {
    return pricePaid.multiply(new BigDecimal(numberOfShares));
  }

  public void split(int splitFactor) {
    numberOfShares *= splitFactor;
    pricePaid = pricePaid.divide(new BigDecimal(splitFactor));
  }
}
```

In order to perform a two-for-one split for Oracle stock, we have to find all the positions with the ORCL ticker symbol, invoke the `split` method on them, and update the cache.

An obvious way to do it is to retrieve all the matching positions using a filter, iterate over them, and update them one by one. The code to do that might look similar to the following:

```
Set keys = positions.keySet(
                new EqualsFilter("getTickerSymbol", "ORCL"));

for (Object key : keys) {
  positions.lock(key, 0);
  try {
    PortfolioPosition pp = (PortfolioPosition) positions.get(key);
    pp.split(2);
    positions.put(key, pp);
  }
  finally {
    positions.unlock(key);
  }
}
```

While this will work from a purely functional standpoint, it is a terribly inefficient way to do it. You end up moving a lot of data across the wire. You process it in a single-threaded fashion, item by item. Finally, you have to push the data back into the cluster, which again results in a lot of unnecessary network traffic. You also need to worry about concurrency. This is because it slows things down even further by requiring few more round trips to the server owning a piece of data to lock it and unlock it.

What you could do instead is implement an entry processor that performs a stock split and distribute it across the cluster to do the job in parallel, fully utilizing the processing power of all the servers in the cluster. In order to do that, you need to create a class that implements the `com.tangosol.util.InvocableMap.EntryProcessor` interface. The easiest way to achieve that is to extend a `com.tangosol.util.processor.AbstractProcessor` base class and implement the `process` method. In the case of our `StockSplitProcessor`, the final result might look similar to this:

```
public class StockSplitProcessor
        extends AbstractProcessor
        implements PortableObject {

    private int splitFactor;
```

```
public StockSplitProcessor() {
  // deserialization constructor
}

public StockSplitProcessor(int splitFactor) {
  this.splitFactor = splitFactor;
}

public Object process(InvocableMap.Entry entry) {
  PortfolioPosition pp = (PortfolioPosition) entry.getValue();
  pp.split(splitFactor);
  entry.setValue(pp);

  return null;
}

// serialization methods omitted for brevity
}
```

There are several things worth pointing out in the code above:

- If your processor needs any arguments to do the work, you can pass the arguments as instance members of the processor itself, as we did with the splitFactor in this example.

- An entry processor needs to be serializable because it has to be marshaled across the network in order to do its work. It also needs to be in the classpath of all Coherence nodes, so it can be deserialized and executed on the storage node.

- Within the process method, you don't need to worry about concurrency – Coherence guarantees that the individual entry processors against the same entry will execute atomically and in the order of arrival, which greatly simplifies the processing logic. It also guarantees that the processor will be executed even in the case of server failure, by failing it over to the node that becomes the new owner of the entry it needs to process.

- If you want to modify the value of a target entry within a processor, you need to call the setValue method on the entry itself. Similarly, you can remove a target entry from the cache by invoking the remove method on the entry.

Now that we have an entry processor, the only remaining questions are how to execute it, and more importantly, how to specify which cache entries it should execute against.

The answer to both of these questions is in the remaining methods of the InvocableMap interface. (We have already covered the aggregate method in the previous chapter.)

```
public interface InvocableMap extends java.util.Map {

  Object invoke(Object key,
                InvocableMap.EntryProcessor entryProcessor);

  Map invokeAll(Collection keys,
                InvocableMap.EntryProcessor entryProcessor);

  Map invokeAll(Filter filter,
                InvocableMap.EntryProcessor entryProcessor);

}
```

As you can see, there are three methods you can use to execute an entry processor. The first one, invoke, allows you to execute a processor against a single entry by specifying the entry's key and the processor to execute, and returns the result of the processor's process method.

The two invokeAll methods allow you to execute a processor against multiple entries, either by specifying a collection of keys to execute against, or by specifying a filter that should be used to determine the target entries. In both cases, you will get a Map as a result. The Map contains the results of every executed processor keyed by the entry key it was executed against. That way you can determine how many entries have been processed, by simply checking the size of the returned Map, as well as what the results of individual processor executions were.

To complete the example, here is the code that is functionally equivalent to the iterative example we saw earlier, but which uses an entry processor instead:

```
positions.invokeAll(new EqualsFilter("getTickerSymbol", "ORCL"),
                    new StockSplitProcessor(2));
```

I believe you will agree that the code above is much easier to read than the earlier iterative example, but that is not the only, or even the biggest, benefit of entry processors.

In the example above, the StockSplitProcessor will be executed in parallel by all cluster members, significantly reducing the latency of the stock split operation—no data other than the entry processor itself needs to be moved across the wire, and each node needs to process only a small subset of the data.

This also allows us to scale because there is no single point of bottleneck. As the data set grows, we can add more nodes to the cluster to ensure that each individual node still owns approximately the same number of objects. This would ensure that the duration of the operation remains constant as the size of the data set increases.

On the other hand, we can also scale the system to reduce the latency even further and improve performance. By splitting a data set of any given size across more nodes, we ensure that each node has less data to process.

In-place processing

We began this chapter by describing entry processors as one of the ways to perform processing in parallel across the cluster, only to learn later that the `InvocableMap` interface also provides a method that allows you to execute an entry processor against a single entry. If you are wondering why you would ever want to do that, it's a perfectly valid question.

The reason why this feature is useful has to do with cluster-wide concurrency and data modification. If you want to update the value of a cache entry using the `put` method, you need to obtain an explicit lock first. The typical pattern you will use when performing explicit locking is similar to this:

```
if (cache.lock(key, timeout)) {
  try {
    Object value = cache.get(key);
    // modify value
    cache.put(key, value);
  }
  finally {
    cache.unlock(key);
  }
}
else {
    // decide what to do if unable to obtain the lock:
    // retry, raise an exception, or something else
}
```

While the code above is fairly straightforward (even though it's definitely not the prettiest code ever written), think about the impact of the four highlighted method calls. Each of these calls will require a round trip to a remote cache server: first one to lock the entry, second to retrieve the value, third to update it and finally, fourth to unlock it. That's eight network hops in order to perform the update, plus six more that are not immediately obvious—two to create a backup of the lock, two to create a backup of the updated value, and two to remove the lock backup when the object is unlocked. That's 14 network hops for an update of a single object!

On the other hand, we can execute an entry processor carrying all the information we need to perform the update. It will eliminate the need for the explicit concurrency control, so we are saving eight network hops right there. It also won't require us to move the data object across the network in order to update it, which might be a huge saving if the object is large and the amount of information that needs to be updated is small. In the end, we will have two network hops for the entry processor (one to send the processor to the target node and one to send the result back to the client), plus two more to create a backup copy of the updated entry. As each network hop introduces latency into the system, reducing their number as much as possible will ensure that the system performs well.

Implementing WithdrawalProcessor

In *Chapter 4, Implementing Domain Objects*, we implemented the domain model for our sample application. One of the classes we created is the `Account` class, which has a method that allows us to withdraw the money from the account:

```
public Money withdraw(Money amount, String description)
                                throws InsufficientFundsException {
  Money balance = m_balance;

  // currency conversion code omitted for brevity

  if (amount.greaterThan(balance)) {
    throw new InsufficientFundsException(balance, amount);
  }

  m_balance = balance = balance.subtract(amount);
  postTransaction(TransactionType.WITHDRAWAL,
                  description,
                  amount,
                  balance);

  return balance;
}
```

As highlighted above, this method mutates the internal state of the `Account` instance, so we need to provide some kind of concurrency control. Using explicit locking is an option, but for the reasons discussed earlier we will create and use a custom entry processor instead:

```
public class WithdrawalProcessor
       extends AbstractProcessor
       implements Serializable {
```

```
    private Money  m_amount;
    private String m_description;

    public WithdrawalProcessor(Money amount, String description) {
      m_amount      = amount;
      m_description = description;
    }

    public Object process(InvocableMap.Entry entry) {
      Account account = (Account) entry.getValue();

      Money balance = account.withdraw(amount, description);
      entry.setValue(account, false);

      return balance;
    }
  }
```

It might be obvious by now that entry processors are my favorite way to perform *any* mutating operations on cached objects, but the example above also shows my favorite way to invoke such operations. All the business logic is completely encapsulated within domain classes, and the entry processor is simply used to control the location of execution.

I have also seen people implement business logic within the entry processor, but I don't personally like that approach. I don't believe that a Coherence-specific infrastructure component, such as the entry processor, is the best place to put business logic.

Cache service re-entrancy

As currently implemented, our `WithdrawalProcessor` has a problem.

The problem is not in the processor itself, but in the way Coherence internally processes requests submitted to a cache service. Even though the Coherence API is mostly synchronous, Coherence is internally very much asynchronous and each cache service has a request queue that stores all incoming requests. The cache service thread then dequeues and processes requests one by one.

An entry processor, from a cache service perspective, is just another request that needs to be processed. When a processor is dequeued, the cache service retrieves the target object from the cache and passes it as an argument to the entry processor's `process` method. So far so good—that's exactly what it should do, so you might be wondering what the problem with that is.

The problem is that you can easily deadlock the cache service thread by simply submitting another request to it within the entry processor. Any get or put, or any other API call for that matter, to a cache that belongs to the same cache service within the entry processor will effectively enqueue the request and block, and wait for the response. The problem is that the response will never arrive because it needs to be sent by the same cache service thread that is waiting for it!

Coherence guards against this scenario. So if you try to make a re-entrant call into a cache service, you will see an exception on the console saying that "`poll()` is a blocking call" and that the most likely reason is that you attempted to access cache that belongs to the cache service from the cache service thread.

In our case, the problem is caused by the attempt to post a transaction within the `Account.withdraw` method. Even though the actual call is buried deep within the `CoherenceTransactionRepository` implementation, it is still executed on the same cache service thread that is executing the processor, which makes it a re-entrant call.

There are several ways to deal with the problem. The obvious one is to use explicit locking and execute the `withdraw` method on the client, and that might be the easiest and the most straightforward approach in many cases. However, for the benefit of the discussion, let's agree that in this case that is not the option. That's because withdrawal is one of the critical operations in the system and we need to maximize the throughput as much as possible.

Another possible option is to map the cache we need to access to a different cache service. If the transactions cache belonged to a different cache service from the one accounts cache belongs to, we wouldn't have the problem as each cache service has its own request queue. However, in this case that is not an option either—data affinity can only be used if both caches belong to the same cache service, and we really, really want to have data affinity between accounts and transactions in order to optimize query performance.

However, the fact that we have data affinity between accounts and transactions gives us a third option, and the one we will use to solve the problem—direct backing map access.

Accessing the backing map directly

We have discussed data affinity, so we know that the new transaction should be stored on the same node (and within the same partition) as the account it is related to. Because the entry processor by definition executes on that same node, we can access the backing map for the transactions cache directly and put the transaction into it.

We can easily achieve this by overriding the save method within the `CoherenceTransactionRepository` implementation:

```
public void save(Transaction tx) {
    CacheService service = getCache().getCacheService();

    BackingMapManager bmm = service.getBackingMapManager();
    BackingMapManagerContext ctx = bmm.getContext();

    Converter keyConverter = ctx.getKeyToInternalConverter();
    Converter valueConverter = ctx.getValueToInternalConverter();

    Map backingMap = ctx.getBackingMap(getCache().getCacheName());
    backingMap.put(keyConverter.convert(tx.getId()),
                                    valueConverter.convert(tx));
}
```

As you can see, accessing the backing map directly is significantly more complex than accessing named cache, but it is not rocket science. You first need to obtain a `BackingMapManager` from the cache service and get its context. The backing map stores entries in an internal (binary) format, so you also need converters for both the key and the value, which can be obtained from the `BackingMapManagerContext`. Finally, you need to get the backing map itself and put the converted entry into it.

This effectively bypasses the cache service completely and avoids re-entrancy issues. However, keep in mind that direct backing map access is a very advanced feature and don't use it unless you know exactly what you are doing and are absolutely certain that no simpler solution is available.

Built-in entry processors

You will probably be writing custom entry processors more often than custom filter predicates, or even aggregators, which is why we have discussed how to do that first. However, just as in the case of filters and aggregators, Coherence ships with a number of useful entry processors you can use out of the box:

Class Name	Description
CompositeProcessor	Executes an array of entry processors sequentially, against the same cache entry
ConditionalProcessor	Wraps another entry processor and executes it only if the target entry satisfies the specified criteria
ConditionalPut	Updates an entry value only if the target entry satisfies the specified criteria

Class Name	Description
ConditionalPutAll	Updates the values of multiple entries only if they satisfy the specified criteria
ConditionalRemove	Removes an entry if it satisfies the specified criteria
NumberIncrementor	Increments a numeric property by a specified amount and returns either the old or the new value
NumberMultiplier	Multiplies a numeric property by a specified multiplier and returns either the old or the new value
VersionedPut	Updates an object implementing the Versionable interface, but only if the version of the specified value matches the version of the current value in the cache
VersionedPutAll	Updates multiple objects implementing the Versionable interface, but only if the versions of the specified values match the versions of the current values in the cache
PriorityProcessor	A wrapper processor that allows you to control scheduling priority and execution timeout for other entry processors
ExtractorProcessor	A processor that uses a ValueExtractor to extract one or more properties from the target entry
UpdaterProcessor	A processor that uses a ValueUpdater to update one or more properties of the target entry

We are not going to spend much time on most of these, as their purpose is fairly obvious and you can fill in the blanks using API documentation. That said, a few of them do deserve a further discussion and we'll cover them in the following sections.

VersionedPut and VersionedPutAll

These two processors allow you to implement optimistic concurrency for your objects.

Unlike the NamedCache.put method, which will simply overwrite the existing value with the new value even if it has been changed in the meantime, the VersionedPut method will update the entry only if the versions of the existing and the new value match.

In order to be able to use one of these processors, your objects need to implement a com.tangosol.util.Versionable interface, which defines the following methods:

```
public interface Versionable {
  public Comparable getVersionIndicator();
  public void incrementVersion();
}
```

By default, VersionedPut will not return anything and will only update an entry if it is already in the cache. However, you can change this behavior to return the existing value if the versions do not match, or to insert new value into the cache if it doesn't already exist.

PriorityProcessor

The PriorityProcessor allows you to explicitly control the scheduling priority and execution timeout of any entry processor.

This is an advanced feature that should be used judiciously. It can come in very handy in situations where you need to ensure that the processor is executed as soon as possible, or to override a default timeout value for a long-running processor.

ExtractorProcessor

The ExtractorProcessor allows you to extract a value from a cache entry using a ValueExtractor.

This processor is important because it can use available indexes to avoid deserialization of a value, which can significantly improve performance.

UpdaterProcessor

The UpdaterProcessor uses a ValueUpdater to modify one or more properties of a target object without sending the whole object across the wire.

This can be very useful when you need to update only a few properties on a large object, as it can significantly reduce the amount of network traffic. It essentially allows you to send only a small delta containing changes and update the target object on the node that owns it.

Invocation service

The **invocation service** allows you to execute an *agent* on one or more cluster members. Unlike entry processors, which are always a target for execution against specific cache entries, invocation service agents are targeted for execution on one or more cluster members. This makes them more suitable for cluster-wide management tasks than for the actual processing of data.

Another difference is that that the invocation service agents can be executed both synchronously and asynchronously, while the entry processors are always executed synchronously.

Unfortunately, the invocation service has one significant downside as well—unlike entry processors, which automatically fail-over to the backup node if the primary node fails and provide a 'once and only once' execution guarantee, invocable agents provide an 'at most once' guarantee. If an invocable agent or the node it is executing on fails, it is up to you to react to such an event, either by retrying agent execution on another node or by simply ignoring the failure.

This makes them suitable only for idempotent tasks, which can be retried in the case of failure, or for "best effort" tasks where it isn't critical that the execution ever occurs.

Configuring the invocation service

In order to be able to use the invocation service, you first need to configure it within the cache configuration file. To do that, simply add the following child element to the `caching-schemes` section:

```
<invocation-scheme>
  <scheme-name>invocation-service</scheme-name>
  <service-name>InvocationService</service-name>
  <thread-count>5</thread-count>
  <autostart>true</autostart>
</invocation-scheme>
```

Of course, you can specify any values you want for the configuration elements above. If you specify the `thread-count` element, the invocation service will be able to execute multiple agents in parallel using a thread pool of the specified size. You can also omit that particular element if you want the agents to be executed by the main invocation service thread itself.

Implementing agents

Invocation service agents need to implement the `com.tangosol.net.Invocable` interface:

```
public interface Invocable extends Runnable, Serializable {
  void init(InvocationService service);
  void run();
  Object getResult();
}
```

As you can see, the `Invocable` interface extends standard `java.lang.Runnable` by adding the `init` and `getResult` methods. The former can be used for one-time agent initialization, while the latter should return the result of agent execution after the `run` method completes.

Finally, notice that `Invocable` also extends `java.io.Serializable`. This is necessary because agents need to be serialized in order to be sent across the wire to the target node for execution, just like the entry processors.

Invocable versus Callable

You might've noticed that the `Invocable` interface is functionally very similar to the `java.util.concurrent.Callable` interface introduced in Java 5. They are both essentially `Runnable` extensions that can return the result of execution. So you might be wondering why the Coherence team didn't simply use `Callable` instead.

The reason is that the `Invocable` interface in Coherence predates Java 5 and `Callable` by several years, and has to remain part of the API both for backwards compatibility reasons and because Coherence supports Java 1.4 as well. However, it is fairly simple to implement an adapter that will allow you to pass any `Callable` to the Coherence invocation service as long as it is serializable.

As a matter of fact, you don't even have to write it yourself; you can simply use the one provided by the Coherence Tools project.

However, you don't have to implement the `Invocable` interface directly. Coherence provides `AbstractInvocable`, an abstract base class that you can extend in order to implement a custom invocable agent. This class provides the default implementations of the `init` and `getResult` methods, as well as the protected `setResult` method. All that you need to do is to implement the `run` method and invoke `setResult` from it to set the result of agent execution.

The following example shows a custom invocable agent that returns the amount of free memory on the target node:

```
public class FreeMemoryAgent extends AbstractInvocable {
  public void run() {
     Runtime rt = Runtime.getRuntime();
     setResult(rt.freeMemory());
  }
}
```

Executing agents

As I mentioned at the beginning of the section, the Invocation Service allows both synchronous and asynchronous agent execution:

```
public interface InvocationService extends Service {
  Map query(Invocable agent, Set members);
  void execute(Invocable agent, Set members,
              InvocationObserver observer);
}
```

The query method enables synchronous agent execution. You simply pass the agent to execute and the set of target members as arguments, and it returns a map of results that are keyed by the member. If you specify null as a second argument, the agent will be executed on all the members that are running the invocation service.

The following example invokes FreeMemoryAgent synchronously on all the members and prints the results:

```
InvocationService is =
    (InvocationService) CacheFactory.getService("invocation-service");

Map<Member, Integer> freeMemMap =
    is.query(new FreeMemoryAgent(), null);

for (Map.Entry<Member, Integer> freeMem : freeMemMap.entrySet()) {
    System.out.println("Member: " + freeMem.getKey() +
                       " Free: " + freeMem.getValue());
}
```

The execute method, on the other hand, allows you to invoke agents asynchronously. It does not have a return value, but it allows you to specify an observer that will be notified as the agents are executed on target members.

In order to implement the same functionality as in the previous example, we need to create an observer that will print out the result for each completed agent execution:

```
private static class LoggingInvocationObserver
        implements InvocationObserver {

    public void memberCompleted(Member member, Object result) {
        System.out.println("Member: " + member + " Free: " + result);
    }

    public void memberFailed(Member member, Throwable throwable) {
    }

    public void memberLeft(Member member) {
    }

    public void invocationCompleted() {
    }
}
```

In this case, we only care about the agent completion. However, you can see from the example above that you can also provide event handlers that will be invoked if an exception occurs during agent execution, or if the member leaves the cluster or invocation service during agent execution. Finally, the `invocationCompleted` method will be called after all the agents have either finished or the members they were targeted to have left the service.

Now that we have the logging observer, we can invoke `FreeMemoryAgent` asynchronously and use `LoggingInvocationObserver` to print the results:

```
InvocationService is = (InvocationService)
        CacheFactory.getService("invocation-service");

is.execute(new FreeMemoryAgent(), null,
        new LoggingInvocationObserver());
```

CommonJ Work Manager

The CommonJ Work Manager specification was developed jointly by BEA and IBM in order to overcome the limitations of the J2EE specification and provide a model for concurrent task execution in the managed environment. The work is currently under way to formalize this specification under *JSR 236: Concurrency Utilities for Java EE* and make it an official part of Java EE, but at the time of this writing this is still not the case and you will have to include `commonj.jar` as well as `coherence-work.jar` (both of which can be found within the Coherence `lib` directory) if you want to use it within your application.

The CommonJ Work Manager provides a simple API that allows applications to schedule work to be executed on their behalf within a managed environment. One of the common usage scenarios is to pull data from several backend data sources in parallel within a servlet in order to minimize the time it takes to render the page.

Coherence provides a clustered implementation of Work Manager, which allows you to execute work in parallel across all the nodes in the cluster, while still being able to use the same simple API for work scheduling.

In this section, we will use Work Manager to send email alerts to customers if their account balance falls under the minimum amount they configured, but first let's take a look at the Work Manager API basics.

Work Manager API basics

The CommonJ Work Manager API revolves around three main interfaces: WorkManager, Work, and WorkItem. While there are a few more, such as WorkEvent and WorkListener, you will only need to use them if you want to receive event notifications as the status of the scheduled work changes, which is typically not the case.

Defining work

You can define the task that you want to execute in parallel by implementing the Work interface. For the most part, this boils down to implementation of the run method defined by the Runnable interface, which Work extends. However, there are two more methods you need to implement: isDaemon and release.

The isDaemon method is ignored by the Coherence implementation of Work Manager, so you can simply return false from it. The release method is called indirectly when you invoke the method with the same name on the related WorkItem instance. If your run method is iterative and could potentially execute for a long time, you should use the release method to set a flag that can be used to interrupt the iteration and perform necessary cleanup.

That said, the run method is where you will implement the custom logic your task should execute. For example, if you need to send e-mail alerts to customers when their account balance falls below a predefined amount, you might want to implement a task for that purpose:

```
public class LowBalanceAlertTask
        implements Work, PortableObject {

    private Account account;
```

```
   public LowBalanceAlertTask() {
       // deserialization constructor
   }

   public LowBalanceAlertTask(Account account) {
     this.account = account;
   }

   public void release() {
   }

   public boolean isDaemon() {
     return false;
   }

   public void run() {
     SimpleMailMessage message = new SimpleMailMessage();
     message.setFrom("alerts@coherentbank.com");
     message.setTo(account.getCustomer().getEmailAddress());
     message.setSubject("ALERT: Low Balance");
     message.setText("Your account balance is " +
                     account.getBalance());

     JavaMailSenderImpl sender = new JavaMailSenderImpl();
     sender.setHost("mail.coherentbank.com");

     sender.send(message);
   }

   public void readExternal(PofReader pofReader) throws IOException {
     account = (Account) pofReader.readObject(0);
   }

   public void writeExternal(PofWriter pofWriter) throws IOException {
     pofWriter.writeObject(0, account);
   }
 }
```

As you can see, the `run` method simply uses the information from the account,
such as customer's e-mail address and current balance, to create and send an e-mail
message. In this example we used utility classes provided by Spring Framework
in order to make the code more readable, but you could use plain JavaMail API to
achieve the same thing.

You should also note that our task implements the `PortableObject` interface. This is necessary because the task will likely be executed by a remote cluster member, so Coherence needs to be able to serialize it in order to send it across the network.

Scheduling work

Now that we have a `Work` implementation defined, we need to schedule it for execution. In order to do that, we need to obtain an instance of a `WorkManager` and pass our task to its `schedule` method:

```
WorkManager wm = new WorkManager("NotificationManager", 3);
wm.schedule(new LowBalanceAlertTask(acct1));
wm.schedule(new LowBalanceAlertTask(acct2));
```

The first argument passed to the `WorkManager` constructor is the name we want to use for this work manager.

Coherence `WorkManager` is implemented on top of Invocation Service, so the specified name will also be used as the name of the underlying `InvocationService`. One important caveat you should be aware of when creating `WorkManager` instances is that the `WorkManager` constructor can only be called once per Coherence node for any given work manager name. Any attempt to create an instance of a `WorkManager` that already exists will throw an exception. For that reason, you should store the reference to a created `WorkManager` in a static final variable, which will ensure that the constructor is called only once when the client class is initialized. If that's not possible, or you need to access the same `WorkManager` from multiple client classes, you can obtain it indirectly from the `InvocationService` it runs on top of:

```
Service service = CacheFactory.getService(managerName);
WorkManager wm = (WorkManager) service.getUserContext();
```

The second constructor argument is the number of worker threads the work manager should use to execute tasks. If you specify zero for this argument, `WorkManager` will be created in the "client" mode. This implies that it will only be able to schedule the work to be executed by the remote cluster members that belong to the same `InvocationService`. If you specify a negative integer, the default number of threads as defined in the cache configuration file will be used. This allows you to configure the thread pool size externally and is probably the best way to initialize `WorkManager` in your code.

When deciding on the number of threads to use, you should keep in mind that all work managers across the cluster that share a common name essentially form a cluster-wide thread pool to execute tasks on. That means that if we have a cluster of 10 nodes, each of which initializes our `NotificationManager` to use three threads, we will be able to execute 30 tasks simultaneously.

Once WorkManager is created, you can schedule tasks to execute by calling the schedule method, as we did in the example earlier. In addition to the method used in the example, there is an overload of the schedule method that allows you to pass a WorkListener to be notified as the status of the task changes.

The schedule method returns a WorkItem instance that can be used to determine the result of Work execution and to wait for completion of one or all tasks. In the example earlier, we didn't really care if the tasks have completed and what the result of each one was, so we simply ignored the return values. In cases when you do care about the results, you will need to do things a bit differently.

Processing the results

Coherence Work Manager implementation allows you to process the results of distributed Work execution using the same simple API you would use in a single-server application. All you need to do is to capture each WorkItem returned by the schedule method and use them to wait for the execution to finish and to get the result for each task.

For example, if we wanted to modify the example earlier to wait for all the notifications to be sent, we could implement it like this:

```
Set items = new HashSet();

WorkManager wm = new WorkManager("NotificationManager", 3);
items.add(wm.schedule(new LowBalanceAlertTask(acct1)));
items.add(wm.schedule(new LowBalanceAlertTask(acct2)));
...

wm.waitForAll(items, WorkManager.INDEFINITE);
```

As you can see, all we had to do was to add each WorkItem returned by the schedule method to the items collection and pass that collection to the WorkManager.waitForAll method. The second argument to waitForAll is the time in milliseconds to wait for all the tasks to complete. In this example, we have used one of the constants defined in the WorkManager interface to wait indefinitely until all the tasks are completed.

If you wanted to wait until any one of the scheduled tasks is completed, you could use the `waitForAny` method instead. An example of when this would be useful is when you have multiple ways to accomplish some task. For example, you might want to implement an alert notification that can be sent either via e-mail or SMS, but you only need to ensure that one of them is complete before proceeding. To achieve that, you would schedule both e-mail and SMS notification tasks and use `waitForAny` to block until at least one of them completes.

Once the task is marked as completed, you need to check what the result of its execution was by calling the `getResult` method on the related `WorkItem`. This method will either return the final `Work` instance, which might have been modified during execution, or will throw an exception if the task's `run` method threw an exception.

Coherence Work Manager limitations

The main limitation of the Coherence Work Manager is the same as for the Invocation Service — there are no guarantees that a task will be executed at all, so you shouldn't use Work Manager to execute tasks that need stricter execution semantics than 'at most once', which is essentially what both the Invocation Service and Work Manager provide.

Coherence Incubator

Coherence Incubator, an Oracle-sponsored open source project led by Brian Oliver, provides a few more alternatives for distributed execution such as Command, Functor, and Processing patterns.

In addition to that, it also provides the implementation of store and forward messaging on top of Coherence, as well as the push replication framework, which can be used to synchronize multiple Coherence clusters across data centers.

Detailed discussion of Coherence Incubator is out of the scope of this book, but you should definitely check out the official website for the project (`http://coherence.oracle.com/display/INCUBATOR/Home`) and Brian's blog (`http://brianoliver.wordpress.com`) for more details.

Summary

In this chapter we have looked at three powerful ways to leverage the processing power of the whole cluster to execute tasks in parallel.

We discussed entry processors, which provide a way to bring processing closer to the data and significantly reduce the network bandwidth requirements of the application. When used properly, they can have a huge impact on both performance and scalability of the application. You should always look for the opportunities to replace inefficient client-side code with entry processors.

We also talked about the Invocation Service, which allows you to encapsulate custom logic into agents that can be targeted for execution on one or more members of the cluster.

Finally, we discussed clustered implementation of the CommonJ Work Manager specification that allows you to schedule tasks for execution using simple Work Manager API while fully leveraging processing power of the cluster to execute scheduled tasks in parallel.

While each of these mechanisms comes with some limitations, they are all important when building scalable applications and you should keep them in mind when designing various features of your application. There will be many situations where one of them could be used to significantly improve both performance and scalability.

7
Processing Data Grid Events

So far we have used Coherence in a somewhat imperative way. We used the API to store and retrieve data from it, to run queries, and to execute entry processors, invocable agents, and Work Manager tasks. In many cases, a typical application will require us to use Coherence in this way; however, there are situations where we want our application to simply observe what's going on within the cluster and to react only when an event of interest occurs. Fortunately, Coherence makes this a breeze.

There are a number of different events that Coherence raises, to which any interested application can subscribe. As a matter of fact, many of the core features of Coherence, such as creation of backup copies of data and cluster repartitioning are driven by events, so the messaging infrastructure required for reliable event delivery is extremely robust and well tested.

Your application can listen to events such as service startup and shutdown, cluster membership changes, cache repartitioning, and modifications to data in the cache. The first three event types are fairly advanced features, which require deep understanding of the Coherence internals, so we will not discuss them further in this book. The remainder of this chapter will focus on the last, but for most practical purposes, the most important type of event in Coherence—cache events.

Cache events

If your application is interested in the current state of the data in the data store, you have two options:

- You can poll the data store for updates at regular intervals
- You can register a listener that will be notified by the data store when the data changes

Obviously, the first option doesn't scale well, as it puts a significant burden on both the client application and the data store, even when there are no changes. Imagine a desktop trading application that queries a database, or even Coherence, every second or so to retrieve current stock prices. It wouldn't take very many of those applications to bring even the most powerful database server or a large Coherence cluster to a halt.

Unfortunately, most data sources do not support the second option, or you have to jump through the hoops to do it. For example, with most relational databases you can create a trigger that will raise the event, typically using some kind of an asynchronous messaging system. While this might provide a better solution than polling in many cases, it increases the complexity of the system as a whole and the events are still fairly expensive from a performance standpoint.

Coherence, on the other hand, provides an out-of-the-box event mechanism that is both easy-to-use and efficient. Events are delivered using the same fast and reliable protocol that is used for all other communication within the cluster, so there is no additional messaging infrastructure that needs to be set up.

From a development perspective, all that you need to do is to create a class that implements a `com.tangosol.util.MapListener` interface and register it with the cache you want to observe, as shown next:

```
public interface MapListener
        extends java.util.EventListener {
   void entryInserted(MapEvent mapEvent);
   void entryUpdated(MapEvent mapEvent);
   void entryDeleted(MapEvent mapEvent);
}
```

In the common case that you are not interested in all three types of events, you can simply extend the `com.tangosol.util.AbstractMapListener` class and override the methods from the `MapListener` interface you are interested in.

The `MapEvent` object, which each of the event handling methods accepts as an argument, carries detailed information about the event that occurred, such as the event type, a reference to a cache that event occurred on, the key of the entry that triggered the event, as well as the old and new values of an entry, if applicable.

In some cases, you might be interested in an event, but not necessarily in either the old or the new value. Therefore Coherence gives you an option of registering a listener for **lite** events, in which case old and new value will not be set within the `MapEvent` instance. For default, non-lite events, they will be set according to the following table:

Event Type	Old Value	New Value
Inserted	`null`	Inserted value
Updated	Old entry value	New entry value
Deleted	Old entry value	`null`

Registering map listeners

There are two ways to register map listeners:

- Programmatically, within your application's code
- Within the cache configuration file

While the latter approach allows you to ensure that every node is automatically registered for events, it only allows you to register for all of the events occurring in a cache. As you'll see soon, programmatic registration gives you more options and is typically used to register client-side event listeners.

Programmatic listener registration

You can register map listeners programmatically, using one of the methods defined by the `com.tangosol.util.ObservableMap` interface:

```
public interface ObservableMap extends java.util.Map {
  void addMapListener(MapListener mapListener);

  void addMapListener(MapListener mapListener,
                      Object key, boolean fLite);

  void addMapListener(MapListener mapListener,
                      Filter filter, boolean fLite);

  void removeMapListener(MapListener mapListener);

  void removeMapListener(MapListener mapListener, Object key);

  void removeMapListener(MapListener mapListener, Filter filter);
}
```

As you can see, there are three overloads of the `addMapListener` method, as well as the matching variants of the `removeMapListener` method, which is used to unregister a listener.

The first method registers a cache-wide listener that receives all cache events, as well as the old and new values. This method is also called when you register a listener in the configuration file.

The second overload of `addMapListener` allows you to register for events on a single cache entry by specifying the entry key as the second argument. You can also choose whether to receive standard or lite events by specifying `fLite` flag as the third argument.

Finally, using the third overload you can register for events based on filter evaluation, and this is probably the most interesting of the three. What it basically allows you to do is to register interest in events that occur within a subset of cache entries that satisfy certain criteria. For example, you could register to be notified whenever a withdrawal exceeding a certain amount is posted for a specific account.

This method can also be used to listen for lite events on the cache as a whole, which the first method doesn't allow you to do. You can achieve this by passing `AlwaysFilter.INSTANCE` as the `filter` argument.

Listening for events based on a filter presents some interesting challenges. For instance, when you update a cache entry, that update could impact whether that entry satisfies the filter or not. When an entry that didn't match the filter is modified so it does, should that be treated as an update or as an insert event? Similarly, when an entry that did match the filter is modified so it doesn't anymore, should that be treated as update or a delete event?

The answer is that Coherence only raises insert and delete events when an entry is physically inserted into or removed from the cache, so the answer to both of the above questions is that an update event will be raised. However, because it is sometimes important to know whether an update happened *within* the filter, or caused an entry to *enter* or *leave* the filter, Coherence provides a special filter type, `MapEventFilter`, which allows you to more selectively register for events.

Listening to specific events

The `MapEventFilter` is a wrapper implementation of the `Filter` interface that gives you more control over the exact set of events you want to receive. In addition to the regular filter that will determine the set of entries to observe, you can specify a mask that will determine which specific events to raise.

You can combine one or more of the following constants, defined in the
MapEventFilter class, to create a mask:

Constant	Description
E_ALL	Indicates that all events should be evaluated.
E_INSERTED	Indicates that insert events should be evaluated.
E_DELETED	Indicates that delete events should be evaluated.
E_UPDATED	Indicates that all update events should be evaluated.
E_UPDATED_ENTERED	Indicates that update events that caused an entry to *enter* the filter should be evaluated. An entry is deemed to have entered the filter if the filter evaluates to false for its old value and to true for its new value.
E_UPDATED_LEFT	Indicates that update events that caused an entry to *leave* the filter should be evaluated. An entry is deemed to have left the filter if the filter evaluates to true for its old value and to false for its new value.
E_UPDATED_WITHIN	Indicates that update events *within* the filter should be evaluated. An entry is considered updated within the filter if the filter evaluates to true for both its old value and its new value.
E_KEYSET	Indicates that all events that change the observable entry set should be evaluated. This is essentially a simpler way to register for a combination of inserted, deleted, updated (entered) and updated (left) events – basically everything except for updated (within) events.

As you can see, MapEventFilter allows you to register only for specific events,
so you should use it to limit what events are sent to the client whenever you are
interested in only some of them.

As mentioned earlier, you can extend AbstractMapListener if you are interested
in some events, but that's just a coding convenience that will help you keep your
listeners free from empty method implementations. It will not impact in any way
on which events actually get sent across the network, so unless you limit those
using MapEventFilter, even the events you are not interested in will be sent to
your listener, only to be discarded by it. This will create unnecessary network traffic,
even if you use lite events, and especially if you use the standard events and have
large objects in the cache you are observing, as each event will also carry either the
old or the new value with it, or both in the case of an update event.

By using MapEventFilter to register a listener only for the events you actually
care about, you can significantly reduce network traffic and improve your
application's throughput.

Listening for specific property changes

Another filter that can come in handy to reduce the number of update events that are sent to the listening client is the `ValueChangeEventFilter`.

By default, an update event is raised when any property of the cached object changes. However, you might only be interested in changes to a specific property of an object, such as account balance, or a stock price. In those cases you can use `ValueChangeEventFilter` to pinpoint which property you are interested in and to receive notifications only when that property changes.

For example, if you wanted to receive a notification only when the account's balance changes, you could register a listener like this:

```
NamedCache accounts = CacheFactory.getCache("accounts");

accounts.addMapListener(new BalanceChangedListener(),
                new ValueChangeEventFilter("getBalance"), false);
```

Notice that there is no need to wrap `ValueChangeEventFilter` with a `MapEventFilter`, as it will only return update events. You just need to make sure that your event listener implements the `entryUpdated` method.

Transforming map events

In most situations, you can get by using either standard or lite events, but sometimes you need something in between: you might need the information about the old and new values. However, you don't need the whole, potentially large, values. For example, our `BalanceChangedListener` might not care about the accounts themselves, but only about the old and new balance amounts.

Coherence uses `MapEventTransformer` interfaces as a way to transform a `MapEvent` before it's raised. The `MapEventTransformer` is an interface with the single method:

```
public interface MapEventTransformer {
    MapEvent transform(MapEvent event);
}
```

There are two event transformers that ship with Coherence:

- `ExtractorEventTransformer`: This uses value extractors to replace old and new value with the property values extracted from them
- `SemiLiteEventTransformer`: This removes the old value from the `MapEvent`

If we wanted to implement a custom event transformer that causes only balances to be returned instead of the `Account` instances, we could use the following code snippet:

```
public class BalanceChangedEventTransformer
        implements MapEventTransformer, PortableObject {

    public MapEvent transform(MapEvent mapEvent) {
        Account oldAccount = (Account) mapEvent.getOldValue();
        Account newAccount = (Account) mapEvent.getNewValue();

        return new MapEvent(mapEvent.getMap(), mapEvent.getId(),
                            mapEvent.getKey(), oldAccount.getBalance(),
                            newAccount.getBalance());
    }

    // serialization methods omitted for brevity
}
```

As you can see, the implementation of a transformer is trivial. You create a new `MapEvent` instance using map, event type identifier, and entry key from the original event, and replace old and new value appropriately.

You can also use a transformer to prevent an event from being raised in a first place. All you need to do is return `null` from the `transform` method.

In order to tell Coherence to apply our transformer to events we are interested in, we need to use `MapEventTransformerFilter`:

```
NamedCache accounts = CacheFactory.getCache("accounts");

Filter filter = new MapEventTransformerFilter(
                    new ValueChangeEventFilter("getBalance"),
                    new BalanceChangedEventTransformer());

accounts.addMapListener(new BalanceChangedListener(),
                        filter, false);
```

The `MapEventTransformerFilter` is another special filter type that wraps a filter to evaluate and the transformer to apply to the events. You can optionally pass `null` as a filter, in which case you will listen for all events on the cache and the specified transformer will be applied to them.

As a final note, while the preceding code demonstrates how to implement a custom transformer, we could've used the built-in `ExtractorEventTransformer` to achieve the same result:

```
NamedCache accounts = CacheFactory.getCache("accounts");

Filter filter = new MapEventTransformerFilter(
                    new ValueChangeEventFilter("getBalance"),
                    new ExtractorEventTransformer("getBalance"));

accounts.addMapListener(new BalanceChangedListener(), filter, false);
```

Cache topology warning
Event transformers are currently supported by the partitioned cache service only.

Registering listeners within the cache configuration file

As mentioned at the beginning of this section, you can also register cache listeners by specifying them in the cache configuration file. All you need to do is add a `listener` element to the cache scheme configuration, and specify the fully qualified name of the class implementing a listener:

```
<distributed-scheme>
  <scheme-name>example-distributed</scheme-name>
  <service-name>DistributedCache</service-name>
  <listener>
    <class-scheme>
      <class-name>BalanceChangedListener</class-name>
    </class-scheme>
  </listener>

  <backing-map-scheme>
    <local-scheme>
      <scheme-ref>unlimited-backing-map</scheme-ref>
    </local-scheme>
  </backing-map-scheme>

  <autostart>true</autostart>

</distributed-scheme>
```

While this allows us to register a listener automatically on every node in the cluster, it has several major drawbacks:

- It can only be used to register a cache-wide listener, not a key-based or a filter-based one

- There is no way to register for lite events, which means that old and new value will always be sent as a part of the event

- There is no way to register for a specific event, which means that all events will be sent to the client

- It tends to make cache configuration more complex, as it often requires that you create separate configuration for caches that could otherwise be configured exactly the same

For all these reasons, you should register listeners within the cache configuration file only when you have a listener that can be applied to multiple caches and needs to listen for all events and receive old and new value. Otherwise, you are better off registering a more specifically targeted listener programmatically, as described in the previous sections.

Making any map observable

If you like the way map events are implemented in Coherence, you might want to utilize the same mechanism even for other maps within your application.

The good news is that there are several ways to make the features of `ObservableMap` available to your application even outside the cluster. The first one is to use one of the `Map` implementations that ship with Coherence and implement the `ObservableMap` interface directly, such as the `com.tangosol.util.ObservableHashMap` class.

The second, and usually more appropriate way for existing applications, is to wrap your application's map with a `com.tangosol.util.WrapperObservableMap`, or, if you need map concurrency features as well, a `com.tangosol.util.WrapperConcurrentMap`, which extends it.

Either way, you can use the same event mechanism both with the clustered maps within Coherence and with the local, in-process maps within your application.

Backing map events

So far, we have discussed client-side event listeners that receive notifications when something happens in the cluster. One of the main characteristics of client-side listeners is that many of them can register to receive the same event, which is great when you need to use the event payload on each client. For example, you could use client-side event listeners to update the UI in many desktop applications as the data in the cluster changes.

However, there are cases when you want to react to an event only once, and in those cases you typically want to handle the event on the server it originated from.

In the previous chapter, we implemented a Work Manager task that allows us to send an e-mail alert to the customer if the balance in his or her account falls under a certain amount. However, we never discussed how to integrate that feature into the application.

Now that you have learned about event listeners, it is probably obvious that we can use an event listener to receive notification when the account balance changes, check if the balance is low, and if it is low, schedule an alert task for execution within our event handler.

The problem is that if we use client-side event listeners, we will be sending as many alerts to a customer as we have listeners that are registered for that particular event. Each listener will receive an event, decide that the balance is low, and schedule the e-mail alert task for execution. Needless to say, even if you don't care too much about the unnecessary strain you are putting on your e-mail server, your customers probably won't be very pleased when you flood their inbox with alerts.

Fortunately, Coherence provides an effective way to solve this problem, in the form of a **backing map listener**. For the most part, a backing a map listener is exactly the same as the client-side listener we discussed earlier. It is nothing more than a class that implements the `MapListener` interface.

However, there are several caveats that make backing map listeners more difficult to implement, and most of them stem from the fact that they are executed on the cache service thread, which imposes a certain set of requirements and limitations on them.

For one, just like entry processors, backing map listeners are not allowed to make a re-entrant call into the cache service that they are part of. That means that you cannot access from them any cache that belongs to that same cache service.

Second, because they are executed synchronously on a cache service thread, it is of paramount importance that you do not do anything time consuming within the event handler or you might cause all sorts of delays across the cluster. If you need to do anything that might take longer, you need to delegate it to Invocation Service, Work Manager, or an external messaging system. This is exactly the reason why we implemented our e-mail alert sender as a Work Manager task instead of directly within the backing map listener.

Finally, because backing map listeners are essentially the same mechanism that is used internally for backup of cache entries, the `MapEvent` instances they receive are not quite what you would expect and calls to `getKey`, `getOldValue`, and `getNewValue` will return values in internal, serialized binary format, not the nice object format you know how to work with.

All that said, backing map listeners are still extremely useful and will probably be the best way to solve many problems in a typical Coherence application. You just need to keep the caveats above in mind when you are designing them.

Implementing a low-balance listener

Now that we are aware of the limitations, let's get our hands dirty and implement an event listener that will send an alert if the balance falls below a certain amount. In a real-world application, you would probably allow customers to specify the threshold that should be used as a trigger for the alert for each account individually, but we'll keep things simple and configure our listener with the amount that should be used as a threshold for all the accounts in the system.

In the previous chapter, we discussed `BackingMapManagerContext` and learned how to convert cache keys and values from their internal representation into their standard Java representation. We will use that knowledge now to implement a base class for our backing map listeners, which will make the implementation of our low-balance listener much easier and more direct.

AbstractBackingMapListener

What we want is an abstract base class that provides convenience methods that allow us to extract key and values from the internal representation of a `MapEvent` and convert them to their standard object form. We will also implement a method that allows us to convert a whole `MapEvent` instance at once, which might be more convenient if you need to convert both the key and the values. Finally, because backing map events can be triggered not only by regular inserts, updates, and deletes, but also by cache evictions or distributions, we will add a few methods that allow us to differentiate among these event causes.

Anyway, to cut long story short, here is what our base class for backing map listeners might look like:

```java
public abstract class AbstractBackingMapListener
        extends AbstractMapListener {

  private BackingMapManagerContext context;

  protected AbstractBackingMapListener(
                                BackingMapManagerContext context) {
    this.context = context;
  }

  protected BackingMapManagerContext getContext() {
    return context;
  }

  protected MapEvent convertFromInternal(MapEvent event) {
    return ConverterCollections.getMapEvent(
                event.getMap(), event,
                context.getKeyFromInternalConverter(),
                context.getValueFromInternalConverter());
  }

  protected Object getKey(MapEvent event) {
    return context.getKeyFromInternalConverter()
                .convert(event.getKey());
  }

  protected Object getOldValue(MapEvent event) {
    return context.getValueFromInternalConverter()
                .convert(event.getOldValue());
  }

  protected Object getNewValue(MapEvent event) {
    return context.getValueFromInternalConverter()
                .convert(event.getNewValue());
  }
  protected boolean isEviction(MapEvent event) {
    return context.isKeyOwned(event.getKey())
            && event instanceof CacheEvent
            && ((CacheEvent) event).isSynthetic();
  }

  protected boolean isDistribution(MapEvent event) {
    return !context.isKeyOwned(event.getKey());
  }
}
```

The `getKey`, `getOldValue`, and `getNewValue` methods should be self-explanatory, as we discussed usage of backing map converters in the previous chapter, so let's focus on the topics we haven't covered yet.

The `com.tangosol.util.ConverterCollections` class is a utility class that provides a number of methods that either allow you to convert items stored in various collection types, or in the case of a `getMapEvent` method, a wrapper implementation of a `MapEvent` that lazily converts the key and the values.

Finally, let's look at the methods that allow us to determine the cause of an event. The `isEviction` method returns true if the `MapEvent` is an instance of a more specific `CacheEvent` class and is a synthetic event, meaning that it didn't occur as a result of direct cache manipulation by the application.

The `isDistribution` method returns true if the key of the entry that raised the event does not belong to the backing map we are working with anymore, which implies that Coherence had to repartition data due to changes in cluster membership.

That pretty much concludes our discussion of the base class for backing map listeners, so we are ready to extend it and implement our first real backing map listener.

Low-balance listener

Now that we have both the base class and the `LowBalanceAlertTask` implemented, the implementation of the actual `LowBalanceListener` is quite simple:

```
public class LowBalanceListener extends AbstractBackingMapListener {

  private static final WorkManager lowBalanceAlertManager =
          WorkManagerFactory.getInstance("LowBalanceAlertManager", 3);

  private int lowBalance;

  public LowBalanceListener(BackingMapManagerContext context,
                            int lowBalance) {
    super(context);
    this.lowBalance = lowBalance;
  }

  public void entryUpdated(MapEvent event) {
    Account account = (Account) getNewValue(event);

    if (account.getBalance().intValue() < lowBalance) {
      try {
```

```
        lowBalanceAlertManager.schedule(
          new LowBalanceAlertTask(account));
      }
      catch (WorkException e) {
        log(e);
      }
    }
  }
}
```

The first thing we do is obtain a reference to a `WorkManager` instance. In this case, we have done that using the `WorkManagerFactory.getInstance` method, which allows us to specify the number of worker threads we want our Work Manager to use.

Our constructor accepts both the `BackingMapManagerContext` instance and the threshold amount we should use when checking if the balance is too low. We will see shortly how both of these arguments are passed to the constructor.

Finally, we implement the `entryUpdated` method to obtain a converted `Account` instance from the event, and to schedule `LowBalanceAlertTask` for execution if the balance is lower than the threshold.

In this case we don't really care if the alert tasks execute or not, so we simply log any exceptions that might occur when scheduling the task for execution, and we don't wait for its completion, which would in this case defeat the purpose of using `WorkManager` for asynchronous execution in the first place.

That's really all there is to it, so we are ready to connect the dots by registering our listener with the backing map.

Registering a backing map listener

While you technically could register a backing map listener programmatically, this requires a good understanding of advanced APIs and tends to be somewhat convoluted. Much easier, and in this case the preferred way to register a listener is by specifying it in the cache configuration file.

The way you do it is similar to the registration of the client-side listeners we covered earlier in the chapter, with two main differences:

- You configure a listener within a `backing-map-scheme` element for the cache scheme, instead of within the top-level element for the scheme.

- You pass one or more arguments to the constructor using `init-param` elements. At the very least, you need to pass the `BackingMapManagerContext` to it.

So, in order to register the LowBalanceListener we just implemented, we would add the following to the cache scheme for the accounts cache:

```xml
<distributed-scheme>
  <scheme-name>accounts-scheme</scheme-name>
  <scheme-ref>default-partitioned</scheme-ref>

  <backing-map-scheme>
    <local-scheme>
      <scheme-ref>unlimited-backing-map</scheme-ref>
      <listener>
        <class-scheme>
          <class-name>
            ...LowBalanceListener
          </class-name>
          <init-params>
            <init-param>
              <param-type>
                ...BackingMapManagerContext
              </param-type>
              <param-value>
                {manager-context}
              </param-value>
            </init-param>
            <init-param>
              <param-type>int</param-type>
              <param-value>500</param-value>
            </init-param>
          </init-params>
        </class-scheme>
      </listener>
    </local-scheme>
  </backing-map-scheme>

</distributed-scheme>
```

I have abbreviated class names above to better accommodate the page size, but you need to specify the fully qualified class names for both the listener class and the BackingMapManagerContext.

You should also notice how `init-param` elements are used to pass constructor arguments to our listener. For the first parameter we use a {manager-context} macro defined by Coherence to pass `BackingMapManagerContext`, while for the second one we simply specify the integer value of the balance threshold.

That's all there is to it. Assuming that the configuration above is used on all the nodes, we will be listening for the account modifications locally on each node and schedule alerts for execution if the balance falls below 500.

Also, notice that with backing map listeners we don't have to worry about the network utilization as all the events are raised locally, in-process, so we don't need a mechanism such as `MapEventFilter` to limit the events that are sent to the listener. In this case, our listener will simply discard the ones it doesn't need.

Map triggers

Another Coherence feature that relies on cache events is **map triggers**.

Unlike map listeners, which execute *after* an event occurs in the cache, map triggers execute *before* any mutating operation is committed and allow you to validate, modify, or even reject the operation.

You can create a trigger by implementing a class that fulfils the `com.tangosol.util.MapTrigger` interface:

```
public interface MapTrigger
       extends Serializable {

  public void process(MapTrigger.Entry entry);
}
```

The `MapTrigger` interface defines a single method, `process`, which is invoked by Coherence before the result of a mutating operation is committed into the underlying map. The `process` method accepts a single argument of the `MapTrigger.Entry` type, which is an extension of `InvocableMap.Entry` that allows you to access both the information about the pending change and the original value that will be replaced.

You can do a number of things within the process method of your trigger that will ultimately determine if and how the original value is replaced:

- You can do nothing, which will allow the pending change to be committed as if there was no trigger
- You can undo the change by resetting the entry value to the original value
- You can override the change by modifying the pending value

- You can remove the entry from the cache

- You can prevent the change from happening by throwing a `RuntimeException`, which will be propagated to the caller that performed the mutating operation on the cache.

There are numerous situations where triggers might be appropriate. For example, you could write a trigger that sanitizes new data to ensure that all the properties are in the correct format, populates an incomplete object before committing it, or checks if the caller has the necessary permissions to modify the object, thus allowing you to implement object-level, or even property-level security.

The example we are going to implement is a `ValidatorTrigger`, which allows you to validate an object before it is accepted into the cache.

Using map triggers for data validation

Any non-trivial application requires data validation to be performed before the data is accepted and stored within the persistent storage. Unfortunately, while validating data is conceptually a fairly simple task, it tends to become a thorny issue in many applications.

What makes data validation complex is the fact that you likely have to perform it multiple times. If you are building a web application, you need to decide if you are going to perform validation on the client, using JavaScript, but even if you do you will still have to perform it on the server as well, for several reasons:

- You likely won't be able to fully validate data on the client

- You might have additional entry points into the application, such as a web service layer

- Client-side validation can be easily disabled by the user

To complicate things even further, whether you like it or not some of the validation rules will be defined within your data store. For example, if you are using a relational database, your database schema will determine the maximum length of your string properties, and it might also impose further restrictions on your objects via referential integrity constraints.

Even though these rules are already defined in the database, you will have to replicate them in your middle tier as well in order to ensure that an object that passes the middle-tier validation will be successfully written into the database. That means that you are likely to end up with the validation logic scattered across the tiers, and will have to keep it in sync.

To reduce that complexity, some people recommend that you perform all data validation in a database, so you can keep all your validation logic in one place and ensure that the invalid data is never stored in the system, even if someone attempts to insert it directly into the database, using raw SQL. There is an excellent article by Robyn Page on how to accomplish that in SQL Server 2005 that you can find at `http://www.simple-talk.com/sql/learn-sql-server/robyn-pages-sql-server-data-validation-workbench/`, and I heartily recommend it, especially if you are also interested in a proof that hot soap opera actresses are smart and can sling T-SQL code, but I digress.

However, while I agree with the approach in principle, I see two major flaws in it:

- Going to the database in order to determine if the data is valid will put even more strain on the resource that is the most difficult and most expensive to scale.

- While most individual validation rules are very simple, such as checking if the property is set, or is within a certain range, or that it doesn't exceed a certain length, many real-world validation scenarios tend to be quite complex, and include conditional validations (A should be X, but it should only be checked if B is Y), data lookups, and sometimes even complex business rules driven by the rules engine. This is much easier to do in the middle tier, using the full expressiveness and rich libraries of a higher-level language, than in the database.

The nice thing about Coherence triggers is that they are written in Java and execute within the highly scalable cluster, so neither of the two objections above apply to them. That makes them a perfect candidate for the implementation of a data validation mechanism that is very close to the data store but doesn't suffer from the problems associated with database-based validation.

Enough talk—let's roll our sleeves up and implement a simple data validation framework and the map trigger that uses it to perform validation when the data is either inserted or modified in the cache.

Data validation framework

There are many existing validation frameworks out there, either as independent utilities or within larger frameworks, such as Spring or XWork/Struts 2. There is also a soon-to-be-final *JSR-303: Bean Validation*, which is based on Hibernate Validation and aims to standardize validation of JavaBeans. The result of JSR-303 will likely be included in the future release of Java SE, so the natural question is why we don't just use that, instead of building another, non-standard validation framework.

The answer is: we won't build a whole framework. We will simply build a thin abstraction layer that uses JSR-303 validation under the hood by default, but also allows us to perform data validation using a hand-coded Java class or even a script written in one of the languages supported by the Scripting API, which has been a standard part of Java SE since version 6.

The reason that we want this flexibility is that JSR-303 is purely metadata driven, which has some inherent limitations. One of them is that you cannot easily perform conditional validation, where certain properties of an object are either not validated or are validated differently based on the state of other properties. An example would be validation of an account transaction where we want to make sure that the transaction amount is not more than $300, but only if the transaction type is ATM withdrawal. While you can achieve this to a certain extent using JSR-303 validation groups, it requires you to validate a specific group explicitly, instead of adapting constraints dynamically based on the state of the `TransactionType` property.

Second, being able to implement a validator using a custom Java class or a script makes it much easier to integrate things such as rules engines into your validations.

The first step we need to take is to define an interface that will allow us to initiate validation of an object and obtain the result:

```
public interface Validator
        extends Serializable {

    ValidationResult validate(Object target);
}
```

The result of the validation should include two things—whether or not it was successful and a collection of error messages if it wasn't:

```
public interface ValidationResult
        extends Serializable {

    boolean isValid();
    Collection<String> getErrorMessages();
}
```

That's really all we need from the API perspective. In the sample code for the book, you will also find two concrete implementations of the `Validator` interface—`DefaultValidator`, which uses JSR-303 validation and `ScriptValidator`, which uses Java Scripting API to execute script-based validators. Of course, you can also create custom Java classes that implement the `Validator` interface, if that's what you prefer.

Also, notice that both validators and results must be serializable, as they will need to be moved across the wire when registering a trigger or throwing a validation exception.

Implementing validation trigger

Now that we have a validation framework in place, implementing ValidationTrigger is fairly straightforward:

```
public class ValidationTrigger
        implements MapTrigger, PortableObject {

  private Validator validator;

  public ValidationTrigger() {
    validator = Validator.DEFAULT;
  }

  public ValidationTrigger(Validator validator) {
    this.validator = validator;
  }

  public void process(Entry entry) {
    ValidationResult result = validator.validate(entry.getValue());

    if (!result.isValid()) {
      throw new ValidationException(result);
    }
  }

  // serialization methods omitted for brevity
}
```

As you can see, all we need to do is perform the validation using the specified validator and throw a ValidationException if the object is not valid.

One final thing to note is that map triggers must be serializable and override the equals and hashCode methods. Otherwise, if you register the same trigger multiple times (which is highly probable considering that you will likely invoke the registration method from each cluster node, as you'll see shortly) there will be multiple redundant registrations inside the cluster that will be performing the same processing and have the same ultimate result.

Registering map triggers

The final thing we need to do in order to activate the `ValidationTrigger` we just implemented is to register it with the cache. In order to do that, we need to register a special map listener called `MapTriggerListener`:

```
NamedCache transactions = CacheFactory.getCache("transactions");

transactions.addMapListener(
                new MapTriggerListener(new ValidationTrigger()));
```

The previous code snippet would register our `ValidationTrigger` with the `transactions` cache and would use the default JSR-303-based validator to validate `Transaction` objects when they are inserted into the cache.

If we wanted to validate transactions using Groovy script instead, we could accomplish that by simple registering the trigger slightly differently:

```
transactions.addMapListener(
        new MapTriggerListener(
            new ValidationTrigger(
                new ScriptValidator(
                    "groovy",
                    "validators/transaction.groovy"))));
```

It should be noted that the `MapTriggerListener` is really more of a hack whose only purpose is to register a map trigger with the cache service. It is never used as a true map listener, and it has to be registered globally, using single-argument `addMapListener` overload.

My personal preference is to bury `MapTriggerListener` and its registration deep under the hood by providing a utility `registerMapTrigger` method in the `AbstractCoherenceRepository` class. That way all I need to worry about is how to create a trigger instance, and the `registerMapTrigger` method takes care of the rest.

Continuous query cache

It should be fairly obvious by now that you could use Coherence cache events to implement a local, in-process view of the partitioned cache (or a subset of it) that is automatically kept up to date as the data in the cluster changes.

The good news is that such a thing already exists and is available for you to use, in the form of a `ContinuousQueryCache`, often referred to as **CQC** in Coherence circles.

The CQC is an extremely powerful feature that is frequently used to bring a subset of the data to users' desktops and update them in real time, which can be very useful in trading or logistics applications, for example.

Unlike other cache types, which are typically defined in the cache configuration file, the CQC can only be created programmatically, because you need to specify the filter to use to create the live view of the data. For example, if we wanted to create a view of all open trade orders assigned to a particular trader, we would create the CQC instance like this:

```
NamedCache tradeOrders = CacheFactory.getCache("tradeOrders");

Filter myOrdersFilter = new FilterBuilder()
                            .equals("status", "Open")
                            .equals("traderId", myId)
                            .toAnd();

ContinuousQueryCache myOpenOrders =
        new ContinousQueryCache(tradeOrders, myOrdersFilter);
```

The preceding code will result in a locally materialized view of the cache data that satisfies the specified filter. By default, both keys and values will be cached locally. If you want to cache only keys and retrieve values from the back cache as needed, which might be the best option if the values are large and accessed infrequently, or if you only care about having an up-to-date keyset locally, you can pass `false` as the third argument to the CQC constructor.

Observing a continuous query cache

The CQC implements `ObservableMap` interface, so you can subscribe for cache events just as with any other observable cache implementation. As the data is delivered to the CQC from the back cache, it will raise events locally that your application can handle in order to update the UI or perform some other processing.

If you register a listener with the CQC using `ObservableMap` methods, as described earlier in the chapter, you will receive only the events that are raised after the initial synchronization. If you want to receive the events during initial synchronization as well, you can pass your listener as the third argument to the CQC constructor.

Using a continuous query cache as a substitute for a replicated cache

As we briefly discussed in *Chapter 3, Planning Your Caches*, CQC can also be used as a replacement for a replicated cache. For example, let's say that we have a cache holding current exchange rates that we need to be able to access at in-process speed on all cluster nodes.

One option would be to configure exchange rates as a replicated cache, but then we might not be able to use certain features that are only available to partitioned caches, such as read-through caching, which will be discussed in the next chapter.

What we might do instead is configure the exchange rates cache as a partitioned cache and use CQC to bring data in-process. All we need to do is create an instance of the CQC using `AlwaysFilter` to bring all data locally and to keep it up to date as it changes in a back cache:

```
NamedCache forexRates = CacheFactory.getCache("forexRates");

ContinuousQueryCache localRates =
            new ContinousQueryCache(forexRates, AlwaysFilter.INSTANCE);
```

Summary

The ability to raise and respond to events as the data changes is an extremely powerful concept that can lead to better architectural solutions for many problems.

In this chapter, we looked into the set of features Coherence provides that make implementation of event-driven applications not only feasible, but simple and enjoyable as well.

We discussed the core concept of map listeners, which allow any application to observe cache events and react when an event of interest occurs. We talked about both client-side listeners, which allow many applications or processes to receive the same event, and backing map listeners, which allow you to ensure that the event is handled only once, and as close to the data that caused it as possible.

Then we talked about map triggers, which allow us to intercept mutating cache operations and decide if and how they are going to be performed. Along the way, we implemented a small validation framework that uses triggers to validate our objects as they are inserted into or updated within the Coherence cache.

Finally, we discussed the Continuous Query Cache, which allows you to bring all or a filtered subset of the data from the partitioned cache in-process, providing a near real-time, fully synchronized view into the cache as well as lightning fast read access.

8

Implementing the Persistence Layer

Coherence was originally conceived as a reliable and scalable distributed cache for J2EE applications connected to relational databases. It has since evolved to become the market leader in data grid technologies. Today many users of Coherence forego the database and store the entire data set for their applications in memory.

However, in spite of the innovation that makes this architecture possible, these applications are still vastly outnumbered by applications that use a database as the system of record. Relational databases continue to be the workhorse of today's enterprise IT; the need for reliable persistence, along with the number of applications and reporting tools that use databases, indicate that they won't be going away anytime soon.

Coherence contains a rich set of features that make it an ideal caching layer for applications that rely on an external data source as the system of record. Relational databases are the most common data source used with Coherence; however, you have the ability to use any data source, including mainframes, web services, SAN file systems, and so on. We will use the term 'database' in the remainder of the chapter for simplicity, but keep in mind that you can put Coherence in front of pretty much any data source you can think of.

Although any type of data source can be used, the one requirement is that it must be a shared resource that all storage members have access to.

This means that the persistence API described in this chapter should not be implemented with technologies requiring the use of local disk (writing to the local file system, embedded databases such as Berkeley DB, and so on).

In this chapter, we will explore persistence patterns offered by Coherence, including **cache aside**, **read through**, **write through**, and **write behind**. We will discuss the pros and cons of each approach, common issues that often come up, and features in Coherence that resolve these issues.

Cache aside

Perhaps the most common caching pattern in use today is **cache aside**. If you have ever used a standard map to implement primitive caching yourself, you are already familiar with this approach—you check if a piece of data is in the cache and if it isn't then you load it from the database and put it in the cache for future requests. When the data is subsequently updated, it is up to the application to either invalidate the cache or update it with the new value.

Applications that have a well-defined data access object (DAO) layer can easily treat caching as a cross-cutting concern. The DAO can be wrapped by a proxy that performs the cache-aside operations. This can be as simple as the use of `java.util.Proxy` or as advanced as the use of AspectJ or any other AOP framework.

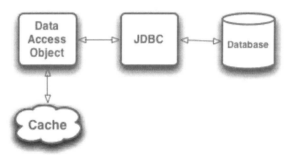

There are some consequences of cache aside that should be kept in mind:

- If multiple threads require access to the same piece of data that is not in the cache, it may result in multiple redundant reads to the database.

- When an application writes directly to the database, concurrency concerns are handled by the database, whether via optimistic or pessimistic locking. When writing to a cache in memory, data integrity must be maintained via some explicit concurrency control mechanism.

In the case of a single JVM, these problems are not too difficult to overcome although it will take some effort. However, when you start to add more JVMs (each with its own cache) things become complicated very quickly. The likelihood of these caches containing overlapping and inconsistent data is very high.

At this point we should mention that for some types of data this incoherency across JVMs might be acceptable, especially for small amounts of reference data that can easily fit within the allocated heap of the JVM. For data that must be consistent across JVMs and/or is updated often, cache aside in a local cache is clearly not the right solution.

To solve some of these cache-aside problems in a multi JVM environment, Coherence provides the following tools:

- Distributed concurrency control, either through the use of distributed locking using the `ConcurrentMap` API or optimistic updates using `EntryProcessor` using the `InvocableMap` API.

- Coherent consistent view of the data from any JVM in a cluster.

Although Coherence provides these tools to ease the implementation of a distributed cache-aside solution, it also provides tools that enable much more efficient and easier-to-implement persistence patterns.

Read-through caching

When using cache aside, the application has to check both the cache and (potentially) the database when reading data. Although these operations can be abstracted away for most of the part, it would be easier if the developer could deal with just one source of data.

This is exactly what the read-through pattern provides. With the read-through pattern, the cache is the single interface the application deals with when reading data. If the requested piece of data exists in the cache it will be returned, thus avoiding a hit to the database. If the data is not in the cache, the cache itself will fetch the data from the database, store it, and return the value to the client. This approach has the following advantages:

- The responsibility of connecting to the data source is pushed away from the client tier, thus simplifying client code.

- Reads to the database are coalesced, meaning that multiple requests for a piece of data absent from the cache will result in one request to the database. This eliminates redundant reads to the database when multiple threads attempt to access the same piece of data simultaneously.

- Moving the responsibility of database connectivity to the cache allows for optimizations, such as pre-fetching of the data to avoid having a client wait for data retrieval.

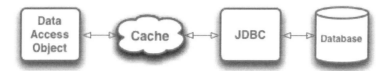

Implementing read through

Enabling read through in Coherence requires the implementation of an interface called CacheLoader. The CacheLoader interface in its entirety is as follows:

```
public interface CacheLoader {
  Object load(Object key);
  Map loadAll(Collection keys);
}
```

The load method is responsible for retrieving the value from the database, based on the specified key. The loadAll method accepts a collection of keys that may be bulk loaded; it returns a map of the keys and their corresponding values loaded from the database. If one of the requested keys does not exist in the database, that key should be excluded from the result map. As can be observed via the key-based API, read through will only work with key-based access, that is, queries executed via the QueryMap API will not use CacheLoader.

> The loadAll method in CacheLoader will not be invoked by Coherence unless **operation bundling** is configured. This topic falls outside the scope of this book; however, this feature is documented in the Coherence user guide on OTN under the operation-bundling section.

Note that the interface does not dictate in any way what type of data store can be used. In the following example we will use the H2 database available at http://www.h2database.com/html/main.html.

Accessing a NamedCache from a CacheLoader

In *Chapter 5, Querying the Data Grid*, we discussed the dangers of reentrant entry processors and the potential for deadlock. The same caveat also applies here; a `CacheLoader` or `CacheStore` (introduced later in this chapter) should not access its own cache or any other caches that belong to the same cache service.

Here is a simple implementation of `CacheLoader` for our `Account` class. Note that it extends `AbstractCacheLoader`, which provides a simple implementation of `loadAll` that delegates to `load`.

```
public class AccountCacheLoader
       extends AbstractCacheLoader {

  public AccountCacheLoader() throws Exception {
    JdbcDataSource ds = new JdbcDataSource();
    ds.setURL("jdbc:h2:tcp://localhost/db/coherent-bank-db");
    ds.setUser("sa");
    ds.setPassword("");

    this.dataSource = ds;
  }

  @Override
  public Object load(Object oKey) {
    Connection        con = null;
    PreparedStatement ps  = null;
    ResultSet         rs  = null;
    Account           act = null;

    try {
      con = dataSource.getConnection();
      ps = con.prepareStatement(
          "SELECT id, description, balance, " +
                          "currency, last_tx, customer_id " +
          "FROM accounts WHERE id = ?");
      ps.setLong(1, (long) oKey);
      rs = ps.executeQuery();
      if (rs.next()) {
        act = new Account(rs.getLong("id"),
                    rs.getString("description"),
                    new Money(rs.getLong("balance"),
                    rs.getString("currency")),
```

```
                              rs.getLong("last_tx"),
                              rs.getLong("customer_id"));
      }
    }
    catch (SQLException e) {
      throw new RuntimeException("Error loading key " + oKey, e);
    }
    finally {
        // clean up connection, etc
    }

    return act;
  }

  private DataSource dataSource;
}
```

In order to use this `CacheLoader`, we must configure a **read-write backing map**.

Introducing the read-write backing map

The use of `CacheLoader` or `CacheStore` requires the backing map for the partitioned cache to be configured as a read-write backing map. A read-write backing map provides many configuration options for `CacheLoader` and `CacheStore` that will soon be covered in detail.

 A read-write backing map can only be used with partitioned caches; replicated caches are not supported.

The following is a sample configuration for the `CacheLoader`:

```
<distributed-scheme>
  <scheme-name>partitioned</scheme-name>
  <backing-map-scheme>
   <read-write-backing-map-scheme>
     <internal-cache-scheme>
       <local-scheme />
     </internal-cache-scheme>
     <cachestore-scheme>
       <class-scheme>
         <class-name>
           com.seovic.coherence.book.ch8.AccountCacheLoader
         </class-name>
       </class-scheme>
```

```
      </cachestore-scheme>
    </read-write-backing-map-scheme>
  </backing-map-scheme>
  <autostart>true</autostart>
</distributed-scheme>
```

Some points to note:

- The `<internal-cache-scheme>` indicates the data structure that will be used for managing the data in memory; this will normally be `<local-scheme>`

- Under `<cachestore-scheme>`, a `<class-scheme>` is used to configure the name of the `CacheLoader` implementation class

- When the backing map is instantiated for the cache, an instance of the `CacheLoader` will be created by Coherence and held in memory

Although this `CacheLoader` will work perfectly well in development, it has several flaws that make it unsuitable for use in production, which are as follows:

- The `DataSource` configuration is hard coded, thus requiring a recompile for any changes

- It is not configured to use a connection pool, thus a new connection will be created each time `load` is invoked

- The addition of another `CacheStore` will require the `DataSource` configuration to be copied/pasted, or refactored so that it can be shared

Due to these issues, it may be desirable (but not required) to use a container to manage the configuration and shared infrastructure required for database connectivity. This can be accomplished with a standard JEE container such as Oracle WebLogic Server or Apache Tomcat.

It can also be accomplished with a non-JEE container such as the Spring Framework. For the remainder of this chapter, we will use Spring to manage cache stores and related artifacts.

Using Spring Framework with a read-write backing map

Spring is a popular dependency injection framework that provides utility classes that make it easy to write JDBC code and manage a `DataSource`. A full tutorial on Spring is beyond the scope of this chapter; if you are unfamiliar with Spring please refer to the user guide at `http://www.springsource.org/documentation`.

The Coherence Tools project provides several useful classes that make both the implementation and configuration of `CacheLoader` and `CacheStore` classes much more convenient.

The first one is `ConfigurableCacheStore`, which allows you to configure cache stores within a Spring application context. The main benefit is that you can have a single backing map configuration for all persistent caches in your application. You configure Coherence to use `ConfigurableCacheStore`, which in turn delegates to the concrete `CacheStore` implementation defined within the Spring application context.

For example, we can add the following backing map definition to our cache configuration file and reuse it for all the caches that require persistence, as shown next:

```
<read-write-backing-map-scheme>
  <scheme-name>persistent-backing-map</scheme-name>
  <internal-cache-scheme>
    <local-scheme>
      <scheme-ref>unlimited-backing-map</scheme-ref>
    </local-scheme>
  </internal-cache-scheme>
  <cachestore-scheme>
    <class-scheme>
      <class-name>
        c.s.coherence.util.persistence.ConfigurableCacheStore
      </class-name>
      <init-params>
        <init-param>
          <param-type>string</param-type>
          <param-value>{cache-name}</param-value>
        </init-param>
      </init-params>
    </class-scheme>
  </cachestore-scheme>
  <write-delay>
    {write-delay 0}
  </write-delay>
  <write-batch-factor>
    {write-batch-factor 0}
  </write-batch-factor>
  <write-requeue-threshold>
    {write-requeue-threshold 0}
  </write-requeue-threshold>
```

```
  <refresh-ahead-factor>
    {refresh-ahead-factor 0}
  </refresh-ahead-factor>
</read-write-backing-map-scheme>
```

The `ConfigurableCacheStore` constructor takes a single string argument, which is used to retrieve the concrete `CacheStore` to delegate to from the associated Spring context. In this example we are simply passing cache name, which implies that we will need to define a Spring bean with a matching name for each concrete cache store within the persistence context.

You should also notice that we use macro arguments to configure several read-write backing map settings at the bottom. This will allow us to change the persistence behavior of individual caches without having to create separate backing map configurations. These settings will be covered in the upcoming sections.

Now that we have a backing map definition, we can use it to configure the cache scheme for accounts, as is done in the following code:

```
<distributed-scheme>
  <scheme-name>accounts-scheme</scheme-name>
  <scheme-ref>default-partitioned</scheme-ref>
  <service-name>AccountsCacheService</service-name>
  <backing-map-scheme>
    <read-write-backing-map-scheme>
      <scheme-ref>persistent-backing-map</scheme-ref>
    </read-write-backing-map-scheme>
  </backing-map-scheme>
  <autostart>true</autostart>
</distributed-scheme>
```

Another important benefit of `ConfigurableCacheStore` is that it allows us to use all the existing Spring constructs when configuring our cache stores, including transaction managers, data sources, connection pools, and so on. This makes cache store configuration significantly easier, as you'll see shortly.

The second useful class provided by the Coherence Tools project is `AbstractJdbcCacheStore`. This class uses Spring's `JdbcTemplate` to implement all necessary data access code, which makes implementation of concrete JDBC-based cache stores trivial; all you need to do is to define the SQL statements and `RowMapper` that will be used for object retrieval and persistence.

The following is a snippet of `AbstractJdbcCacheStore` relevant to the `load` operation:

```
@Transactional
public abstract class AbstractJdbcCacheStore<T>
        extends AbstractBatchingCacheStore {

  public AbstractJdbcCacheStore(DataSource dataSource) {
    m_jdbcTemplate = new SimpleJdbcTemplate(dataSource);
  }

  protected abstract String getSelectSql();

  protected abstract RowMapper<T> getRowMapper();

  @Transactional(readOnly = true)
  public Object load(Object key) {
    List<T> results = getJdbcTemplate().query(
                  getSelectSql(), getRowMapper(),
                  getPrimaryKeyComponents(key));
                  return results.size() == 0 ? null : results.get(0);
  }
  protected Object[] getPrimaryKeyComponents(Object key) {
    return new Object[] {key};
  }

  protected SimpleJdbcTemplate getJdbcTemplate() {
    return m_jdbcTemplate;
  }

  private final SimpleJdbcTemplate m_jdbcTemplate;
}
```

The following is an implementation of the `AccountJdbcCacheStore` from our sample application, which leverages features provided by `AbstractJdbcCacheStore`. The parts relevant to `load` are included, as shown in the following code:

```
public class AccountJdbcCacheStore
        extends AbstractJdbcCacheStore<Account> {

  public AccountJdbcCacheStore(DataSource dataSource) {
    super(dataSource);
  }

  @Override
```

```java
protected String getSelectSql() {
  return SELECT_SQL;
}

@Override
protected RowMapper<Account> getRowMapper() {
  return ROW_MAPPER;
}

private static final RowMapper<Account> ROW_MAPPER =
                                  new RowMapper<Account>() {
  public Account mapRow(ResultSet rs, int i)
    throws SQLException {
      return new Account(rs.getLong("id"),
                    rs.getString("description"),
                    new Money(rs.getLong("balance"),
                    rs.getString("currency")),
                    rs.getLong("last_tx"),
                    rs.getLong("customer_id"));
    }
};

private static final String SELECT_SQL = "SELECT id, description,
                balance, currency, " + "last_tx, customer_id " +
                "FROM accounts WHERE id = ?";
}
```

Now that we have both the `CacheStore` and necessary cache configuration, the last thing we need to do is add the `CacheStore` bean definition to the Spring context defined in the `persistence-context.xml` file, which should be located in the root of the classpath:

```xml
<?xml version="1.0" encoding="UTF-8"?>
<beans xmlns=...>

  <tx:annotation-driven transaction-manager="txManager"/>

  <bean id="txManager"
        class="o.s.j.d.DataSourceTransactionManager">
    <property name="dataSource" ref="dataSource"/>
  </bean>

  <!-- H2 DataSource connection pool -->
  <bean id="dataSource"
        class="org.h2.jdbcx.JdbcConnectionPool"
```

```
             factory-method="create">
      <constructor-arg value="jdbc:h2:tcp://localhost/db/
                              coherent-bank-db"/>
      <constructor-arg value="sa"/>
      <constructor-arg value=""/>
      <property name="maxConnections" value="5" />
   </bean>


   <!-- cache store definitions -->


   <bean name="accounts"
         class="c.s.s.bank.persistence.AccountJdbcCacheStore">
     <constructor-arg ref="dataSource"/>
   </bean>


</beans>
```

Note that the JDBC `DataSource` in this example is configured using the connection pool that ships with the H2 database we used for the sample application. If your JDBC driver does not provide its own connection pool you can use a third-party pool such as Apache DBCP (`http://commons.apache.org/dbcp/`) or C3P0 (`http://sourceforge.net/projects/c3p0/`). The Oracle Universal Connection Pool (UCP) is another free option for connection pooling, which is available at `http://www.oracle.com/technology/tech/java/sqlj_jdbc/UCP_dev_guide.pdf`.

The configuration above should be self-explanatory — the `accounts` bean is injected with a data source, which is the only dependency it requires.

Refresh ahead

Many Coherence applications do not have exclusive access to the database. In several cases the database and its contents outlive several generations of applications that create and access that data. For these types of applications, Coherence caches can be configured to expire after a configurable amount of time to limit data staleness.

The expiration of heavily accessed cached entries may cause inconsistent response times, as some requests will require a read through to the database. This is especially true for applications that have aggressive expiry configured in order to minimize the amount of time for which cache entries may remain stale. However, a read-write backing map can be configured to fetch these items from the database in a background thread before they expire from the cache.

This setting is controlled by `<refresh-ahead-factor>`, which is a fraction of the expiry time. If an entry is accessed from the cache during the configured refresh-ahead period, it will be refreshed from the data source in a background thread.

Using refresh ahead to pre-fetch exchange rates

Our sample banking application uses an external REST web service to obtain exchange rates for currency conversion. In order to retrieve the rate on a cache miss, we have implemented a simple `CacheLoader` that uses Spring's `RestTemplate` to invoke the web service, as shown next:

```
public class ExchangeRateRestCacheLoader
        extends AbstractCacheLoader {

  public Object load(Object key) {
    Map<String, String> params =
                Collections.singletonMap("instrument", (String) key);

    RestTemplate client = new RestTemplate();
    String rate = client.getForObject(m_url, String.class, params);

    return new BigDecimal(rate);
  }

  public void setUrl(String url) {
    m_url = url;
  }

  private String m_url;
}
```

While this works well for the most part, the issue is that the external web service has non-deterministic latency. In most cases latency is minimal, but during peak periods it can be several seconds (which, for arguments sake, is not acceptable in our case).

Fortunately, we can use refresh ahead to solve the problem. The code snippet is as follows:

```
<cache-mapping>
  <cache-name>exchange-rates</cache-name>
  <scheme-name>exchange-rates-scheme</scheme-name>
  <init-params>
    <init-param>
      <param-name>refresh-ahead-factor</param-name>
      <param-value>.75</param-value>
```

```
        </init-param>
      </init-params>
    </cache-mapping>


    ...


    <distributed-scheme>
      <scheme-name>exchange-rates-scheme</scheme-name>
      <scheme-ref>default-partitioned</scheme-ref>
      <service-name>ExchangeRatesCacheService</service-name>
      <backing-map-scheme>
        <read-write-backing-map-scheme>
          <scheme-ref>persistent-backing-map</scheme-ref>
          <internal-cache-scheme>
            <local-scheme>
              <scheme-ref>unlimited-backing-map</scheme-ref>
              <expiry-delay>1m</expiry-delay>
            </local-scheme>
          </internal-cache-scheme>
        </read-write-backing-map-scheme>
      </backing-map-scheme>
      <autostart>true</autostart>
    </distributed-scheme>
```

By configuring the exchange rate cache to expire entries after one minute (which is the degree of staleness we are willing to tolerate), and setting refresh ahead factor to .75, we can ensure that any requests for entries that have been in the cache between 45 and 60 seconds will trigger an automatic refresh by invoking our cache loader (and consequently, the external web service).

However, keep in mind that refresh ahead only works for frequently accessed entries; if no requests are made for the entry after it has been in the cache for 45 seconds, it will be automatically evicted once it expires (after 60 seconds). In other words, refresh ahead is triggered by reads during the refresh-ahead interval, but not by evictions.

Another important thing to realize is that the read that initiates refresh ahead, as well as all the reads that come after it, will not block—refresh ahead is asynchronous, so all read requests will simply return the old value until it is updated by the loader.

Additional considerations

There are a few additional items that should be configured in the read-write backing map to support read through. First, a `<high-units>` setting should be configured for the `<local-scheme>` in `<internal-cache-scheme>`. This will ensure that the storage-enabled cluster member does not run out of memory while storing cached data.

Additionally, a thread pool should be configured for the partitioned cache service. Normal partitioned caching does not require a thread pool. This is because a thread pool will cause the service thread to queue up a cache request and a context switch will be required for a worker thread to process the request. Since reading from memory is such a low-overhead operation, there will be less overhead if the service thread simply processes the request.

However, the inevitability of a cache request through the read-write backing map resulting in a blocking I/O call over the network makes it a requirement to configure a thread pool. The service thread is the lifeblood of the partitioned cache; it should be kept as free as possible so it can service requests coming from other cluster members.

To start with, configure the thread count to be equal to the number of connections in the connection pool. Your application may be able to handle more threads and/or less connections; be sure to load test your configuration before going to production.

In order to configure a thread pool for the `AccountsCacheService` we defined earlier, we need to add a `thread-count` configuration element to it, which is shown next:

```
<distributed-scheme>
  <scheme-name>accounts-scheme</scheme-name>
  <scheme-ref>default-partitioned</scheme-ref>
  <service-name>AccountsCacheService</service-name>
  <thread-count>5</thread-count>
  <backing-map-scheme>
    <read-write-backing-map-scheme>
      <scheme-ref>persistent-backing-map</scheme-ref>
    </read-write-backing-map-scheme>
  </backing-map-scheme>
  <autostart>true</autostart>
</distributed-scheme>
```

Finally, when using read through, it may be desirable to maintain a set of cache misses. This information can be used to avoid reading through to the `CacheLoader` if the likelihood of the value existing in the database immediately after a cache miss is low.

This cache can be configured via the `<miss-cache-scheme>` in the read-write backing map. This setting requires the use of `<local-scheme>`, which would ideally be configured with an expiry that indicates how long the read-write backing map will wait before reissuing a load request for a given key to the `CacheLoader`.

Write through

The pattern of accessing the cache exclusively for reading data can be extended for writing data as well. Write through inherits all of the benefits associated with read through, but it adds a few of its own as well, which are as follows:

- A single point of data update simplifies the handling of concurrent updates.
- While write through is synchronous by default, it could easily be made asynchronous by changing a configuration option, which will be covered in the next section.

The biggest benefit of synchronous (as opposed to asynchronous) writes is that failed operations to the database will cause the cache update to roll back, and an exception will be thrown to the client indicating the failure of the store operation.

Prior to Coherence 3.6, the default handling of write through failure was to log the exception on the storage cluster member and allow the cache write to succeed. In order to propagate the store exception to the client and roll back the cache update, the `<rollback-cachestore-failures>` element in the read-write backing map configuration should be set to `true`.

To enable writes to the database via the cache, the `CacheStore` interface must be implemented. The `CacheStore` interface in its entirety is as follows:

```
public interface CacheStore extends CacheLoader {
    void store(Object oKey, Object oValue);
    void storeAll(Map mapEntries);
    void erase(Object oKey);
    void eraseAll(Collection colKeys);
}
```

Note that `CacheStore` extends `CacheLoader`. As is the case with `CacheLoader`, Coherence provides an `AbstractCacheStore` class that implements the bulk operation methods by iterating each entry and invoking the respective corresponding single entry methods.

The store implementation of `AbstractJdbcCacheStore` is as follows:

```
protected abstract String getMergeSql();

public void store(Object key, Object value) {
  getJdbcTemplate().update(getMergeSql(),
          new BeanPropertySqlParameterSource(value));
}
```

The `AccountJdbcCacheStore` class including the code required for `store` is as follows:

```
public class AccountJdbcCacheStore
        extends AbstractJdbcCacheStore<Account> {

public AccountJdbcCacheStore(DataSource dataSource) {
    super(dataSource);
  }

  ...

  @Override
  protected String getMergeSql() {
    return MERGE_SQL;
  }

  ...

  private static final String MERGE_SQL =
                  "MERGE INTO accounts (id, description, "+
                  "balance, currency, last_tx, customer_id) " +
                  "VALUES (:id, :description, :balance.amount, "+
                  ":balance.currency.currencyCode, " +
                  ":lastTransactionId, :customerId)";
}
```

Write through is an excellent choice in many situations, but unfortunately it will only scale as far as the underlying database scales. If you need to scale data writes beyond that, you will need to use the asynchronous cousin of write through—**write behind**.

Write behind

Most users of Coherence choose the write behind pattern for updating data through the cache. Write behind offers the following benefits over write through:

- The response time and scalability of updates will be decoupled from the database

- Multiple updates to the same entry are coalesced, thus resulting in a reduction in the number of updates sent to the database

- Multiple updates to different entries can be batched

- The application can continue to function upon database failure

In order to configure write behind, modify the `<write-delay>` setting in the read-write backing map configuration to the amount of time the data should live in the cache before being flushed to the database.

Upon insertion into a read-write backing map configured with write behind, an entry will be queued until it is time to write it out to the `CacheStore`. An entry that has lived in the queue for the amount of time specified by the write delay setting is considered to be **ripe**. Once a cache entry becomes ripe, a dedicated write-behind thread will dequeue that entry and other ripe entries, and write them out to the `CacheStore`.

A read-write backing map can also be configured to write queued entries that have not reached ripe status via `<write-batch-factor>`. This value is a percentage of the `<write-delay>` time and is specified as a `double` (between 0.0 and 1.0). Entries in the write behind queue that reach this threshold are considered **soft-ripe**. A value of 1.0 will store all entries that are currently in the queue, whereas 0.0 (the default) will only store ripe entries.

Using write behind for accounts and transactions

Accounts and transactions are the most heavily used objects in our banking applications. To make things worse, they are also heavily write-biased, that is, whenever a new transaction is posted, it is inserted into the transaction cache and the corresponding account is updated.

While we would prefer the reliability of a synchronous write through, the transaction volume is so high that our database simply cannot cope with it. Thus, we will use write behind to increase throughput, which means we will simply write transactions and account updates into Coherence and allow the database to catch up in the background.

There are two reasons why write behind is a good fit. In the case of accounts, a single account object might be updated several times a second. Instead of writing each update into the database, write behind will allow us to coalesce them and perform a single database update for many cache updates. In the case of transactions, it will allow us to perform bulk inserts by batching many transactions into a single database call (this feature is introduced in a subsequent section). Both of these features will allow us to significantly reduce the database load, while at the same time reducing latency and improving throughput from the end-user perspective.

You have seen earlier that we defined macro parameters for `write-delay` and `write-batch-factor` within the `persistent-backing-map` definition, which makes it simple to enable write behind for accounts and transactions. We just need to define these two parameters within the corresponding cache mappings, as shown next:

```
<cache-mapping>
  <cache-name>accounts</cache-name>
  <scheme-name>accounts-scheme</scheme-name>
  <init-params>
    <init-param>
      <param-name>write-delay</param-name>
      <param-value>10s</param-value>
    </init-param>
    <init-param>
      <param-name>write-batch-factor</param-name>
      <param-value>.25</param-value>
    </init-param>
  </init-params>
</cache-mapping>

<cache-mapping>
  <cache-name>transactions</cache-name>
  <scheme-name>accounts-scheme</scheme-name>
```

```
  <init-params>
    <init-param>
      <param-name>write-delay</param-name>
      <param-value>10s</param-value>
    </init-param>
    <init-param>
      <param-name>write-batch-factor</param-name>
      <param-value>.25</param-value>
    </init-param>
  </init-params>
</cache-mapping>
```

This configuration will enable write behind for these two caches and will persist all entries between 2.5 and 10 seconds old.

Write behind and storeAll

As previously mentioned, Coherence ships with AbstractCacheStore, which provides a default implementation of storeAll that iterates the map passed to it and invokes store on each entry. Although this implementation works, it may not be the optimal way of storing multiple entries to the database.

With a write through configuration, this method will never be invoked by Coherence (unless operation-bundling is enabled, see the previous note on loadAll). Each entry will be written to the database via the store method, even if using putAll from the client.

On the other hand, write behind does invoke storeAll when there are multiple entries in the queue that need to be stored. Therefore, a CacheStore configured to use write behind should take advantage of any batching functionality provided by the database. Many databases and other data stores have batching features that allow for a much more efficient (in terms of both latency and throughput) storeAll implementation.

The AbstractJdbcCacheStore base class being used for our CacheStore implementations extends AbstractBatchingCacheStore, and implements an abstract method storeBatch, as shown next:

```
public void storeBatch(Map mapBatch) {
    SqlParameterSource[] batch =
            SqlParameterSourceUtils.createBatch(
                            mapBatch.values().toArray());

    getJdbcTemplate().batchUpdate(getMergeSql(), batch);
}
```

This implementation uses batching via Spring's `SimpleJdbcTemplate.batchUpdate` method, whose underlying implementation uses JDBC `PreparedStatement` batching, to execute the updates. Depending on the JDBC driver implementation and latency to the database, batching updates in this manner can yield an order of magnitude performance improvement over sending one update at a time, even within the same database transaction.

 If you implement a `CacheStore` using a JPA implementation such as TopLink or Hibernate, refer to their respective documents on batching.

In turn, `storeBatch` is invoked by `AbstractBatchingCacheStore` as follows:

```
public void storeAll(Map mapEntries) {
  int batchSize = getBatchSize();
  if (batchSize == 0 || mapEntries.size() < batchSize) {
    storeBatch(mapEntries);
  }
  else {
    Map batch = new HashMap(batchSize);

    while (!mapEntries.isEmpty()) {
      // since entries will be removed from mapEntries,
      // the iterator needs to be recreated every time
      Iterator iter = mapEntries.entrySet().iterator();

      while (iter.hasNext() && batch.size() < batchSize) {
        // retrieving the entry will force
        // deserialization
        Map.Entry entry = (Map.Entry) iter.next();
        batch.put(entry.getKey(), entry.getValue());
      }

      storeBatch(batch);

      // remove the entries we've successfully stored
      mapEntries.keySet().removeAll(batch.keySet());
      batch.clear();
    }
  }
}
```

`AbstractBatchingCacheStore` gives us more control over batching granularity, by allowing us to chunk the map passed by the write-behind thread to `storeAll` into batches of configurable size.

Let's say that we have determined during load testing that batches of 500 objects work best for our application. Although you can use the write batch factor to roughly determine the percentage of queued entries that will be persisted at a time, there is no way to tell Coherence exactly how many objects to send in each batch. You might get 50, or you might get 10,000.

Smaller batches are usually not a problem—they simply lighter load on the system. However, writing out a large number (thousands) of items to a database in a single batch may be suboptimal for various reasons (very large transactions requiring a large transaction/rollback log in the database, memory consumption by the JDBC driver, and so on). It will also cause Coherence to consume more memory in the storage member.

As mentioned in the previous chapters, data is stored in binary format in the backing map. This is also the case for data stored in the write-behind queue. The map passed to `storeAll` will deserialize its contents lazily. If a large amount of data is passed in the map and it is deserialized in its entirety to perform a batch store, the JVM may experience very long GC pauses or even run out of heap. Therefore, it is a good idea to cap the number of items written to the database in a single batch.

Fortunately, the solution is simple—implement chunking within the `storeAll` method and persist large batches in multiple database calls. This is exactly what `AbstractBatchingCacheStore` does for us; all we need to do is configure the batch size for accounts and transactions within our cache store bean definitions, as shown next:

```xml
<bean name="accounts"
      class="c.s.s.b.persistence.AccountJdbcCacheStore">
  <constructor-arg ref="dataSource"/>
  <property name="batchSize" value="500"/>
</bean>

<bean name="transactions"
      class="c.s.s.b.persistence.TransactionJdbcCacheStore">
  <constructor-arg ref="dataSource"/>
  <property name="batchSize" value="500"/>
</bean>
```

Handling write-through/write-behind failures

Both Coherence cluster members and persistent data stores that Coherence writes data to could fail at any time. That means that we need to be prepared to deal with such failures.

Cluster member failures

In order to handle member failover correctly, `store` and `storeAll` implementations must be idempotent, which means that invoking these methods multiple times for the same entry will not yield undesired effects.

To demonstrate why this is necessary, consider the case where a primary storage member receives a `put` request, calls `store` to write it to the database, and fails before sending the entry to the backup member. The client will detect the failure of the storage member and repeat the operation, as it never received confirmation from the failed member that the operation did in fact succeed. If the `store` operation is idempotent, the backup member can invoke the operation again without any ill side effects.

Store failures

Handling a `store` failure in write-through mode is fairly straightforward. If an exception is thrown by `store`, the exception will be propagated to the client inserting the cache entry (see the previous section on write through for caveats).

Dealing with `store` failures in a write behind scenario is more complex. The client performing the write to the cache will not have an exception thrown to it upon failure, so it is incapable of handling the exception. Therefore we will explore several strategies and configuration options intended to deal with write behind store failures.

The first thing to note is that there are no guarantees as far as ordering of writes to the database goes. Therefore, it is not advised to have `store` or `storeAll` implementations with external dependencies, including referential integrity, or data validation on the database tier that is not performed on the application tier.

If a store operation does fail, the entry will not be requeued by default. Requeuing can be enabled by setting `<write-requeue-threshold>` to the maximum number of entries that should exist in the queue upon failure. When another attempt is made to store the failed entries, the entire set of requeued entries will be passed to the `storeAll` method, thus the intention of `<write-requeue-threshold>` is to cap the size of the map sent to `storeAll` after a `storeAll` failure. This limitation is in place to protect against `storeAll` implementations that attempt to write the contents of the entire map at once. For properly implemented `storeAll` implementations (such as the one provided by `AbstractBatchingCacheStore`) the `<write-requeue-threshold>` setting can be set very high to ensure that all failed entries are requeued.

 This behavior has changed in Coherence 3.6. The read-write backing map will now limit the number of entries sent to `storeAll` regardless of how many entries are in the write-behind queue. By default this limit is set to 128, but it can be modified via the `<write-max-batch-size>` setting. To enable requeuing in Coherence 3.6, `<write-requeue-threshold>` should be set to a value greater than 0.

If `storeAll` throws an exception, the read-write backing map will requeue all entries that are still present in `mapEntries`. Therefore, removing entries that are successfully stored will reduce the number of entries that need to be requeued in case of failure.

Write behind and eviction

It is considered a good practice to configure backing maps with size limits to prevent an `OutOfMemoryError` in the cache server tier. This can present interesting challenges in a write-behind scenario.

Consider the case where a client thread performs a put into a cache that causes evictions to occur to avoid exceeding high units. What will happen if the eviction policy dictates that we evict an entry from the backing map that is still in the write-behind queue (and therefore has not been flushed to the database)?

In this situation, the read-write backing map will synchronously invoke the `store` operation on any entries about to be evicted. The implication here is that the client thread performing the put operation will be blocked while evicted entries are flushed to the database. It is an unfortunate side effect for the client thread, as its operation will experience a higher than expected latency, but it acts as a necessary throttle to avoid losing data.

This edge condition highlights the necessity to configure a worker thread pool even for caches that are strictly performing write behind in order to prevent this flush from occurring on the service thread. It is important to keep in mind that the `store` operation won't always necessarily be performed by the write-behind thread.

Note that this can also occur with caches that have expiry configured. The likelihood of this occurring will decrease if there is a large difference between expiry time and write-behind time.

Write behind and deletes

The `CacheStore` interface defines `erase` and `eraseAll` for removing entries from a backing store. These operations are always performed synchronously, even if write behind is enabled.

That said, most enterprise databases never allow the execution of `DELETE` statements. Instead, records no longer in use are flagged as inactive. It is therefore expected that `erase` and `eraseAll` will be implemented sparingly.

The `erase` implementation of `AbstractCacheStore` throws `UnsupportedOperationException` to indicate that the method is not implemented. This is also optional for `store` and `storeAll` implementations. If the read-write backing map detects that any of these methods are not implemented, it will refrain from invoking them in the future.

Configuring backup with a read-write backing map

By default Coherence distributed caches will maintain one backup copy of each cache entry. When using a read-write backing map, other backup options may be considered that will reduce overall memory consumption across the cluster and allow for greater storage capacity.

Backup with read through

Applications that use read through are most likely using a database as the system of record. If a storage member is lost, the data can be retrieved from the database when needed. Therefore, this type of application may be a good candidate for a distributed cache with backups disabled.

Disabling backups will slightly improve read through performance (as a backup copy will not be made when the object is loaded from the database) and it will increase the storage capacity of the distributed cache. The downside is increased latency to retrieve lost items from the database
if a storage member fails.

To disable backups, add the following to `<distributed-scheme>`:

```
<backup-count>0</backup-count>
```

Backup with write behind

Although disabling backups with read through is a good combination, disabling backups with write behind is not a good idea, as it can result in data loss if a storage member fails while cache entries are in the write behind queue.

However, once the queued entries are flushed, it may be desirable to remove the backup copy for the reasons mentioned previously. This can be enabled in `<distributed-scheme>` with the following setting:

```
<backup-count-after-writebehind>
   0
</backup-count-after-writebehind>
```

Built-in CacheStore implementations

Coherence ships with a number of `CacheStore` implementations that work with popular commercial and open-source **object relational mapping (ORM)** tools including JPA, TopLink, and Hibernate.

This section will highlight the steps required to configure the JPA `CacheStore` with EclipseLink (`http://www.eclipse.org/eclipselink/`). Please refer to the Coherence User Guide for configuration details regarding TopLink and Hibernate. If you are using TopLink, it is recommended to investigate TopLink Grid (`http://www.oracle.com/technology/products/ias/toplink/tl_grid.html`), as it ships with custom `CacheLoader` and `CacheStore` implementations that auto-configure a persistence unit for use in a `CacheStore` context.

Using the Coherence JPA CacheStore

The first step is to modify the `Account` object with the required JPA annotations, as shown next:

```
@Entity
@Table(name="accounts")
public class Account
       implements Serializable {

  public Account() {
  }
  ...
  @Id
  private long id;
  ...
}
```

There are several ways of mapping a Java class to a relational database using JPA. The previous example uses field-level mapping and specifies the table and column names that deviate from the defaults. There is no @GeneratedValue annotation as JPA will not be responsible for key generation. In general, optimistic locking should not be enabled, especially when combined with write behind.

The next step is to create the META-INF/persistence.xml file that JPA requires for configuration:

```
<persistence xmlns="http://java.sun.com/xml/ns/persistence"
    xmlns:xsi="http://www.w3.org/2001/XMLSchema-instance"
    xsi:schemaLocation="http://java.sun.com/xml/ns/persistence
        http://java.sun.com/xml/ns/persistence/persistence_1_0.xsd"
    version="1.0">

  <persistence-unit name="CoherentBankUnit"
                    transaction-type="RESOURCE_LOCAL">

    <provider>
      org.eclipse.persistence.jpa.PersistenceProvider
    </provider>

    <class>com.seovic.coherence.book.ch8.Account</class>

    <properties>
      <property name="javax.persistence.jdbc.driver"
                value="oracle.jdbc.OracleDriver"/>
      <property name="javax.persistence.jdbc.url"
                value="jdbc:oracle:thin:@10.211.55.4:1521:XE"/>
      <property name="javax.persistence.jdbc.user"
                value="scott"/>
      <property name="javax.persistence.jdbc.password"
                value="tiger"/>

      <property name="eclipselink.cache.shared.default"
                value="false"/>
      <property name="eclipselink.jdbc.read-connections.min"
                value="1"/>
      <property name="eclipselink.jdbc.read-connections.max"
                value="3"/>
      <property name="eclipselink.jdbc.write-connections.min"
                value="2"/>
      <property name="eclipselink.jdbc.write-connections.max"
                value="5"/>
```

```
        <property name="eclipselink.jdbc.batch-writing"
                value="JDBC"/>

        <property name="eclipselink.logging.level"
                value="FINEST"/>
      </properties>

  </persistence-unit>

</persistence>
```

As EclipseLink is running outside of a JEE container, the only supported transaction type is RESOURCE_LOCAL. Note that JPA entities should be listed in <class> elements.

By default L2 caching is enabled; this should be disabled (via the eclipselink.cache.shared.default property) when using EclipseLink in a CacheStore, as L2 caching would be redundant.

EclipseLink ships with a connection pool suitable for JPA applications running outside of a container, the settings for which are configured via the eclipselink.jdbc.*-connections properties indicated in persistence.xml previously. To enable batching for storeAll operations, the eclipselink.jdbc.batch-writing property is set for JDBC PreparedStatement batching. For development/testing purposes, logging is set to the highest setting (to produce the most output); this should be adjusted accordingly when deploying to production.

Finally, the following modifications should be made to coherence-cache-config.xml:

```
<class-scheme>
  <class-name>
    com.tangosol.coherence.jpa.JpaCacheStore
  </class-name>
  <init-params>
    <!-- Entity name -->
    <init-param>
      <param-type>java.lang.String</param-type>
      <param-value>account</param-value>
    </init-param>
    <!-- Fully qualified entity class name -->
    <init-param>
```

```
        <param-type>java.lang.String</param-type>
        <param-value>
          com.seovic.samples.bank.domain.Account
        </param-value>
      </init-param>
      <!-- Persistence unit name -->
      <init-param>
         <param-type>java.lang.String</param-type>
         <param-value>CoherentBankUnit</param-value>
      </init-param>
    </init-params>
  </class-scheme>
```

Note the name of the `CacheStore` class, `com.tangosol.coherence.jpa.`
`JpaCacheStore`. This class ships with Coherence, but in order to use it, you
will need to add `coherence-jpa.jar` to the classpath.

The `JpaCacheStore` constructor requires the following parameters:

- The name of the JPA entity. By default this is the unqualified name of the
  entity class.

- The fully qualified name of the JPA entity class.

- The name of the persistence unit as defined in `persistence.xml`.

As we are using `ConfigurableCacheStore`, we can optionally leave the Coherence
cache configuration alone, and simply change the definition of our `accounts` bean
within `persistence-context.xml`, as shown next:

```
<bean name="accounts"
      class="com.tangosol.coherence.jpa.JpaCacheStore">
  <constructor-arg value="Account"/>
  <constructor-arg value="com.seovic.samples.bank.domain.Account"/>
  <constructor-arg value="CoherentBankUnit"/>
</bean>
```

This simplified configuration for `JpaCacheStore` is a further demonstration of the
benefits of using `ConfigurableCacheStore` in Spring-based Coherence applications.

Summary

Relational databases, web services, and even mainframes are permanent fixtures in today's IT ecosystem. The need to persist data to disk will never go away; however the demand for reliable, scalable, and fast access to data increases with each passing day.

The advanced caching features provided by Coherence render it an excellent choice to bridge the gap between legacy systems and producers/consumers of data hosted by these systems.

This chapter gave you enough information to choose the most appropriate persistence approach for your caches. You can easily integrate Coherence into existing applications using the cache-aside pattern.

However, if you want to take it a step further and reap the benefits of coalesced reads and a single data source for application developers to deal with, you can switch to read through by implementing and configuring the necessary cache loaders. When working with a high-latency data source, you can use refresh-ahead functionality to ensure that frequently accessed data is automatically updated before it expires.

If you also need to write data into the database, you can chose between synchronous write through and asynchronous write behind. The later is especially attractive if you need to minimize latency and maximize throughput, and will allow you to keep the database load within comfortable boundaries as you scale into extreme transaction processing (XTP).

In the next chapter we will look at Coherence support for remote grid clients, a feature that allows you to extend Coherence to users' desktops and to connect Coherence clusters across the WAN.

9

Bridging Platform and Network Boundaries

So far we have assumed that all of the components of an application are written in Java and collocated on the same high-speed network. However, that is not always the case.

For example, you might have a desktop application that needs to access a Coherence grid, and that application could be written in a language other than Java, such as C++ or any one of the number of languages supported by Microsoft's .NET platform. Some of these client applications might be physically located on the same network as the Coherence grid, but more likely than not, there will also be some that are in a remote location and connect to the Coherence grid over the **WAN (Wide Area Network)**.

If your client application is written in Java you have an option of making it a full-blown, although possibly storage-disabled, member of the cluster. This is what you will likely do for a long-running, web-based application that is collocated with the data grid, and that is exactly what we have done so far. However, even though you can do the same for a desktop Java application, it is probably not a good idea.

Desktop applications, by their nature, will likely connect to and disconnect from the Coherence cluster several, or in some cases, many times a day. Even when they are storage-disabled it results in some overhead, as cluster membership information needs to be maintained. When you have a large number of client applications connecting to and disconnecting from the cluster, this overhead might be significant. The negative effect is further compounded if your clients access the cluster across an unreliable, high-latency WAN link, if they have long garbage collection cycles, or if, God forbid, you make your clients storage-enabled, as each membership change would then also trigger cluster repartitioning.

In general, you want to keep cluster membership as stable as possible, and the amount of network traffic caused by repartitioning to a minimum. In order to allow you to achieve this in situations where you have remote or unstable clients, Coherence provides a TCP-based messaging protocol called **Coherence*Extend**. Coherence*Extend is also your only option when you need to access data grid from non-Java applications, such as .NET or C++ clients.

In the remainder of this chapter, we will cover Coherence*Extend in detail and show you how to configure both Coherence cluster and Java clients to use it. However, before we do that we need to take a step back and discuss the networking protocols Coherence uses, in order to better understand how Coherence*Extend fits into the whole picture.

Coherence networking

The Internet as a whole, as well as the vast majority of private networks in operation today, uses IP as a protocol of choice in the **networking layer**, so it is of no surprise that Coherence is an IP-based system as well.

IP is by design a best-effort delivery protocol and on its own does not provide any reliability guarantees. This means that **transport layer** protocols implemented on top of it must decide whether to support reliability or not, and to what extent.

The most popular transport layer protocol within the Internet Protocol Suite is the **Transmission Control Protocol**, or **TCP**. TCP is a *reliable* protocol—it guarantees that the messages sent from one computer to another will be transmitted and received successfully and in order. TCP is also a connection-based protocol, and requires connection between the two endpoints to be established before the message exchange begins.

The main benefit of TCP is its reliability—any lost messages are automatically retransmitted and duplicate messages are discarded by the protocol itself. This makes TCP very easy to use from the application developer's perspective, when a reliable point-to-point message delivery is required.

Another popular transport protocol is **User Datagram Protocol**, or **UDP**. Unlike TCP, UDP does not provide any reliability guarantees—messages can get lost on the way to the recipient and there is no built-in mechanism for retransmission. They can also be received out of order by the recipient, although this typically only happens under heavy traffic conditions. The main benefit of UDP is that it is very fast and does not require connection to be established in order to exchange the messages.

A Coherence cluster requires reliable message delivery between all members, so on the surface TCP seems like a better choice. Unfortunately, the fact that TCP requires connections to be established is a deal breaker. Coherence uses full-mesh peer-to-peer architecture, which means that whenever a new node joins the cluster, it would have to establish TCP connections with all other nodes. Imagine a cluster of a few hundred nodes and think about the implications of the last statement.

This would effectively prevent Coherence from scaling past a handful of nodes, which leaves us with UDP as an alternative. As far as scaling goes, UDP is great. It is a connectionless protocol, so there are no connections to establish when new members join the cluster. All that a new member needs to do is to send a single message to anyone who happens to be listening, effectively saying "I'm here to help out, let me know what you want me to do". It also doesn't require the sender to wait for the acknowledgment from the recipient, so it allows for a much higher throughput. Unfortunately, as we discussed earlier, UDP does not provide the reliability guarantees that Coherence requires.

In order to solve that problem, Coherence engineers created **Tangosol Cluster Messaging Protocol** (**TCMP**), an **application layer** protocol on top of UDP that ensures reliable, in-order delivery of UDP datagrams. TCMP is used for most of the communication between the cluster members, with TCP being used only for fast death detection of members and for Coherence*Extend support, as we'll discuss shortly.

TCMP makes certain assumptions about its environment that are typically true for a Coherence cluster within a data center, but would not necessarily be true in a general case. For one, it is optimized for the common scenario where all cluster members are on the same, reliable, low latency network, and the packet loss and the number of datagrams received out-of-order are minimal.

This is not necessarily true as soon as you move your clients to a different network switch, which will typically be the case with desktop applications, and is definitely not true if your clients connect to the Coherence cluster over WAN. In those cases, TCP-based Coherence*Extend is a much better choice.

Coherence*Extend overview

Just like the TCMP, Coherence*Extend is a proprietary application layer protocol that can be used to communicate with the Coherence cluster. However, unlike TCMP, which is UDP-based, Coherence*Extend is a TCP-based protocol.

 Actually, Coherence*Extend is designed to be protocol independent, and there are two implementations provided out of the box: the TCP-based implementation and a JMS-based implementation.

However, Extend-JMS has been deprecated in Coherence 3.5, so in the remainder of this chapter, we will focus on the Extend-TCP implementation.

Coherence*Extend allows you to access remote Coherence caches using standard Coherence APIs you are already familiar with, which means that with some care you can make your applications protocol-agnostic and be able to switch between TCMP and Extend using configuration. It also allows you to submit entry processors and invocable agents for execution within the cluster, which is particularly useful when you need to overcome some of the inherent limitations of Coherence*Extend that we will discuss shortly.

In order to allow client applications to connect to the cluster via Coherence*Extend, you need to ensure that one or more **proxy servers** are running within the cluster. While you could easily turn all cluster members into proxy servers, this is probably not the best thing to do as proxy servers will be competing for CPU resources with cache services and other code executing on your storage nodes, such as filters, entry processors, and aggregators.

What you should do instead is configure Coherence*Extend proxy servers on a dedicated set of machines that serve no other purpose. This will allow you to scale your proxy servers independently from the storage-enabled members of the cluster. It is important to remember, however, that Coherence*Extend proxy servers are full-blown TCMP members, so they should have fast and reliable communication with the rest of the cluster. Ideally, they should be on the same network switch as the cache servers.

A typical Coherence*Extend deployment using the recommended architecture described previously will be similar to the following diagram:

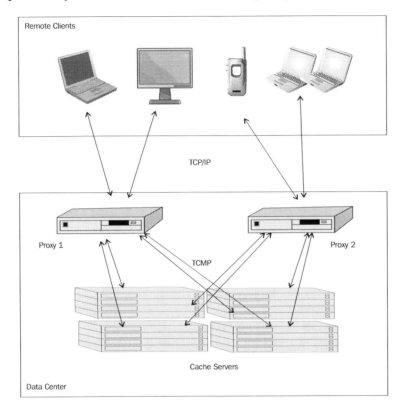

Configuring Coherence*Extend

So much for the theory and background, let's get more practical and learn how to configure Coherence*Extend both within the cluster and on the client.

Configuring proxy servers

In order to configure a Coherence node to serve as a Coherence*Extend proxy server, you need to add a scheme similar to the following to your cache configuration file:

```
<cache-config>
  <caching-scheme-mapping>
  ...
  </caching-scheme-mapping>

  <caching-schemes>
```

```
<proxy-scheme>
  <scheme-name>extend-tcp-proxy</scheme-name>
  <service-name>ExtendTcpProxyService</service-name>
  <thread-count>50</thread-count>

  <acceptor-config>
    <tcp-acceptor>
      <local-address>
        <address>localhost</address>
        <port>9099</port>
      </local-address>
    </tcp-acceptor>
  </acceptor-config>

  <autostart>true</autostart>
</proxy-scheme>

      </caching-schemes>
    </cache-config>
```

Within the `proxy-scheme` element, you need to configure the number of threads the proxy server should use to process client requests, as well as the address and port number the server should listen on for client connections.

The proxy server threads are I/O-bound—they spend most of their lifetime waiting for the response from the cluster, so you can configure a high number of threads per CPU core. Ideally, you should have as many threads in the proxy server pool as there are client threads accessing proxy server. In the example above, the proxy server would be able to serve up to fifty single-threaded clients without any request blocking.

You can also configure a number of TCP-specific settings within the `tcp-acceptor` element, such as send and receive buffer size, the size of the backlog queue, whether to reuse the socket (it is not reused by default), as well as whether to use "keep-alives" (enabled by default) and TCP delay/Nagle algorithm (disabled by default). The detailed discussion of these topics is out of the scope of this book, so you should consult *Coherence User's Guide* and documentation within `cache-config.dtd` for details.

If you want to use POF for serialization, but don't have enabled POF globally for all the services, you also need to configure the serializer that the proxy server should use:

```
<acceptor-config>

  <tcp-acceptor>
    <local-address>
      <address>localhost</address>
      <port>9099</port>
    </local-address>
  </tcp-acceptor>

  <serializer>
    <class-name>
      com.tangosol.io.pof.ConfigurablePofContext
    </class-name>
    <init-params>
      <init-param>
        <param-type>string</param-type>
        <param-value>
          my-pof-config.xml
        </param-value>
      </init-param>
    </init-params>
  </serializer>

</acceptor-config>
```

By default the proxy server will serve as a proxy for both the cache services and the invocation services running within the cluster, and will allow you to both read from and write into Coherence clustered caches. However, you can modify the defaults by adding a `proxy-config` element similar to the following within your proxy scheme definition:

```
<proxy-config>
  <cache-service-proxy>
    <enabled>true</enabled>
    <read-only>true</read-only>
  </cache-service-proxy>
  <invocation-service-proxy>
    <enabled>false</enabled>
  </invocation-service-proxy>
</proxy-config>
```

Once you are satisfied with the configuration, you can test it by starting Coherence node as you normally would. If everything is configured correctly, you should see the `ExtendTcpProxyService` in the list of running services:

```
Services
  (
  TcpRing{...}
  ClusterService{...}
  InvocationService{...}
  DistributedCache{...}
  ReplicatedCache{...}
  ProxyService{Name=ExtendTcpProxyService, State=(SERVICE_STARTED),
     Id=5, Version=3.2, OldestMemberId=1}
  )
```

Congratulations! You are ready to use Coherence*Extend to connect to the cluster.

Configuring clients

Once you have one or more proxy servers up and running, you are ready to configure your client application to use Coherence*Extend. In order to do so, you need to configure a *remote cache scheme* on the client and map cache names to it. If you want to be able to send invocable agents for processing within the cluster, as we discussed in *Chapter 6, Parallel and In-Place Processing*, you will also need to configure a *remote invocation scheme* on the client.

In this section, you will learn how to do both. We will also discuss the closely related topic of *address providers*, which gives you full control over the selection of the proxy server that a client should connect to, but first things first.

Configuring remote cache scheme

In order to allow your client application to connect to a Coherence*Extend proxy server, you need to add a `remote-cache-scheme` definition to your client's cache configuration file:

```
<cache-config>
  <caching-scheme-mapping>
    ...
  </caching-scheme-mapping>

  <caching-schemes>

    <remote-cache-scheme>
      <scheme-name>extend-tcp</scheme-name>
      <service-name>ExtendTcpCacheService</service-name>
```

```
<initiator-config>
  <tcp-initiator>
    <remote-addresses>
      <socket-address>
        <address>proxy1.mycompany.com</address>
        <port>9099</port>
      </socket-address>
      <socket-address>
        <address>proxy2.mycompany.com</address>
        <port>9099</port>
      </socket-address>
      ...
    </remote-addresses>
  </tcp-initiator>
  <outgoing-message-handler>
    <request-timeout>30s</request-timeout>
  </outgoing-message-handler>
</initiator-config>

  </remote-cache-scheme>

 </caching-schemes>
</cache-config>
```

As you can see, you need to specify the IP addresses of your proxy servers within the `remote-addresses` element. In the example above, we have specified a static list of remote addresses using `socket-address` elements, but this is just one of the ways to achieve the goal, as you'll see shortly.

In addition to proxy server addresses, the `tcp-initiator` element allows you to specify a number of TCP-specific configuration parameters, just as the `tcp-acceptor` element does on the server, as well as the client-specific connection timeout.

Finally, the `outgoing-message-handler` element allows you to configure the timeout for individual requests, as well as the heartbeat interval and timeout, which are used to detect network connection or proxy server failure, as we'll discuss soon.

Mapping cache names to caches

The next thing you need to do in order to configure the client is to map cache names to the appropriate cache schemes by adding the necessary elements to the `caching-scheme-mapping` section of the cache configuration file, just like within the cluster. You can map cache names either directly to the remote cache scheme, or to a near cache scheme that uses the remote cache as a back cache.

The latter is especially interesting, as it allows you to bring frequently or recently used objects into the client's process, and can significantly improve read performance. For example, we can access the `accounts` cache through a near cache, while accessing all other caches directly:

```
<cache-config>

  <caching-scheme-mapping>

    <cache-mapping>
      <cache-name>accounts</cache-name>
      <scheme-name>accounts-scheme</scheme-name>
    </cache-mapping>

    <cache-mapping>
      <cache-name>*</cache-name>
      <scheme-name>extend-tcp</scheme-name>
    </cache-mapping>

  </caching-scheme-mapping>

  <caching-schemes>

    <near-scheme>
      <scheme-name>accounts-scheme</scheme-name>

      <front-scheme>
        <local-scheme>
          <eviction-policy>HYBRID</eviction-policy>
          <high-units>1000</high-units>
        </local-scheme>
      </front-scheme>

      <back-scheme>
        <remote-cache-scheme>
          <scheme-ref>extend-tcp</scheme-ref>
        </remote-cache-scheme>
      </back-scheme>

      <autostart>true</autostart>
    </near-scheme>

    <remote-cache-scheme>
      <scheme-name>extend-tcp</scheme-name>

      <!-- configuration details omitted for brevity -->

    </remote-cache-scheme>

  </caching-schemes>
</cache-config>
```

Configuring a remote invocation service

If you want to be able to submit invocable agents from a client, you also need to configure a remote invocation service. This is very similar to the remote cache scheme we configured earlier—the only difference really is the name of the top-level configuration element:

```
<remote-invocation-scheme>
  <scheme-name>extend-tcp-invocation</scheme-name>
  <service-name>ExtendTcpInvocationService</service-name>
  <initiator-config>
    <tcp-initiator>
      <remote-addresses>
        <socket-address>
          <address>192.168.1.5</address>
          <port>9099</port>
        </socket-address>
      </remote-addresses>
      <connect-timeout>30s</connect-timeout>
    </tcp-initiator>
    <outgoing-message-handler>
      <heartbeat-interval>1s</heartbeat-interval>
      <heartbeat-timeout>10s</heartbeat-timeout>
      <request-timeout>30s</request-timeout>
    </outgoing-message-handler>
  </initiator-config>
</remote-invocation-scheme>
```

The rest of the configuration should look fairly familiar by now, so let's move to the more interesting topic of address providers.

Address providers

When specifying the list of proxy server addresses that a client can connect to, you can either specify a static list, as we did in the examples above, or you can implement and configure an *address provider* to use.

Address providers are a very interesting option, as they allow you to externalize the information about the available proxy servers. For example, you might find it easier from a maintenance perspective to keep a list of proxy server addresses in a text file on network share than to embed them into the cache configuration file, especially if the number of proxy servers is significant.

In order to create a custom address provider, you need to create a class that implements the `com.tangosol.net.AddressProvider` interface, either directly or by extending one of the base classes available in the sample code for this book. Once you implement it, configuring clients to use it is quite simple—all you need to do is replace the static address list with the `address-provider` element in the cache configuration file:

```
<tcp-initiator>
  <remote-addresses>
    <address-provider>
      <class-name>
        com.mycompany.MyAddressProvider
      </class-name>
    </address-provider>
  </remote-addresses>
  <connect-timeout>30s</connect-timeout>
</tcp-initiator>
```

Before we conclude this section, we should also mention that an address provider is actually used even in the static configuration examples we've seen so far. One of the address providers that ships with Coherence is `ConfigurableAddressProvider`, which accepts configuration in the form of the `socket-address` XML elements we've seen earlier.

When a `ConfigurableAddressProvider` is instantiated on the client, it will randomize the list of available proxy server addresses during initialization. That way each client will attempt to connect to proxy servers in a slightly different order, which provides a somewhat crude, but in practice quite effective, load balancing algorithm for proxy servers.

Handling connection or proxy server failure

If the connection to a proxy server fails at some point, whether because of the network or proxy server failure, the client will automatically attempt to reconnect to the next proxy server returned by the address provider. It is important to note that reconnection only occurs the next time client actively attempts to access the cluster, which is acceptable for most client applications.

However, some real-time client applications are completely passive—they simply register event listeners with a remote cache and react to event notifications, without ever issuing another active request to the cluster. In situations like these, reconnection will not occur automatically and has to be forced, either by running a low-priority background thread that periodically calls a lightweight method, such as `size()`, on each cache, or by listening for membership changes in the cluster and actively accessing the cache when the `MemberEvent.MEMBER_LEFT` event is received.

Coherence*Extend limitations

Now that we have both the cluster and the clients configured to use Coherence*Extend, we are ready to access remote Coherence caches from the client. For the most part, you already know how to do that, as the API is exactly the same whether you use TCMP or Coherence*Extend for communication: you use CacheFactory to obtain a reference to a NamedCache instance, and then use methods defined by the NamedCache interface to access or manipulate cached data, register listeners, execute queries, invoke entry processors, and so on.

However, even though the API is exactly the same, there are some major architectural differences between TCMP and Extend-based applications that have a significant impact on how certain things can be achieved.

Explicit concurrency control

Cluster-wide concurrency control using explicit locking is one such example. Explicit locking is disabled by default on a proxy server, which means that any attempt to lock a cache entry from a client will result in an exception. While you can enable it by setting the lock-enabled element of the cache-service-proxy to true, that is probably not a good idea.

Locks within the clustered cache are managed by the service the cache belongs to, and they are associated either with a thread or a member that requested a lock. The exact behavior is controlled using the lease-granularity option within cache scheme definition, and its value is thread by default.

The problem with that is that the proxy server uses a pool of threads to process client requests, and there are no guarantees that the same thread will be used to process subsequent requests from the same client. In other words, if the default, thread-scoped lease granularity is used, the chances are that an unlock request will fail because it will likely be executed by a different thread than the one that issued the original lock request, even though both requests originated from the same client.

This is exactly why Coherence *User's Guide* states that if you enable locking on the proxy server you must set lease granularity for the affected cache scheme to member as well. Unfortunately, this doesn't really help much either – while setting lease granularity to member will prevent the problem described above, it creates another one, which is not so obvious. In my opinion, this makes the situation even worse.

Consider the following scenario, step by step:

- Client A connected to a proxy server X requests a lock on a cache entry with a key '123' in the `accounts` cache

- Proxy server X forwards the lock request to the owner of the specified entry

- The owner obtains the lock, registers member X (proxy server) as the lock owner because the lease granularity is set to `member`, and returns `true` to the proxy server to let it know that the lock was acquired successfully

- The proxy server returns `true` to Client A, to notify it that the lock was acquired successfully

So far, so good—client A successfully obtained the lock and can go about modifying account '123' any way it wants, working under the assumption that it holds an exclusive lock on it and that any other client that wants to modify the same entry will have to wait until it releases the lock. However, things can get a bit dicey from here:

- Client B connected to proxy server X requests a lock on the cache entry with a key '123' in the `accounts` cache

- The proxy server X forwards the lock request to the owner of the specified entry

- The owner sees that member X already holds the lock and simply returns `true`, as it should—multiple locks against the same entry by the same lock owner should always succeed

- The proxy server returns `true` to Client B, to notify it that the lock was acquired successfully

Yup, I'm sure you can see the problem from miles away—both clients, A and B, believe that they hold an exclusive lock on the same piece of data and proceed accordingly. To make things worse, the first one to unlock the entry will succeed, while the second one will fail and the unlock method will return `false`. Unfortunately, that means that the client-side locking will work reliably only in the unlikely scenario that each client connects to its own, dedicated proxy server.

While you could try to handle the situation gracefully by checking the result of the `unlock` call and retrying the operation if necessary, this is very error-prone and will not work in all possible cases, so my advice is to leave locking disabled and use an alternative approach for mutating cache operations.

One option is to use an entry processor, as we discussed in *Chapter 6*. In addition to performance advantages we discussed earlier, entry processors eliminate the need for the explicit lock, as they execute on the entry owner and are guaranteed to execute atomically.

Another possibility is to let an invocable agent do the work. The agent will execute on the proxy server the client is connected to, which behaves like any other member of the cluster, and will be able to obtain and release locks successfully. You should be careful though and ensure that the lease granularity is set to the default, `thread` level, or you might run into the same issue you are trying to avoid.

Executing invocable agents via Coherence*Extend

For the most part, executing invocable agents from a Coherence*Extend client is no different than executing them from a normal cluster member. However, just as with the explicit concurrency controls, functionality is somewhat limited due to architectural differences.

For one, an agent submitted from an Extend client will always be executed on the proxy server the client is connected to. You cannot influence this by passing a set of members to execute the agent on to a `query` method, as you normally could, because Coherence*Extend client has no direct knowledge of the cluster and the members within it. Therefore, you should always pass a `null` member set to a `query` method.

Second, the remote invocation service only supports synchronous task execution, because of the limitations in the underlying Coherence*Extend protocol. That means that you can use `query`, but not the `execute` method of the `InvocationService` interface.

Even with these limitations, the remote invocation service is extremely useful, especially when the concurrency limitations described above are taken into account, so you should look for the opportunities to use it when building Coherence*Extend-based client applications.

Securing proxy servers

Whether you use TCMP within the data center, or Coherence*Extend to allow access to your application from remote desktops, across the WAN, or even across the Internet, Coherence allows you to secure your application by limiting access based on the client's IP address.

While you typically don't need to do that when your whole application, including the Coherence cluster, is hidden behind a firewall, you might want to consider it when you open it up for access from remote Coherence*Extend clients.

In order to achieve that, you need to add an `authorized-hosts` section to the `tcp-acceptor` configuration element of your proxy server scheme:

```
<proxy-scheme>
  <scheme-name>extend-tcp-proxy</scheme-name>
  <service-name>ExtendTcpProxyService</service-name>
  <thread-count>5</thread-count>

  <acceptor-config>
    <tcp-acceptor>
      <local-address>
        <address>localhost</address>
        <port>9099</port>
      </local-address>
      <authorized-hosts>
        ...
      </authorized-hosts>
    </tcp-acceptor>
  </acceptor-config>

  <autostart>true</autostart>
</proxy-scheme>
```

Within that section, you can specify:

- One or more `host-address` elements, which allow you to specify individual names or addresses of the hosts that should be allowed access
- One or more `host-range` elements, which allow you to grant access to all the hosts whose addresses fall into a specific range, with the typical example being access from a whole subnet
- Or finally, a `host-filter` element, which allows you to the evaluate client address using a built-in or custom implementation of a Coherence filter, as discussed in *Chapter 5, Querying the Data Grid*.

The last option is quite interesting as it allows you to dynamically determine if a particular host should be allowed to access the Coherence cluster or not. This can come in very handy if you are building a SaaS solution, for example, and need to be able to provision it for new customers as they sign up.

While you could just add a new customer's IP address using `host-address` or `host-range` elements, that would require you to restart all proxy servers in order for the change to take effect, which is not very convenient.

What you can do instead is implement a custom filter that simply checks if the address is present in the cache of allowed addresses. Once you have that in place, all you need to do when a new customer signs up is to add their IP address into that cache.

Keep in mind that any custom logic that you implement as part of your filter should execute as quickly as possible, so you will probably not want to perform database lookups or any other high-latency operations. Even with the caching approach described above, you might want to use either a replicated cache or a partitioned cache fronted by a CQC to store allowed IP addresses, in order to eliminate one network call and keep latency to a minimum.

For example, we could implement `AuthorizedHostsFilter` like this:

```
public class AuthorizedHostsFilter implements Filter {

  private static final NamedCache hosts =
                      new ContinuousQueryCache(
                              CacheFactory.getCache("auth-hosts"),
                              AlwaysFilter.INSTANCE, false);

  public boolean evaluate(Object o) {
    InetAddress address = (InetAddress) o;
    return hosts.containsKey(address.getHostAddress());
  }
}
```

The important part is initialization of the static `hosts` field, which is set to an instance of a CQC that caches locally all the keys from the `auth-hosts` partitioned cache in order to improve access performance.

Now that we have that in place, the implementation of the `evaluate` method that will perform access checking is trivial—it simply casts the argument to `java.net.InetAddress` instance, which is what is always passed as an argument to a host filter, and checks if the `auth-hosts` cache contains the matching key.

The last thing we need to do is configure our proxy servers to use the host filter we just created:

```
<authorized-hosts>
  <host-filter>
    <class-name>
        ...security.AuthorizedHostsFilter
    </class-name>
  </host-filter>
</authorized-hosts>
```

We have now secured the access to a Coherence cluster by ensuring that only hosts that are explicitly registered in the `auth-hosts` cache can access it.

However, that is only one part of the complete security solution — while it will not be possible for unauthorized hosts to connect to the cluster, they can still eavesdrop on the network traffic between the authorized clients and the proxy server and obtain the data they shouldn't be allowed to see. This would also allow them to impersonate one of the authorized hosts and gain direct cluster access.

In order to prevent them from doing that (or at least to make the task much more difficult and time consuming), we need to encrypt the traffic between the client and the proxy server. Fortunately, Coherence provides an easy way to do that, and the next section will show you how.

Using network filters

Network filters are another Coherence feature that can be used both with TCMP and Coherence*Extend, but which is much more applicable in a latter case. They are used to modify the contents of the messages exchanged between the client and the proxy server before they are transmitted over the wire.

Two common scenarios that are supported out of the box are encryption and compression. Encryption can be either password or private key-based, and is very useful when you want to address the security concerns described earlier and make network sniffing a non-issue. Unfortunately, as of Coherence 3.5, encryption is supported only by Java clients, and not by .NET and C++ Coherence*Extend clients.

This will hopefully be addressed in a future release, but in the meantime all is not lost if you need encryption support in .NET or C++ — the necessary infrastructure for pluggable network filters is in place, so you can implement one yourself, as we'll do shortly.

In the remainder of this section we will first look at the built-in filters that ship with Coherence and how to configure them. Afterwards, we will implement a custom encryption filter for .NET client using an excellent open source encryption library, Bouncy Castle. You will also learn how to configure custom network filters both within the cluster and on the client.

Built-in network filters

All built-in network filters are configured within the `cluster-config/filters` section of the Coherence deployment descriptor, `tangosol-coherence.xml`. They are assigned unique names, which you need to reference when configuring Coherence*Extend clients and proxy servers to use them.

Each filter can also have one or more configuration parameters, which are defined within the `init-params` configuration section of each `filter` element. For example, the compression filter is configured like this:

```
<filter id="1">
  <filter-name>gzip</filter-name>
  <filter-class>
    com.tangosol.net.CompressionFilter
  </filter-class>
  <init-params>
    <init-param id="1">
      <param-name>strategy</param-name>
      <param-value>gzip</param-value>
    </init-param>
    <init-param id="2">
      <param-name>level</param-name>
      <param-value>default</param-value>
    </init-param>
  </init-params>
</filter>
```

When an instance of a network filter is created, Coherence will convert parameters defined for the filter into an XML element and pass it to the filter's `setConfig` method. In the case of the compression filter defined above, the following XML will be passed to its `setConfig` method:

```
<config>
  <strategy>gzip</strategy>
  <level>default</level>
</config>
```

In some cases, you might want to override the default value specified in the configuration file for one or more parameters. You can do that in Java by allowing parameter override using system properties, just as the built-in symmetric encryption filter defined below does:

```
<filter id="2">
  <filter-name>symmetric-encryption</filter-name>
  <filter-class>
    com.tangosol.net.security.PasswordBasedEncryptionFilter
  </filter-class>
  <init-params>
    <init-param id="1">
      <param-name>password</param-name>
      <param-value
```

```
      system-property="tangosol.coherence.security.password">
      </param-value>
    </init-param>
  </init-params>
</filter>
```

In this case, the default value is an empty string, which is probably not what you want to use as a password, so you need to specify the password using the system property `tangosol.coherence.security.password` when starting a Coherence node.

Now that we have the filter configuration basics out of the way, let's look in more detail into the built-in filters Coherence provides.

Compression filter

The compression filter allows you to compress the network traffic between the nodes in the cluster, or in the case of Coherence*Extend, between the clients and the proxy servers.

Compression rarely makes sense within the cluster, as the network between the nodes will typically have plenty of bandwidth, so compression would only increase the CPU load without providing any real benefits. On the other hand, compression can greatly improve performance over low-bandwidth, high-latency WAN connections, so it might make sense to use it with the remote Coherence*Extend clients, or for cluster-to-cluster communication across the WAN.

In order to configure Coherence*Extend proxy server to use the compression filter, you need to add the `use-filters` configuration section to the `acceptor-config` element of the proxy scheme and specify the filter name within it:

```
<proxy-scheme>
  <scheme-name>extend-proxy</scheme-name>
  <service-name>ExtendTcpProxyService</service-name>
  <acceptor-config>
    <tcp-acceptor>
      ...
    </tcp-acceptor>

    <use-filters>
      <filter-name>gzip</filter-name>
    </use-filters>

  </acceptor-config>

</proxy-scheme>
```

On the client, you need to do the same thing—the only difference is that you need to put the `use-filters` element within the `initiator-config` section of both the remote cache scheme and the remote invocation scheme.

The important thing to understand is that network filters are an all-or-nothing feature. If you decide to use them you need to ensure that all the clients and all proxy servers are configured identically, including the order of the filters within the `use-filters` section. Otherwise, communication between the clients and the proxy servers will not work.

Also, while the compression filter can be configured to use one of several compression strategies supported by Java, such as `gzip`, `huffman-only`, or `filtered`, if you need to use compression between .NET clients and proxy servers you should keep the default value of `gzip`, which is the only strategy supported in the current release of .NET Coherence client.

Symmetric encryption filter

If you look at the filter definitions within the default Coherence deployment descriptor, `tangosol-coherence.xml`, you will notice that there are two encryption filter implementations: `PasswordBasedEncryptionFilter`, which uses a configurable password to perform symmetric encryption of network traffic, as well as the `ClusterEncryptionFilter`, which uses asymmetric encryption to protect the cluster join protocol, but afterwards generates a symmetric encryption key and switches over to a much faster symmetric encryption for data transfer.

The latter is significantly more difficult to configure as it requires that each node in the cluster has access to the public keys of all other nodes. It is also not supported by Coherence*Extend clients at the moment, so in the remainder of this section we will focus on the former: the password-based symmetric encryption filter.

You can configure Coherence*Extend clients and proxy servers to use encryption the same way we configured compression filter earlier—by referencing `symmetric-encryption` filter within the `use-filters` section of `initiator-config` on the client, and `acceptor-config` on the server:

```
<use-filters>
  <filter-name>symmetric-encryption</filter-name>
</use-filters>
```

The Java implementation of encryption filter is based on the **Java Cryptography Extensions (JCE)**, which means that you can use either a standard **Cryptographic Service Provider** that ships with the JDK, or plug in a third-party provider, such as Bouncy Castle (`http://www.bouncycastle.org`).

It also means that the encryption algorithm is configurable—algorithms that are available to you will be determined only by the provider you decide to use. This is the reason why Bouncy Castle is such an attractive alternative to a standard cryptography provider—it supports pretty much any cryptographic algorithm you can think of.

If you are not familiar with password-based encryption, it is important that you understand some basic concepts and terminology. The *password* that you specify is not used directly to encrypt the data. Instead, it is used only as a starting point for the creation of a *secret key*, which is then used to encrypt the data. This provides an additional layer of security—even if the attacker finds out the password itself, he or she will not be able to determine the secret key that should be used the decrypt the data unless he or she knows the remaining parameters used for secret key generation:

- A **salt**, which is combined with the base password
- An **algorithm** that is used to encrypt the combination of the password and salt
- The number of **iterations** for which encryption should be performed

Basically, the secret key is generated by encrypting the combination of the password and salt for the specified number of iterations, using one of the available encryption algorithms.

Oversimplification warning

The process is a bit more complex then described in the preceeding text, as the algorithm mentioned above is actually a combination of two algorithms: a **hashing** or **pseudorandom function**, such as MD5 or HMAC-SHA1, which is used to generate the secret key based on the password, salt, and iteration count, as well as the *encryption algorithm*, such as DES, TripleDES, or Rijndael/AES, which is used to encrypt messages using the generated secret key.

If you are interested in details, please check the RSA PKCS #5 standard or IETF RFC-2898, both of which can be easily found on the Internet.

Coherence provides sensible defaults for salt, algorithm, and the number of iterations, but you can override them by adding `salt`, `algorithm`, and `iterations` parameters to the filter definition and specifying values for them. Just make sure that you configure the filter exactly the same on both the client and the server or your secret keys will not match and the communication between the client and the server will fail.

Now that we understand how the built-in Java encryption filter works, let's see how we can implement one in .NET.

Implementing a custom network filter

In order to create a custom network filter in Java, you need to create a class that implements the `com.tangosol.io.WrapperStreamFactory` interface:

```
public interface WrapperStreamFactory {
    InputStream getInputStream(InputStream stream);
    OutputStream getOutputStream(OutputStream stream);
}
```

Each method should return a new stream that wraps a specified input or output stream and adds necessary behavior. For example, you can implement compression by simply wrapping the original input and output stream with a `java.util.zip.GZIPInputStream` and `java.util.zip.GZIPOutputStream` respectively.

Custom filter implementation in .NET is very similar. The only difference is that your class needs to implement the `Tangosol.IO.IWrapperStreamFactory` interface:

```
public interface IWrapperStreamFactory
{
    Stream GetInputStream(Stream stream);
    Stream GetOutputStream(Stream stream);
}
```

Fortunately for us, the .NET implementation of Bouncy Castle encryption library provides a convenient `Org.BouncCastle.Crypto.IO.CryptoStream` class, so all we need to do is to create a wrapper around it that configures it properly:

```
public class PasswordBasedEncryptionFilter
    : IWrapperStreamFactory, IXmlConfigurable
{
    private char[] m_password;
    private byte[] m_salt;
    private int    m_iterationCount;
    private String m_algorithm;

    public PasswordBasedEncryptionFilter()
       {}

    public Stream GetInputStream(Stream stream)
    {
        return new CipherInputStream(stream, GetCipher(false));
    }

    public Stream GetOutputStream(Stream stream){
        return new CipherOutputStream(stream, GetCipher(true));
    }

    . . .
}
```

The `CipherInputStream` and `CipherOutputStream` classes used in this code are really just thin wrappers around the `CryptoStream` class provided by Bouncy Castle that simplify its configuration and handle few other minor details required by the `IWrapperStreamFactory` implementation, such as keeping track of the current position within the input stream.

The most important piece of code in the preceding example is probably the call to the `GetCipher` method, which is responsible for the creation of a block cipher that should be used for encryption or decryption. However, the details of this method are beyond the scope of this book. If you are interested in implementation details, feel free to review the full implementation of the `PasswordBasedEncryptionFilter` class in the sample code that accompanies the book.

Summary

This chapter addressed some very important topics when it comes to extending the reach of your Coherence-based applications outside of the data center and to platforms other than Java.

At the very beginning we discussed different network protocols Coherence uses and reasons for using Coherence*Extend instead of TCMP across WAN or from remote clients. It is important to choose the right option when architecting your application, as incorrect protocol choice for high-latency or unreliable clients can easily bring the whole cluster to its knees.

We then learned how to configure Coherence*Extend both within the cluster and on the client, and discussed topics such as remote caches, the remote invocation service, address providers, and network filters. We also learned how to secure Coherence*Extend deployments using both host-based access control and data encryption, and implemented a .NET version of a symmetric encryption filter that you can use in combination with a built-in Java encryption filter to encrypt network traffic between .NET clients and Coherence*Extend proxy servers.

However, before I show you how to do that, we need to take a step back and learn a bit more about the implementation of .NET Coherence*Extend clients, which is the subject of the next chapter.

10
Accessing Coherence from .NET

The material we have covered in the previous chapter applies equally to all Coherence*Extend clients, regardless of the platform. However, each platform also has its own idiosyncrasies and conventions, which affect both the API and the client-side configuration to a certain extent. In this chapter we will discuss these differences when it comes to .NET and teach you how to access Coherence from .NET applications.

If you are a Java developer not interested in writing .NET applications, you can safely skip this chapter. However, if you are a .NET developer trying to learn Coherence, keep in mind that the following sections will likely prove to be inadequate if you dive directly into them without reading the prerequisite material in the preceding chapters first.

Coherence, when used properly, is a major foundational component of the application. It is important to understand its role in the overall architecture, as well as its feature set, in order to get the most from the following sections.

Now that you've been warned, let's dig in.

.NET client configuration

One of the first questions you are likely to have when you try to implement a Coherence client in .NET is how to configure everything—how to let .NET application know which operational, cache, and POF configuration files to use.

If you come from the Java world, you are used to placing configuration files with well-known names into a classpath, or telling Coherence explicitly where to find them by setting appropriate system properties. However, neither the classpath nor system properties exist in .NET, so we obviously need a different approach.

The good news is that there are several approaches to .NET client configuration, and which one is most appropriate for your situation will depend mostly on the type of application you are building. For example, while placing files with well-known names into the application directory or specifying them explicitly in the application configuration file might work for a desktop or ASP.NET web application, it is not appropriate for a Microsoft Excel add-in that needs to access Coherence. In the latter case, assembly embedded resources and programmatic configuration are much more appropriate.

We will discuss each of these options in detail, but before we do that let's take a look at how Coherence configuration files in .NET differ from their Java counterparts and create the sample files we will reference throughout the remainder of this chapter.

Coherence configuration files in .NET

Probably the biggest difference between Java and .NET configuration files is that the former use DTD for validation, while the latter use XML Schema. The main reason for this is that Microsoft Visual Studio, by far the most commonly used .NET IDE, can only provide IntelliSense for XML Schema-based XML files.

Enabling Visual Studio IntelliSense for Coherence configuration files

If you installed Coherence for .NET using the Oracle-provided installer, the XML Schema files necessary for the Intellisense support should have been copied to the appropriate Visual Studio directory automatically. However, if for some reason IntelliSense doesn't work when you are editing Coherence configuration files in Visual Studio, you can enable it manually.

In order to do that, you need to copy all three schema files (`coherence.xsd`, `cache-config.xsd`, and `coherence-pof-config.xsd`) from the `config` directory of your Coherence for .NET installation to the `Xml/Schemas` subdirectory of your Visual Studio installation.

Other than that, you will likely notice that you don't have as many configuration options in .NET as you do in Java. For example, out of the myriad of cache schemes available in the Java cache configuration file, you will only be able to configure local, near, and remote schemes in .NET—this makes perfect sense considering the fact that a .NET application is always a Coherence*Extend client and never a full-blown member of the cluster.

So, without any further ado, let's take a look at different configuration artifacts in .NET.

Operational descriptor

The .NET operational descriptor is a significantly trimmed-down version of the Java operational descriptor. Because most of the operational settings are cluster-related, they do not apply to the .NET client, so the only things you can configure in the .NET operational descriptor are the logger, default cache factory, and the network filters.

For details on how to configure the logger please refer to the Coherence *User's Guide*, as there are several options available, including the ability to use one of the popular open source logging frameworks, such as Log4Net, NLog, or Logging Application Block from the Microsoft Enterprise Library by the way of Common.Logging abstraction library.

If you want to use a custom implementation of the configurable cache factory you can specify it within the configurable-cache-factory-config element. However, this is a fairly advanced feature and more likely than not you will never need to use it.

That leaves us with the network filters as the last thing we can configure, so let's see how we can register the PasswordBasedEncryptionFilter we created earlier:

```
<coherence xmlns="http://schemas.tangosol.com/coherence">
  <cluster-config>
    <filters>
      <filter>
        <filter-name>symmetric-encryption</filter-name>
        <filter-class>
          PasswordBasedEncryptionFilter, Coherence.Encryption
        </filter-class>
        <init-params>
          <init-param id="1">
            <param-name>password</param-name>
            <param-value>my!paSSwoRD</param-value>
          </init-param>
        </init-params>
      </filter>
    </filters>
  </cluster-config>
  <logging-config>
    ...
  </logging-config>
</coherence>
```

As you can see, the filter registration is very similar to the one in Java. The only major differences are the namespace declaration within the root element and how the class name is specified. The former is simply the side effect of a switch from a DTD to an XML Schema-based validation, while the latter reflects the difference in class loading mechanisms in Java and .NET.

On a .NET client, you need to include the assembly name the class should be loaded from in addition to the fully qualified class name. In the previous example, `PasswordBasedEncryptionFilter` class will be loaded from the `Coherence.Encryption` assembly. This rule will apply whenever a class name needs to be specified in one of the configuration files for a .NET application.

Cache configuration

As I mentioned earlier, you will only be able to configure a subset of the cache schemes on a .NET client, but this simply reflects the fact that not all of the cache schemes that are available within the cluster make sense on a Coherence*Extend client. For example, it doesn't make any sense to configure a replicated or partitioned scheme on the client.

The schemes that you *can* configure are **local**, **near**, and **remote cache** schemes, as well as the **remote invocation service**. We have already discussed how to configure each of these in the preceding sections, so let's just take a look at the sample .NET cache configuration file.

```xml
<cache-config xmlns="http://schemas.tangosol.com/cache">
  <caching-scheme-mapping>
    <cache-mapping>
      <cache-name>*</cache-name>
      <scheme-name>extend-tcp</scheme-name>
    </cache-mapping>
  </caching-scheme-mapping>
  <caching-schemes>
    <remote-cache-scheme>
      <scheme-name>extend-tcp</scheme-name>
      <service-name>ExtendTcpCacheService</service-name>
      <initiator-config>
        <tcp-initiator>
          <remote-addresses>
            <socket-address>
              <address>localhost</address>
              <port>9099</port>
            </socket-address>
          </remote-addresses>
          <connect-timeout>30s</connect-timeout>
```

```
          </tcp-initiator>
          <outgoing-message-handler>
            <heartbeat-interval>1s</heartbeat-interval>
            <heartbeat-timeout>10s</heartbeat-timeout>
            <request-timeout>30s</request-timeout>
          </outgoing-message-handler>
          <use-filters>
            <filter-name>symmetric-encryption</filter-name>
          </use-filters>
        </initiator-config>
      </remote-cache-scheme>
    </caching-schemes>
  </cache-config>
```

All of this should be familiar by now, aside from the namespace declaration for the root element, so we will not spend any more time discussing it.

POF configuration

Apart from the namespace declaration and the differences in how class names are specified, the POF configuration file is pretty much identical to the one in Java.

```
<pof-config xmlns="http://schemas.tangosol.com/pof">
  <user-type-list>
    <include>
      assembly://Coherence/Tangosol.Config/coherence-pof-config.xml
    </include>

    <user-type>
      <type-id>1000</type-id>
      <class-name>
        BankTerminal.Domain.Account, BankTerminal
      </class-name>
    </user-type>
    <user-type>
      <type-id>1001</type-id>
      <class-name>
        BankTerminal.Domain.Transaction, BankTerminal
      </class-name>
    </user-type>

  </user-type-list>
</pof-config>
```

The important thing is that the type identifiers match the ones configured within the cluster, and that you include the standard `coherence-pof-config.xml` file, which contains definitions for all of the built-in Coherence types that are required either for the Extend protocol itself or for the Coherence API, such as built-in filters, extractors, and aggregators.

You have probably noticed that the `include` element's contents is somewhat different and are probably wondering what this `assembly://` thing is all about, so it is a good time to discuss the resource loading mechanism in Coherence for .NET.

Resource loading in Coherence for .NET

Unlike Java, .NET doesn't have the notion of a classpath, so it is not possible to simply package standard configuration files into an assembly and let the class loader resolve them at runtime.

To complicate things even further, there is no single best place where configuration files should be located. For desktop and web applications it probably makes most sense to store them on the file system, within the application directory, but for other types of applications you might need to embed them into the application assembly.

In order to support a variety of possible sources for configuration files and other resources, Coherence for .NET introduces a higher-level abstraction for resource resolution in the form of the `Tangosol.IO.Resources.IResource` interface and `Tangosol.IO.Resources.ResourceLoader` class.

Resource abstraction

The `IResource` interface represents any resource that an input stream can be obtained from. There are four `IResource` implementations that ship with Coherence for .NET:

Class Name	Description
`FileResource`	Provides access to files on a file system, and is the default resource type in all applications except for ASP.NET web applications.
`WebResource`	Provides access to files within a web application and is the default resource type in ASP.NET web applications.
`EmbeddedResource`	Provides access to assembly-embedded resources.
`UrlResource`	Provides access to HTTP or FTP resources.

While most of the resource implementations mentioned previously should be fairly obvious, the distinction between the file and web resources is not so clear and deserves further discussion. Both file and web resources effectively represent physical files on disk, but they behave quite differently when resolving paths.

The `FileResource` will resolve paths relative to the current working directory, which can lead to some not so pleasant surprises if used in ASP.NET web applications. The problem is that the current working directory for an ASP.NET application is the directory IIS was started from, typically `C:\Windows\System32`, which is probably not where you intend to put configuration files for your application.

The `WebResource`, on the other hand, resolves paths relative to the path of the current HTTP request, but you can force it to resolve them against the application root directory by specifying ~ as a path prefix, as we'll see shortly.

The bottom line is that you should never use `FileResource` within a web application, as paths are likely not going to be resolved the way you expect.

Protocols and resource loader

The `ResourceLoader` is responsible for loading resources using the appropriate `IResource` implementation based on the URI-like resource name. It uses the protocol component of the resource name to determine which `IResource` implementation should be used:

Protocol	Resource	Examples
file	FileResource	file://config/my-pof-config.xml file://c:/config/my-cache-config.xml c:\MyDir\coherence.xml (if file is default)
web	WebResource	web://config/my-pof-config.xml (relative to current) web://~/config/my-pof-config.xml (relative to root) ~/my-pof-config.xml (if web is default)
assembly asm	EmbeddedResource	assembly://MyAssembly/My.Name.Space/pof.xml asm://MyAssembly/My.Name.Space/cache-config.xml
http ftp	UrlResource	http://config.mycompany.com/my-pof-config.xml ftp://user:pass@ftp.mycompany.com/config/pof.xml

The `assembly://Coherence/Tangosol.Config/coherence-pof-config.xml` reference in our POF configuration file should make more sense now, but the knowledge of the resource abstraction and the resource loading mechanism will also come in handy in the next section, when we look into various approaches to .NET client configuration.

Approaches to .NET client configuration

As I mentioned earlier, different application types require different configuration approaches, so Coherence for .NET supports three: convention-based configuration, explicit configuration within the standard .NET configuration files, such as `Web.config` or `App.config`, and finally, programmatic configuration.

In this section we will look into all three approaches and discuss when each one is appropriate.

Convention-based configuration

The convention-based configuration mechanism depends on files with well-known names being placed in the application directory, and works in both desktop and ASP.NET web applications. It is by far the easiest way to configure the Coherence for .NET client and should generally be preferred to other mechanisms.

In order to use it, you need to create the following files:

- `coherence.xml`: This is for the operational descriptor
- `coherence-cache-config.xml`: This is for the cache configuration file
- `coherence-pof-config.xml`: This is for the POF configuration file

Coherence for .NET client library will automatically detect these files on startup and use them to configure itself, unless they are overridden using one of the following two mechanisms.

Explicit configuration

In some cases it might make sense to place configuration files in a shared directory on the network, or to use files with different names. For example, you might need to keep separate sets of configuration files for development, testing, and production.

If you need to do that, you will have to configure the Coherence for .Net client explicitly. This can be accomplished in two ways: either programmatically, which we will discuss in the next section, or using the standard .NET configuration mechanism, and specifying configuration file names within the `App.config` or `Web.config` file.

In order to achieve the latter, you need to register a custom configuration section handler within your main application configuration file, and add a `coherence` section to it:

```
<configuration>
  <configSections>
    <section name="coherence"
    type="Tangosol.Config.CoherenceConfigHandler, Coherence"/>
```

```
    </configSections>

    <coherence>
      <cache-factory-config>
        Config\coherence-dev.xml
      </cache-factory-config>
      <cache-config>
        Config\cache-config-dev.xml
      </cache-config>
      <pof-config>
        Config\pof-config-dev.xml
      </pof-config>
    </coherence>
  </configuration>
```

In the previous example, we are using custom file names and are loading them from a `Config` subdirectory within the main directory of our application.

The previous example will work fine for desktop applications, as the paths specified will be resolved by the `FileResource`, relative to the directory where the application executable is located.

However, in a web application the paths would be resolved relative to the request path, which may or may not be what you expected. To eliminate the guesswork and the possibility for error from the equation, you should always force resolution against the root directory of a web application by prefixing paths with a tilde character:

```
    <coherence>
      <cache-factory-config>
        web://~/Config/coherence.xml
      </cache-factory-config>
      <cache-config>
        web://~/Config/cache-config.xml
      </cache-config>
      <pof-config>
        web://~/Config/pof-config.xml
      </pof-config>
    </coherence>
```

The usage of the `web://` prefix in the previous code snippet is optional, because `WebResource` is the default in ASP.NET applications. That said, it is the best practice to specify it, in order to eliminate any guesswork on the part of an unsuspecting reader.

Programmatic configuration

Finally, in some cases neither of the approaches previously mentioned will work. One of the common examples is a Microsoft Office add-in that depends on Coherence for .NET client library. The problem with an Office add-in is that in order to use the default configuration, you would have to place the configuration files within the directory where the actual Office application's executable is located, which is not very practical. You also don't have the option of specifying paths to configuration files explicitly, as there is no .NET configuration file to speak of.

Fortunately, the solution is quite simple—you can embed configuration files into your add-in's assembly, and configure Coherence client programmatically during add-in initialization:

```
const string baseUrl = "assembly://CoherenceRTD/CoherenceRTD.Config/";

CacheFactory.SetCacheFactoryConfig(baseUrl + "coherence.xml");
CacheFactory.SetCacheConfig(baseUrl + "cache-config.xml");
CacheFactory.SetPofConfig(baseUrl + "pof-config.xml");
```

In this example, we are loading the embedded resources coherence.xml, cache-config.xml, and pof-config.xml, from a CoherenceRTD.Config namespace in a CoherenceRTD assembly.

Coherence integration with Excel

The configuration example mentioned previously is actually taken from a proof-of-concept for an Excel RTD Server that uses Coherence as a data source, originally created by Dave Felcey from Oracle and myself, and subsequently significantly improved by Dave.

While not the focus of this section, this integration is definitely very interesting. I guess there is just something geeky cool about an Excel worksheet and graphs being updated in real-time as the data in the Coherence cluster changes.

Dave was kind enough to provide both the final demo and the instructions for its usage on his blog at http://blogs.oracle.com/felcey/, so you should definitely check it out if Excel integration with Coherence is something you are interested in.

That concludes the section on Coherence for .NET client configuration. It's time to roll up the sleeves and write some real code.

Implementing the client application

In the remainder of this chapter we will do a quick run-down through Coherence for .NET API and cover pretty much the same topics and in the same order as we did in *Chapters* 2 through 7.

Even if you are not particularly interested in .NET, this should provide a quick refresher of the topics we have covered so far, so you should probably not skip this section. You will also see that C# is very much like Java and that the Coherence for .NET API is very similar to the Coherence Java API, so following the examples should be fairly straightforward.

So let's start from the beginning…

Basic Cache Operations

In order to obtain a reference to a named cache, you need to use the `Tangosol.Net.CacheFactory` class and invoke the `GetCache` method on it:

```
INamedCache cache = CacheFactory.GetCache("countries");
```

Once you have a cache instance, you will probably want to put some objects into it and try to read them back. Similar to how `NamedCache` interface extends `java.util.Map`, the `INamedCache` interface extends the standard .NET `System.Collections.IDictionary` interface.

That means that you can use standard members defined by the `IDictionary` interface, such as `Count`, `Add`, `Remove`, and `Clear`, as well as the indexer, to manipulate data in the cache:

```
cache.Add("SRB", "Serbia");
cache.Add("USA", "United States");

cache["USA"] = "United States of America";

cache.Remove("SRB");

Console.WriteLine("USA = " + cache["USA"]);
Console.WriteLine("Cache size = " + cache.Count);

cache.Clear();
```

Following the `IDictionary` contract, the `Add` method will throw an exception if you attempt to add an object with a key that already exists in the cache, so in order to replace an existing entry you need to use an indexer.

Alternatively, you can use one of the methods defined in the `Tangosol.Net.ICache` interface, which extends `IDictionary`:

```
public interface ICache : IDictionary
{
  object Insert(object key, object value);
  object Insert(object key, object value, long millis);
  void InsertAll(IDictionary dictionary);

  IDictionary GetAll(ICollection keys);
}
```

The first three methods behave the same way `put` and `putAll` do in Java—they allow you to both insert new entries and overwrite the existing ones. You also have an option of specifying an expiration time for an entry in milliseconds, or batching multiple entries into a dictionary instance and inserting them into a cache in a single call, which can provide significant performance boost.

Similarly, the `GetAll` method allows you to retrieve multiple entries by key in a single network call, thus significantly improving read performance.

Now that we know how to put objects into the cache and get them back, it is time to implement some Coherence-friendly data objects.

Implementing data objects

In order for the most of the Coherence features to work, your .NET data objects will have to use POF as a serialization format and will probably need to have a parallel Java implementation that is available within the cluster.

While you can technically use .NET binary, or even XML serialization for your data objects, this is strongly discouraged in all but the simplest cases and is a feature that should only be used in early prototyping, if ever, in my opinion.

The problem with non-portable serialization format is that there is no way for a Coherence cluster node to deserialize them, which eliminates most of the cluster-side functionality: you loose the ability to execute queries, aggregators and entry processors, and pretty much turn an extremely powerful piece of software into a distributed hashtable. You will be able to do gets and puts, but unfortunately, that is pretty much all you'll be able to do.

The situation with parallel implementations of Java and .NET classes is somewhat trickier. Up until Coherence 3.5, Java classes were absolutely required if you wanted to do any cluster-side processing, including queries, aggregations, entry processors, and so on.

However, as of Coherence 3.5 this is not strictly necessary, as you can use PofExtractor when creating indexes and executing queries or aggregations. Because PofExtractor works directly with binary data and does not need to deserialize your objects within the cluster, you can get by without the Java classes. You can even use PofUpdater to update binary data within the cluster directly.

That said, if you have the necessary expertise and don't mind a bit of extra work, my opinion is that implementing parallel class hierarchies is still the best approach, for several reasons.

For one, if you want to implement data affinity or to persist cached objects using the read/write-through approach, you will need to have Java classes, as those features depend on them.

It is also much easier to work with strongly typed Java classes within your entry processors and aggregators than with binary data, even though the latter is entirely possible using PofValue, a low-level feature of Coherence 3.5 that both PofExtractor and PofUpdater are based on, but which is also available for direct consumption within your own code.

Finally, having Java classes within the cluster makes debugging much easier, and that is likely where a lot of the activity on a typical project will be spent. Investing some time up-front to create the necessary classes will pay for itself many times over during the course of the project.

With that out of the way, let's see how we can make .NET classes portable and be able to use Coherence to the fullest extent possible.

Implementing the IPortableObject interface

Just as in Java, there are two possible approaches to making your objects portable. The first one is to implement the Tangosol.IO.POF.IPortableObject interface directly within your class:

```
public class Customer : IPortableObject
{
    // ---- data members ------------------------------------

    private long     id;
    private String   name;
    private DateTime dateOfBirth;


    // ---- constructors ------------------------------------
```

```
public Customer()
{
  // deserialization constructor
}

public Customer(long id, String name, DateTime dateOfBirth)
{
  ...
}

// ---- properties omitted for brevity ----------------

// ---- IPortableObject implementation -------------------

public virtual void ReadExternal(IPofReader reader)
{
  id          = reader.ReadInt64(0);
  name        = reader.ReadString(1);
  dateOfBirth = reader.ReadDateTime(2);
}

public virtual void WriteExternal(IPofWriter writer)
{
  writer.WriteInt64(  0, id);
  writer.WriteString(  1, name);
  writer.WriteDateTime(2, dateOfBirth);
}

  // ---- Equals, GetHashCode and ToString (omitted) -------
}
```

As you can see, implementing IPortableObject directly is very straightforward, so let's move on to the second approach.

Implementing the external serializer

The second approach is to create a separate class that implements a Tangosol. IO.Pof.IPofSerializer interface and associate it with your data class within the POF context. To complete the EnumPofSerializer example from *Chapter 4, Implementing Domain Objects*, here is the implementation of its .NET counterpart:

```
public class EnumPofSerializer : IPofSerializer
{
  public void Serialize(IPofWriter writer, object o)
```

```
  {
    if (o == null || !o.GetType().IsEnum)
    {
      throw new ArgumentException(
        "EnumPofSerializer can only be used to serialize enum types.");
    }

    writer.WriteString(0, o.ToString());
    writer.WriteRemainder(null);
  }

  public object Deserialize(IPofReader reader)
  {
    IPofContext pofContext = reader.PofContext;
    Type enumType = pofContext.GetType(reader.UserTypeId);
    if (!enumType.IsEnum)
    {
      throw new ArgumentException(
        "EnumPofSerializer can only be used to deserialize enum
                                                     types.");
    }

    object enumValue = Enum.Parse(enumType, reader.ReadString(0));
    reader.ReadRemainder();

    return enumValue;
  }
}
```

Again, the previous code snippet should be very easy to follow and feel familiar if you remember everything you read about POF in *Chapter 4*.

With serialization out of the way and portable objects in the cache, let's see how we can run the queries from a .NET client.

Executing queries

Executing queries from a Coherence for .NET client is very similar to executing queries from a Java application: you simply create a filter and execute it using one of the methods defined by the `Tangosol.Net.Cache.IQueryCache` interface:

```
public interface IQueryCache : ICache
{
  object[] GetKeys(IFilter filter);
```

```
object[] GetValues(IFilter filter);
object[] GetValues(IFilter filter, IComparer comparer);

ICacheEntry[] GetEntries(IFilter filter);
ICacheEntry[] GetEntries(IFilter filter, IComparer comparer);

void AddIndex(IValueExtractor extractor, bool isOrdered,
              IComparer comparer);
void RemoveIndex(IValueExtractor extractor);
}
```

As you can see, in addition to methods that allow you to retrieve keys and entries based on a filter, the Coherence for .NET library also provides two overloads of the `GetValues` method, which are not present in the Java API at the moment.

Methods that accept an `IComparer` instance as a second argument will sort the results before returning them, either using a specified comparer instance, or in their natural ordering, if null is specified as the second argument and the values within the result implement the `IComparable` interface. The sorting is performed on the client, so asking for the sorted results will not put any additional load on the cache server nodes.

The only exception to the previously mentioned scenario is the `LimitFilter`, which will have to perform the sorting within the cluster in order to determine the first page of the results to return. This is a quite expensive operation in a distributed environment, so you should avoid it if possible, or look for an alternative solution to the problem. Using Coherence Tools `TopAggregator` is one possible approach you should consider if cluster-side sorting is required.

Implementing filters and value extractors

Just as in Java, you need to use value extractors when defining your filters. All of the filters and value extractors described in *Chapter 5, Querying the Data Grid*, are present in Coherence for .NET as well, so you can use them just as easily as you would in Java.

However, there are a few important things you need to understand, especially if you will be writing your own `IFilter` or `IValueExtractor` implementations.

For one, filters and value extractors can execute either within the cluster or on the client, depending on the type of the cache they are used with. If you issue a query against a remote cache, the filter and any value extractors that are part of its state will be serialized and transmitted to the proxy server for execution. The proxy server will then deserialize the filter into the appropriate Java implementation and execute it against the cache servers.

On the other hand, filters that execute against a local or a continuous query cache (unless the CQC is used to cache only keys but not the values) will be evaluated directly on the client, as the scope of the query is well defined and all the objects are already present on the client. This can significantly improve performance and reduce the load on the cache servers.

However, in order for this to work, both the filters and value extractors must have parallel implementations in Java and .NET. The standard filters are all implemented this way, but if you implement your own you will have to ensure that the .NET and Java implementations match and that both are properly registered within the corresponding POF configuration files, using the same type identifier.

In the remainder of this section, we will implement in C# the `PropertyExtractor` and the `StartsWithFilter` we have already implemented in Java in *Chapter 5*. This should provide you with enough guidance to make the implementation of your own filters and extractors a breeze.

Implementing PropertyExtractor in C#

As I mentioned in *Chapter 5*, the main reason I dislike a built-in `ReflectionExtractor` is that it requires you to specify the full name of the accessor method. While this is bearable in Java, it feels really unnatural when working in C#, where properties are a first-class language construct. It also leaks to the very surface the fact that the class the extractor will ultimately be executed against is written in Java, which is not a good thing.

However, what's even worse is that the approach is different depending on whether the extraction needs to be performed locally or within the cluster. For example, when extracting values from the objects in a continuous query cache, you need to specify the .NET property name:

```
IValueExtractor ext = new ReflectionExtractor("Address");
```

However, when using the same extractor within the cluster you will have to specify the name of the Java accessor method:

```
IValueExtractor ext = new ReflectionExtractor("getAddress");
```

Having to write different code based on the type of cache it will be executed against is never a good thing, as it can lead to nasty bugs if you change cache configuration during development. I personally wish that we had spotted and corrected this problem before releasing Coherence for .NET, but better late than never.

Now that we have `PropertyExtractor` on the Java side, all we need to do is to implement its .NET equivalent, which will make this issue go away:

```
public class PropertyExtractor
        : AbstractExtractor, IValueExtractor, IPortableObject
{
  // ---- data members -----------------------------------

  private const BindingFlags BINDING_FLAGS =
                               BindingFlags.Public
                             | BindingFlags.Instance
                             | BindingFlags.IgnoreCase;

  private String m_propertyName;

  [NonSerialized]
  private PropertyInfo m_property;

  // ---- constructors -----------------------------------

  public PropertyExtractor()
  {}

  public PropertyExtractor(String propertyName)
        : this(propertyName, VALUE)
  {}

  public PropertyExtractor(String propertyName, int target)
  {
    if (String.IsNullOrEmpty(propertyName))
    {
      throw new ArgumentNullException(
                 "propertyName", "Property name cannot be null");
    }

    m_propertyName = propertyName;
    m_target       = target;
  }


  // ---- IValueExtractor implementation ------------------

  public override Object Extract(Object target)
  {
```

```
  if (target == null)
  {
    return null;
  }

  Type targetType = target.GetType();
  try
  {
    PropertyInfo property = m_property;
    if (property == null || property.DeclaringType != targetType)
    {
      m_property = property =
      targetType.GetProperty(m_propertyName, BINDING_FLAGS);
    }
    return property.GetValue(target, null);
  }
  catch (Exception)
  {
    throw new Exception("Property " + m_propertyName +
                   " does not exist in the class " + targetType);
  }
}


// ---- IPortableObject implementation -------------------

public void ReadExternal(IPofReader reader)
{
  m_propertyName = reader.ReadString(0);
  m_target       = reader.ReadInt32( 1);
}

public void WriteExternal(IPofWriter writer)
{
  writer.WriteString(0, m_propertyName);
  writer.WriteInt32( 1, m_target);
}

// ---- Equals, GetHashCode and ToString omitted -------
}
```

There are few things worth discussing regarding the previous code snippet. As of Coherence 3.5, value extractors can define the target they should execute against by setting the protected `m_target` field defined in the `AbstractExtractor` class to either the `KEY` or `VALUE` constant, also defined in that class. However, it is important to understand that for backwards compatibility reasons subclasses of the `AbstractExtractor` are responsible for both initialization and serialization of the `m_target` field, which is why we initialize it in the constructor and serialize it as if it was a direct member of the `PropertyExtractor` class.

The name of the field is somewhat unfortunate, as it is very similar to the name of the argument that is passed to the `Extract` method, even though the two have nothing in common—the first one is used to determine if the extractor should be executed against the key or the value of a cache entry, and the second one is the actual target object that the extraction should be performed against.

With the `PropertyExtractor` in place, we can now perform the extraction the same way in both Java and .NET, and regardless of the type of the cache that our code executes against.

Executing the aggregators and entry processors

The Coherence for .NET client library fully supports entry processor execution and cluster-wide aggregations via the `Tangosol.Net.Cache.IInvocableCache` interface, which is pretty much equivalent to the `InvocableMap` Java interface we discussed in *Chapters 5* and *6*:

```
public interface IInvocableCache : ICache
{
  Object Invoke(Object key, IEntryProcessor agent);

  IDictionary InvokeAll(ICollection keys, IEntryProcessor agent);
  IDictionary InvokeAll(IFilter filter, IEntryProcessor agent);

  Object Aggregate(ICollection keys, IEntryAggregator agent);
  Object Aggregate(IFilter filter, IEntryAggregator agent);
}
```

As you can see, the `IInvocableCache` interface defines methods that allow you to invoke `IEntryProcessor` on a single entry or on a collection of entries by specifying either the keys or the filter that will determine a set of target entries for a processor.

There are also two methods that allow you to perform aggregation on a subset of cache entries, using either one of the built-in implementations of IEntryAggregator or a custom one you created.

Aggregators and entry processors can be executed both locally on the client and remotely within the cluster. However, the first scenario is somewhat unlikely—you will typically use them only for remote execution, especially considering the fact that entry processors are by far the best way to implement mutating operations over Extend.

Because of this, even though you still need to have both Java and .NET class for each aggregator and entry processor, it is usually not necessary to implement complete logic on the client. Instead, all you need to do is to capture necessary state on the client and ensure that it is serialized in the format the cluster-side Java aggregator or entry processor expects. Of course, if you do want to be able to execute them locally, you will need to implement the logic within your .NET classes as well.

For example, our sample .NET application uses entry processors to withdraw money from or deposit money into an account. They both extend from the abstract base AccountProcessor class, which implements the IEntryProcessor interface and common serialization code.

This is what the AccountProcessor class looks like:

```
public abstract class AccountProcessor
      : AbstractProcessor, IPortableObject
{
  protected AccountProcessor()
  {
  }

  protected AccountProcessor(Money amount, string description)
  {
    m_amount      = amount;
    m_description = description;
  }

  public override object Process(IInvocableCacheEntry entry)
  {
    throw new NotSupportedException()
  }

  public void ReadExternal(IPofReader reader)
  {
    m_amount      = (Money) reader.ReadObject(0);
```

```
    m_description = reader.ReadString(1);
  }

  public void WriteExternal(IPofWriter writer)
  {
    writer.WriteObject(0, m_amount);
    writer.WriteString(1, m_description);
  }

  protected Money  m_amount;
  protected string m_description;
}
```

As you can see, this class implements the `IEntryProcessor.Process` method by simply throwing `NotSupportedException`. In this case that is perfectly fine—we don't expect this processor to ever be executed on the .NET client. We just need it to capture state (amount and transaction description) that should be transmitted to the server, where it will be deserialized as a fully implemented Java processor and executed.

This makes .NET implementation of the `Deposit/WithdrawProcessor` trivial:

```
public class DepositProcessor : AccountProcessor
{
  public DepositProcessor()
  {}

  public DepositProcessor(Money amount, string description)
                          : base(amount, description)
  {}
}
```

The `WithdrawProcessor` looks pretty much the same, so I will omit it. The only reason we even need these two classes is to let the server know which Java class to instantiate during deserialization, as in this case processor type implies the operation we want to perform.

Listening for cache events

.NET really shines when it comes to desktop application development, so it is completely normal that the Coherence for .NET client is most often used to access a Coherence cluster from Windows Forms or WPF-based desktop applications.

One of the most powerful and interesting Coherence features from a desktop developer's perspective is the ability to register for and receive events as the data in the cluster changes, which can then be used to update the application UI in real time.

In this section we will look at standalone cache listeners and the continuous query cache, as well as the approaches to incorporate them into .NET desktop applications. We will also discuss some of the obstacles related to event handling in desktop applications, and the mechanisms built into Coherence for .NET to overcome them.

Cache listeners

Event handling is one of the areas that are significantly different in Java and .NET. While Java applications typically use classic Observer pattern and define listener interfaces, whose implementations can then be registered with the observed object, .NET promotes events to first-class language constructs and provides the ability to handle events by simply registering delegates with each individual event.

Both approaches have pros and cons. In Java, you are forced to implement all the methods defined by the listener interface even when you only care about one of them, which is why most listener interfaces also have matching abstract base classes that implement event handling methods as no-ops.

On the other hand, in situations when events are closely related and you are expected to handle all of them, the listener class nicely encapsulates all the logic related to event handling.

The situation in .NET is quite the opposite: it is easy to register for a single event, but if you care about multiple events you need to register for each one separately. In the latter case .NET code tends to be scattered across multiple delegate methods, which makes maintenance a bit more difficult.

Fortunately, the Coherence for .NET library supports both approaches. You can register to receive events "the Java way" using the `Tangosol.Net.Cache.IObservableCache` interface:

```
public interface IObservableCache : ICache
{
  void AddCacheListener(ICacheListener listener);
  void RemoveCacheListener(ICacheListener listener);

  void AddCacheListener(ICacheListener listener,
                        Object key, bool isLite);
  void RemoveCacheListener(ICacheListener listener,
                        Object key);

  void AddCacheListener(ICacheListener listener,
```

```
                              IFilter filter, bool isLite);
    void RemoveCacheListener(ICacheListener listener,
                              IFilter filter);
  }
```

As you can see, all variants of Add/RemoveCacheListener methods accept
an instance of the Tangosol.NetCache.ICacheListener interface, which is
identical to the MapListener Java interface we discussed in *Chapter 7, Processing
Data Grid Events*:

```
  public interface ICacheListener
  {
    void EntryInserted(CacheEventArgs evt);
    void EntryUpdated(CacheEventArgs evt);
    void EntryDeleted(CacheEventArgs evt);
  }
```

The usage mechanics of cache listeners are exactly the same as we discussed in
Chapter 7, so we will not repeat the details here. The bottom line is that, just as in
Java, you can register to receive the events for a particular object, a set of objects
defined by the filter, or a cache as a whole.

However, the Coherence for .NET library also provides several helper classes
that allow you to handle the events "the .NET way". The general-purpose one
is Tangosol.Net.Cache.Support.DelegatingCacheListener, which
defines the CacheEventHandler delegate and EntryInserted, EntryUpdated,
and EntryDeleted events:

```
  public delegate void CacheEventHandler(object sender,
                                         CacheEventArgs args);

  public class DelegatingCacheListener : ICacheListener
  {
    public virtual event CacheEventHandler EntryInserted;
    public virtual event CacheEventHandler EntryUpdated;
    public virtual event CacheEventHandler EntryDeleted;
    ...
  }
```

The delegate handling the event will receive two arguments: a reference to a cache
that an event occurred in as a sender argument, and the details about the event as
an args argument. The latter contains all the information related to the event, such
as entry key, as well as the old and new values for non-lite events.

This allows you to easily register for cache events without having to implement the listener interface yourself:

```
IObservableCache cache = CacheFactory.GetCache("accounts");

DelegatingCacheListener listener = new DelegatingCacheListener();
listener.EntryUpdated += AccountUpdated;
cache.AddCacheListener(listener);

private static void AccountUpdated(object sender,
                                   CacheEventArgs args)
{
  // handle event...
}
```

Event marshalling in Windows Forms applications

In addition to the DelegatingCacheListener, Coherence for .NET contains another, more specific ICacheListener implementation that allows you to achieve the same goal and a bit more.

One of the problems with cache events within Windows Forms applications is that all the events received by a client are raised on a background thread, which means that they need to be marshalled to the UI thread if you need to do anything UI-related within the event handlers.

Because one of the main reasons for receiving events in a desktop application is to update the user interface in real time, Coherence provides an ICacheListener implementation that marshals the events for you, in the form of the Tangosol.Net.Cache.Support.WindowsFormsCacheListener class.

All you need to do is to pass the form that the event listener is associated with to its constructor, and the WindowsFormsCacheListener will handle the rest. The code to register for events within the code-behind class for a form will typically look similar to the following:

```
WindowsFormsCacheListener listener =
        new WindowsFormsCacheListener(this);
listener.EntryUpdated += this.AccountUpdated;
cache.AddCacheListener(listener);


private void AccountUpdated(object sender, CacheEventArgs args)
{
  // refresh account details on the UI
}
```

It is worth noting that event marshalling from a background to the UI thread is also required in **Windows Presentation Foundation (WPF)** applications, but it needs to be done in a slightly different way.

Unfortunately, as of Coherence 3.5 there is no built-in listener implementation that does that (primarily because it would create dependency on .NET 3.5), and it is out of the scope of this book to discuss how to create one. However, you can find a `WpfCacheListener` implementation in the sample application, in case you need it.

Continuous Query Cache

As we have seen in *Chapter 7*, a continuous query cache is very useful in all types of applications, as it allows you to bring a subset or even all of the data from a partitioned cache into a client process, while guaranteeing that locally cached data is never stale—as the data within the cluster changes, it is automatically updated within each instance of a continuous query cache as well.

However, a continuous query cache is particularly interesting when used within desktop applications, as it enables easy creation of highly dynamic user interfaces that are automatically updated as the data on a backend changes. Typical examples where this might be useful are trading desktops and logistic applications, but many other applications could benefit from a more dynamic user experience as well.

The reason this kind of functionality is easy to implement with a CQC is that in addition to keeping itself in sync with a back cache, CQC is also observable—as the data within it changes based on events received from a cluster, CQC raises its own events that client applications can listen to and update UI components appropriately.

We have discussed in *Chapter 7* how instances of a continuous query cache are created and the various arguments you can specify to control its behavior. I will not repeat that here, as the mechanics are exactly the same—you simply create an instance of the `Tangosol.Net.Cache.ContinuousQueryCache` class, passing the target cache and a filter to use to its constructor.

Instead, in the remainder of this section we will focus on how you can bind CQC, or any other observable cache, to a Windows Forms `DataGridView` control. It is not as straightforward as I'd like, but fortunately it is not too difficult either.

Data binding with Windows Presentation Foundation (WPF)

We need to show real-time account and transaction information to bank employees using the **BranchTerminal** application, a .NET component of our multi-platform sample application.

We know that we can use CQC to create a live view of the data we are interested in on the client. However, we can't bind UI controls to the CQC directly. While we could bind controls to the Values property of a CQC, this property returns a static, point-in-time snapshot of the CQC contents.

WPF data binding supports dynamic update of UI controls only if the data source they are bound to implements appropriate notification interfaces and raises the change events these interfaces define. Individual objects need to implement the INotifyPropertyChanged interface and raise the PropertyChange event whenever one of their properties changes. Similarly, collections need to implement the INotifyCollectionChanged interface and raise the CollectionChanged event whenever an element is added, updated, or removed from a collection.

CQC does not (and it shouldn't) implement either of these interfaces, so you cannot bind controls to it directly. However, .NET provides the ObservableCollection class, which implements both of these interfaces and is a great source for data binding. So the only thing we need to do is to create an adapter that will expose CQC contents as an ObservableCollection.

In the case of CQC giving us a live view of the accounts cache, we can create the Accounts class that does exactly what we need:

```
public class Accounts :
    ObservableCollection<Account>, IDisposable
{
  private readonly ContinuousQueryCache m_view;

  public Accounts(DispatcherObject control)
  {
    WpfCacheListener listener =  new WpfCacheListener(control);
    listener.EntryDeleted  += OnDelete;
    listener.EntryInserted += OnAdd;
    listener.EntryUpdated   += OnUpdate;

    INamedCache accounts = CacheFactory.GetCache("accounts");
    m_view = new ContinuousQueryCache(accounts,
                          AlwaysFilter.Instance, listener);
  }

  public void OnAdd(object sender, CacheEventArgs evt)
  {
    Add((Account) evt.NewValue);
  }
```

```
public void OnUpdate(object sender, CacheEventArgs evt)
{
  int index = IndexOf((Account) evt.OldValue);
  SetItem(index, (Account) evt.NewValue);
}

public void OnDelete(object sender, CacheEventArgs evt)
{
  Remove((Account) evt.OldValue);
}

public void Dispose()
{
  m_view.Release();
}
}
```

As you can see, our `Accounts` class extends `ObservableCollection` and uses CQC events internally to keep its contents in sync with the CQC it wraps.

There are two important things to notice:

1. We pass the listener that is responsible for keeping a contents of our adapter class in sync with CQC as a third argument to a CQC constructor. This allows us to capture all CQC events, including the ones resulting from initial CQC population.

2. The listener we use is an instance of `WpfCacheListener`. This ensures that all event handlers are invoked on the UI thread, which is necessary because the change event from the underlying `ObservableCollection` will be raised *and handled* on the same thread.

Now that we have an observable `Accounts` collection, we need to bind a `ListView` control on our application's main screen to it.

The first step is to expose it as a property within the window class that contains our `ListView` control. In the case of our sample application, this is `AccountsWindow` class:

```
public partial class AccountsWindow
{
  private readonly Accounts m_accounts;
  private readonly Transactions m_transactions;

  public AccountsWindow()
  {
    try
```

```
        {
          m_accounts      = new Accounts(this);
          m_transactions = new Transactions(this);

          InitializeComponent();
        }
        catch (Exception ex)
        {
        ...
        }
      }

      public Accounts Accounts
      {
        get { return m_accounts; }
      }

      ...

    }
```

As you can see, we are passing the window itself as an argument to the `Accounts` constructor, in order to provide a dispatcher object that `WpfCacheListener` should marshal events to.

The next step is to define the necessary data bindings within the XAML file for the `AccountsWindow`:

```
<Window
  x:Class="Seovic.Samples.Bank.UI.AccountsWindow"
  xmlns="http://schemas.microsoft.com/winfx/2006/xaml/presentation"
  xmlns:x="http://schemas.microsoft.com/winfx/2006/xaml"
  xmlns:cm="clr-namespace:System.ComponentModel;assembly=WindowsBase"
  DataContext="{Binding RelativeSource={RelativeSource Self}}"
  Title="Accounts" Height="600" Width="800" WindowState="Maximized"
  Unloaded="Window_Unloaded">
  <Window.Resources>

    <CollectionViewSource x:Key="AccountsViewSource"
                          Source="{Binding Accounts}">
      <CollectionViewSource.GroupDescriptions>
        <PropertyGroupDescription PropertyName="Customer.Name"/>
      </CollectionViewSource.GroupDescriptions>
      <CollectionViewSource.SortDescriptions>
```

```
              <cm:SortDescription PropertyName="Customer.Name"
                                  Direction="Ascending" />
              <cm:SortDescription PropertyName="Description"
                                  Direction="Ascending" />
       </CollectionViewSource.SortDescriptions>
     </CollectionViewSource>

  </Window.Resources>

  . . .

  <ListView
    ItemsSource="{Binding Source={StaticResource AccountsViewSource}}"
    SelectionChanged="AccountList_SelectionChanged"
    Grid.Row="1" Grid.Column="0"  Name="AccountList"
    Background="White">

    . . .

  </Window>
```

First we specify `DataContext` for the `AccountsWindow` to be the window itself. This allows us to access the `Accounts` property we exposed in the previous step.

That is exactly what we do in the following step by creating a `CollectionViewSource` that defines grouping and sort order for our data, and binding it to the `Accounts` property.

Finally, we specify `CollectionViewSource` as the item source for our `ListView`, which ensures that the items within the view are grouped and sorted properly, and automatically refreshed as the underlying `Accounts` collection changes.

When everything is said and done, the end result looks similar to the following screenshot:

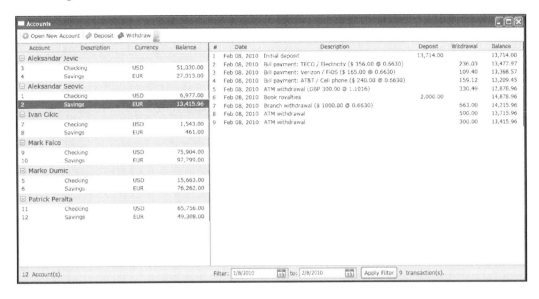

You should ignore the fact that the random number generator wasn't very generous to Ivan and myself, and focus on the functionality.

When you click on the account on the left, the list of transactions on the right is updated based on the selected account and transaction period. Whether you post transactions from the .NET client, Java web application, or C++ command-line client, both the account balance and the list of transactions will be updated in real time.

Unfortunately, it is impossible to show that in print, but don't take my word for it—download the sample application and see for yourself.

Summary

In this chapter we looked at the Coherence for .NET library and how you can use it to allow .NET applications to leverage everything Coherence has to offer. We discussed the configuration of .NET clients and have shown .NET API usage examples for pretty much all the topics we discussed in *Chapters 2* through *7*.

In the next chapter we will go over the same material one more time, but this time from a C++ developer's perspective. I am pleased to say that you are in for a treat, as the chapter that follows was written by Mark Falco, the Oracle engineer who led the implementation of the Coherence C++ client library. Enjoy!

11
Accessing Coherence from C++

Coherence C++ is the latest addition to the Coherence product family. Shipped as a pure native library, Coherence C++ is made available for a select but growing number of platforms. As of Coherence 3.5, support is available for recent versions of Windows, Linux, Solaris, and Apple OS X—in both 32 and 64 bit variants.

Because Coherence C++ is a Coherence*Extend client, the available feature set is virtually identical to what is offered with the Coherence Java and .NET Extend clients. This includes the basic get/put cache access, as well as advanced features such as near cache, continuous query cache, events, entry processors, aggregators, and queries.

The C++ client used the Coherence Java client as a guide in terms of class and method names and signatures. The result is that it is quite easy to transfer your newly acquired Coherence Java knowledge to C++.

Configuring Coherence C++

Coherence C++ supports the same configuration mechanisms, which you've seen being used in the Java and .NET editions. The C++ variants are modeled as a subset of the Java edition, and are DTD-based XML files. Because of this, it is unnecessary to reiterate most of the configuration options; you can reuse the cache and operational configuration files that had been built up for Java Extend clients.

There are exceptions worth noting. For instance, the system property configuration override feature of the Java client is available to C++ clients in a somewhat different form—in that environment variables are used. In some Unix shells, '.' delimited environment variables may not be supported. For this reason, you may also specify the property names in camel case, so `tangosol.coherence.override` and `TangosolCoherenceOverride` are considered to be equivalent. Another notable configuration difference in comparison with Java is that for advanced configurations where custom classes are supplied via configuration, you would make use of C++ naming conventions rather the Java ones, that is, '::' rather than '.' class name delimiters.

POF configuration is where C++ differs from Java and .NET. Currently, C++ POF configuration is programmatic rather then declarative. This means that you will need to include your POF type ID to class registration within your code. This is accomplished via a simple one-line addition to your data object's `.cpp` file. POF configuration will be covered in detail later when we demonstrate how to serialize your data objects.

If included in the application's startup directory, the cache and optional operational configuration files will be automatically loaded without any additional effort. The default filenames are inherited from the Java client, namely `coherence-cache-config.xml` and `tangosol-coherence-override.xml`. If an alternative location or filename is used, you will need to tell Coherence C++ where to look for these files. This can be done programmatically by calling the `CacheFactory::configure` method, which takes up to two `XmlElement` configuration descriptors as input. The first argument is the cache configuration and the optional second argument is the operational configuration. By taking in `XmlElements` rather than file descriptors or names, it allows the application to determine how the configuration content is obtained. As the most likely means of doing so is from a file, convenience helpers are also included so that you can easily load the XML configuration from a file as follows:

```
CacheFactory::configure(
    CacheFactory::loadXmlFile("c:/config/MyCacheConfig.xml"));
```

Alternatively, you can use environment variables to override the default name and location if you wish to avoid specifying them programmatically. The names are again inherited from Java. The `tangosol.coherence.cacheconfig` property specifies the path to the cache configuration, and `tangosol.coherence.override` specifies the path for the operational configuration.

Managed object model

The Coherence C++ API is built on top of a managed object model, which takes on the responsibility for object lifecycle management. This means you will not make explicit calls to `new` or `delete` when dealing with managed objects. A managed object is an instance of any class that derives from `coherence::lang::Object`. This base class is responsible for maintaining the object's reference count, allowing for automatic destruction once the object is no longer being referenced.

This model is useful for Coherence because caches both return and retain references to their cached objects. A cache may be a subset of a larger data set and may evict an item while the application could still be using a previously obtained reference to the same item. The result is that there is no clear owner for cached items, and thus no answer to the question of who should take responsibility for deleting these objects. The managed object model removes this issue by taking over the ownership, ensuring that objects are automatically deleted once they are no longer being referenced.

Application code interacts with these managed objects not via traditional C++ raw pointers, or references, but via smart pointers that transparently update the managed object's reference count, but are otherwise used much the same way as raw pointers. While many C++ smart pointer implementations will declare the smart pointer for a given class `Foo` via templates (that is `smart_ptr<Foo>` and `smart_ptr<const Foo>`), the Coherence managed object model uses nested typedefs to declare the smart pointers for a class (that is `Foo::Handle` and `Foo::View`).

Handles, Views, and Holders

For each managed class, there are three smart pointer typedefs: `Handle`, `View`, and `Holder`.

For a given managed class `Foo`:

- `Foo::Handle` is the functional equivalent of `Foo*`
- `Foo::View` is the functional equivalent of const `Foo*`
- `Foo::Holder` is the functional equivalent of a union of a `Foo*` and const `Foo*`

A `Holder` acts just like a `View`, but allows for a safe cast attempt to a `Handle`. Unlike the standard C++ `const_cast<>` the Coherence `cast<>` is safe and only succeeds if the `Holder` had been assigned from `Handle`. A `Holder` is typically used with containers such as `coherence::util::Collection`, which allows the caller to choose to store either a `Handle` or `View` within the collection.

The assignment rules for the smart pointers follow the same rules as regular pointers:

- A `View` may be assigned from a `Handle`, `View`, or `Holder`.
- A `Holder` may be assigned from a `Handle`, `View`, or `Holder`, and will remember the smart pointer type it has been assigned from.
- A `Handle` may be assigned from a `Handle`, or from a `Holder` via `cast<>`.
- A smart pointer for a parent class may be assigned from the smart pointer of a derived class.
- A smart pointer may only be assigned from a non-derived class via `cast<>`.

Managed object creation

To properly maintain the reference count, it is important that the objects are only referenced via smart pointers, and never via raw pointers. As such, creation is not performed via the traditional `new` operator, but instead by a static `create` factory method (for example, `Foo::create()`). This factory method returns the initial `Handle`, ensuring that raw pointers are avoided from the point of object creation.

The factory methods are auto-generated via inherited template definitions, and take parameter sets matching the class's constructors. The constructors are declared as protected, to ensure that these objects are not allocated by other means.

Casting and type checking

As previously mentioned, the object model also includes a helper function for performing dynamic casts. Its functionality is roughly equivalent to the standard C++ `dynamic_cast`, although it is specialized to work with managed classes and their smart pointers. For example, given an `Object::View`, we can attempt to cast it to a `String::View` as follows:

```
Object::View v  = ...
String::View vs = cast<String::View>(v);
```

If the `View` referenced something other than a `String`, then a `ClassCastException` would be thrown from the `cast<>` function call. There is also a related `instanceof<>` helper function, which will identify if a cast will succeed.

```
Object::View v = ...
if (instanceof<String::View>(v))
    {
    // v references a String
    }
```

These functions work similarly for a `Handle`, `View`, or a `Holder`. In the case of a `Holder`, they are also the mechanism for extracting a stored `Handle`. The following cast will succeed if the `Holder` was assigned from `String::Handle`:

```
Object::Holder oh = ...
String::Handle hs = cast<String::Handle>(oh);
```

Handling exceptions

Error conditions in Coherence C++ are communicated by throwing exceptions. The managed object model defines a hierarchy of managed exceptions, rooted at `coherence::lang::Exception`. A special `COH_THROW` macro is used to throw and re-throw managed exceptions. This macro will, if possible, record a full stack trace into the exception to aid error diagnosis.

The exceptions are caught via their nested (or inherited) `View` type:

```
try
    {
    ...
    COH_THROW (IOException::create("test"));
    ...
    }
catch (IOException::View vexIO)
    {
    // handle IOException
    }
catch (Exception::View vex)
    {
    // print exceptions description and stack trace
    std::cerr << vex << std::endl;
    COH_THROW (vex); // re-throw
    }
```

Managed exceptions may also be caught as `std::exceptions`, allowing pre-existing error handling logic to handle them as well. For instance, a thrown `IOException` could also be caught as follows:

```
try
    {
    ...
    COH_THROW (IOException::create("test"));
    ...
    }
catch (const std::ios_base::failure& exIO)
    {
```

```
        // handle IOException or other
        }
    catch (const std::exception& ex)
        {
        // handle any Exception or std::exception
        std::cerr << ex.what() << std::endl;
        throw;
        }
```

Class hierarchy namespaces

The Coherence classes are organized into a set of namespaces based on their functionality. Their header files are organized similarly. For example, `coherence::lang::Object` is defined in `coherence/lang/Object.hpp`.

For convenience, there is a special header file for each namespace, which includes all headers for that namespace. This mechanism along with a `using namespace` statement is often used to bring the entire `coherence::lang` namespace into your application code, while explicit class headers and `using` statements are preferred for classes outside of the `coherence::lang` namespace:

```
#include "coherence/lang.ns"
#include "coherence/net/CacheFactory.hpp"
#include "coherence/net/NamedCache.hpp"

using namespace coherence::lang;
using coherence::net::CacheFactory;
using coherence::net::NamedCache;
```

For the sake of simplicity, the examples in the remainder of the chapter do not show the `include` or `using` statements.

This basic introduction of the managed object model is enough to get us started with Coherence C++ coding. The object model, internally known as *Sanka*, also contains a large number of generic utility classes, which reside mostly in the `coherence::lang` and `coherence::util` namespaces. You'll find that these classes and the model itself have a noticeable Java inspiration to them. The Coherence C++ cache classes are also inspired by their Java counterparts. The result is that those familiar with Coherence Java should find Coherence C++ quite easy to learn.

There are many more details to the managed object model, but those details are beyond scope of this book. The Coherence C++ product documentation contains an in-depth guide to the object model, and it is recommended that you familiarize yourself with the object model in greater depth as you begin the work of building your Coherence C++ based solutions.

Implementing a Coherence C++ client application

In this section, we will finally write some C++ cache-related code. Let's start by obtaining a `NamedCache` from the `CacheFactory`:

```
NamedCache::Handle hCache = CacheFactory::getCache("accounts");
```

We can then proceed to operate on the cache in much the same way as we did in Java:

```
String::View vsKeySRB = "SRB";
String::View vsKeyUSA = "USA";

hCache->put(vsKeySRB, String::create("Serbia"));
hCache->put(vsKeyUSA, String::create("United States"));

hCache->put(vsKeyUSA, String::create("United States of America"));

hCache->remove(vsKeySRB);

std::cout << vsKeyUSA << " = " << hCache->get(vsKeyUSA) << std::endl;
std::cout << "Cache size = " << hCache->size() << std::endl;

hCache->clear();
```

The C++ `NamedCache` interface contains the full method set from the Java `NamedCache`, allowing access to other standard operations such as `putAll` and `getAll`.

You'll notice that, unlike Java, there is no automatic conversion support from quoted string literals to Coherence managed objects, except for methods whose signature states that they take a `String`, such as `CacheFactory::getCache(String::View)`. Thus to create and pass a `String` to a method such as `NamedCache::put(Object::View, Object:Holder)`, we must explicitly call `String::create()` to produce our managed `String`. `String` objects can also be assigned from and to `std::string` and `std::wstring`.

Implementing Cacheable C++ Data Objects

The previous example demonstrated how to use the basic cache APIs to store strings using C++. Of course, we want to work with more interesting types than just strings. Let's define a simple C++ class that will represent a pre-existing custom data object used in your application, which you'd like to cache.

```cpp
class Account
    {
    // ----- data members -------------------------------------------

    private:
        const long long m_lId;
        std::string      m_sDescription;
        Money            m_balance;
        long long        m_lLastTransactionId;
        const long long m_lCustomerId;

    // ----- constructors -------------------------------------------

    public:
        Account(long long lId, const std::string& sDesc,
            const Money& balance, long long lLastTransId,
            long long lCustomerId)
            : m_lId(lId), m_sDescription(sDesc), m_balance(balance),
              m_lLastTransactionId(lLastTransId),
              m_lCustomerId(lCustomerId)
            {
            }

        Account()
            : m_lId(0), m_lLastTransactionId(0), m_lCustomerId(0)
            {
            }

    // ----- accessors ----------------------------------------------

    public:
        long long getId() const
            {
            return m_lId;
            }

        std::string getDescription() const
            {
```

```
        return m_sDescription;
        }

    void setDescription(const std::string& sDesc)
        {
        m_sDescription = sDesc;
        }

    Money getBalance() const
        {
        return m_balance;
        }

    long long getLastTransactionId() const
        {
        return m_lLastTransactionId;
        }

    long long getCustomerId() const
        {
        return m_lCustomerId;
        }
    };
```

Can we just pass an instance of this into the `NamedCache::put()` method? Unfortunately, it is not quite that simple.

Remember that the caching API deals with managed objects as there is no clear owner for a piece of cached data. Our plain old `Account` class is definitely not managed. Aside from it being a managed class, there are a few other basic requirements for cached data as well:

- It should implement `Object::hashCode/equals` (for keys)
- It should implement `Object::clone` (for values)
- It should be POF serializable

In many cases, it may not be desirable to retrofit your data objects to be managed, as this could impose some far-reaching application-level changes. For this reason, the Coherence API includes a `Managed<>` template adapter, which will adapt pre-existing classes so they may be stored in Coherence.

Managed adapter

In order to be compatible with the `Managed` template, the data object class must have:

- A public or protected zero parameter constructor
- A copy constructor
- An equality comparison operator
- A `std::ostream` output function
- A hash function

The `Managed` adapter will implement the initial set of requirements, delegating where applicable to the previously described functions. Our `Account` class already meets the first two requirements. So all that is needed to make it `Managed`-compatible is to define three functions as follows:

```
bool operator==(const Account& accountA, const Account& accountB)
    {
    return accountA.getId()              == accountB.getId()              &&
           accountA.getDescription()     == accountB.getDescription()     &&
           accountA.getBalance()         == accountB.getBalance()         &&
           accountA.getLastTransactionId() ==
                                        accountB.getLastTransactionId()   &&
           accountA.getCustomerId()      == accountB.getCustomerId();
    }

std::ostream& operator<<(std::ostream& out, const Account& account)
    {
    out << "Account("
        << "Id="                << account.getId()
        << ", Description="     << account.getDescription()
        << ", Balance="         << account.getBalance()
        << ", LastTransactionId=" << account.getLastTransactionId()
        << ", CustomerId="      << account.getCustomerId()
        << ')';
    return out;
    }

size_t hash_value(const Account& account)
    {
    return (size_t) account.getId();
    }
```

As you can see, adding these functions is quite simple and does not require that the data object takes on any awareness of Coherence. Now it becomes possible to use `Managed<Account>` in our code:

```
// construct plain old Account object
Account account(32105, "checking", Money(7374, 10, "USD"), 55, 62409);

// construct managed key and value
Integer64::Handle         hlKey     = Integer64::create(32105);
Managed<Account>::Handle hAccount = Managed<Account>::create(account);

// cache hAccount
hCache->put(hlKey, hAccount);

// retrieve the cached value
Managed<Account>::View vResult = cast<Managed<Account>::View>(
    hCache->get(hlKey));

std::cout << "retrieved " << vResult << " from cache for key "
          << vResult->getId() << std::endl;

// convert the cached value back to a non-managed type
Account accountResult(*vResult);
```

This code demonstrates how a `Managed<Account>` instance is created from a non-managed `Account` data object.

The `create` method delegates to the copy constructor on the `Account` class—thus, the `Managed<Account>` instance is a copy of and retains no references to the `Account` instance it was constructed from. `Managed<Account>` is then inserted into the cache using its identifier as a key. Next, it is extracted from the cache. The `NamedCache::get()` operation returns an `Object::Holder`, which then must be dynamically cast back to the expected data object class. Finally, the `Managed<Account>` instance is used to construct a non-managed `Account`, which can be used by pre-existing application logic.

Note that it is certainly allowed for the application to use the `Managed<Account>` object directly, because all of `Account`'s public methods are still accessible as is demonstrated when we call the `getId` method.

Data object serialization

The requirement to address is serialization, which when using the Managed adapter is accomplished by implementing two additional free functions:

```
template<> void serialize<Account>(PofWriter::Handle hOut,
    const Account& account)
    {
    hOut->writeInt64(0, account.getId());
    hOut->writeString(1, account.getDescription());
    hOut->writeObject(2, Managed<Money>::create(
        account.getBalance()));
    hOut->writeInt64(3, account.getLastTransactionId());
    hOut->writeInt64(4, account.getCustomerId());
    }


template<> Account deserialize<Account>(PofReader::Handle hIn)
    {
    long long              lId        = hIn->readInt64(0);
    std::string            sDesc      = hIn->readString(1);
    Managed<Money>::View vBalance     = cast<Managed<Money>::View>(
        hIn->readObject(2));
    long long              lTransId   = hIn->readInt64(3);
    long long              lCustomerId = hIn->readInt64(4);

    return Account(lId, sDesc, *vBalance, lTransId, lCustomerId);
    }
```

Notice that Account includes a data member Money, which is an instance of another plain old C++ class. To serialize this nested object, we simply write it out as a Managed<Money> object, applying the same patterns as were used for Managed<Account>. The serialization functions obviously have Coherence awareness, and thus it may not be desirable to declare them inside the same source file as that of the Account class. The sole requirement is that they are defined within some .cpp file and ultimately linked into your application. Interestingly, they do not need to appear in any header file, which means that they could be put into something like a standalone AccountSerializer.cpp file, without the need to modify the Account.hpp/cpp that is used in application code.

We must also register our serializable Managed<Account> class with the Coherence C++ library. This is accomplished via a simple call to a macro.

```
COH_REGISTER_MANAGED_CLASS(POF_TYPE_ACCOUNT, Account);
```

The registration statement specifies the POF type ID to class mapping. Unlike the Java and .NET versions, in C++, this mapping is performed at compilation time. The registration statement relies on the declaration of the serialization functions, and is therefore typically part of the same source file. Note the registration macro does not need to be called as part of the application logic — it is triggered automatically as part of static initialization.

The only thing missing now is the definition of POF_TYPE_ACCOUNT, which could just be a #define statement to the numeric POF type ID for the Account class. While you may just choose to embed the ID number directly in the registration line, it is recommended that #define, or some other external constant be used instead. Defining an external constant allows for the creation of a PofConfig.hpp file for the application that includes all the POF type IDs. This results in a single place to perform the ID assignment, so you do not have to search through the various data-object serialization files to adjust any of the IDs. Here is an example of this PofConfig.hpp file:

```
#ifndef POF_CONFIG_HPP
#define POF_CONFIG_HPP

#define POF_TYPE_ACCOUNT              1000
#define POF_TYPE_MONEY                1003
#define POF_TYPE_TRANSACTION          1004
#define POF_TYPE_TRANSACTION_ID       1005
#define POF_TYPE_TRANSACTION_TYPE     1006
#define POF_TYPE_DEPOSIT_PROCESSOR    1051
#define POF_TYPE_WITHDRAW_PROCESSOR   1050
#define POF_TYPE_CURRENCY             2000

#endif // POF_CONFIG_HPP
```

This header file is analogous to the pof-config.xml file we would have used in Java or .NET. With these last pieces in place, our example will now work with both local and remote caches, automatically being serialized as needed.

Implementing managed classes

It is, of course, possible to directly implement a managed class as well, in which case we can also implement the PortableObject interface or, make use of PofSerializer. While it may be unlikely that you would choose to implement your cached data types directly as managed classes, it is the normal pattern for custom implementations of entry processors, map listeners, and other Coherence-related classes.

To demonstrate the process, let's rewrite our `Account` sample class as a managed class. In doing so, we will also choose to make use of the Coherence included types for its data members.

```cpp
class Account
    : public cloneable_spec<Account>
    {
    friend class factory<Account>;

    // ----- data members ---------------------------------------

    private:
        const int64_t       m_lId;
        MemberView<String>  m_sDescription;
        MemberHandle<Money> m_balance;
        int64_t             m_lLastTransactionId;
        const int64_t       m_lCustomerId;

    // ----- constructors ---------------------------------------

    protected:
        Account(int64_t lId, String::View sDesc, Money::View balance,
            int64_t lLastTransId, int64_t lCustomerId)
            : m_lId(lId), m_sDescription(self(), sDesc),
              m_balance(self(), balance),
              m_lLastTransactionId(lLastTransId),
              m_lCustomerId(lCustomerId)
            {
            }

        Account()
            : m_lId(0), m_sDescription(self(), sDesc),
              m_balance(self(), balance), m_lLastTransactionId(0),
              m_lCustomerId(0)
            {
            }

        Account(const Account& that)
            : m_lId(lId), m_sDescription(self(), sDesc),
              m_balance(self(), cast<Money::View>(balance->clone())),
              m_lLastTransactionId(lLastTransId),
              m_lCustomerId(lCustomerId)
            {
            }
```

```
// ----- accessors ----------------------------------------------

public:
    virtual int64_t getId() const
        {
        return m_lId;
        }

    virtual String::View getDescription() const
        {
        return m_sDescription;
        }

    virtual void setDescription(String::View sDesc)
        {
        m_sDescription = sDesc;
        }

    virtual Money::View getBalance() const
        {
        return m_balance;
        }

    virtual int64_t getLastTransactionId() const
        {
        return m_lLastTransactionId;
        }

    virtual int64_t getCustomerId() const
        {
        return m_lCustomerId;
        }

// ----- Object methods --------------------------------------

virtual bool equals(Object::View vThat) const
    {
    if (!instanceof<Account::View>(vThat))
        {
        return false;
        }
    Account::View that = cast<Account::View>(vThat);
```

```
    return this == that || (
        getId()                == that->getId()               &&
        getLastTransactionId() == that->getLastTransactionId() &&
        getCustomerId()        == that->getCustomerId()         &&
        getDescription()->equals(that->getDescription())        &&
        getBalance()->equals(that->getBalance));
    }

//optional ostream output function
virtual void toStream(std::ostream& out) const
    {
    out << "Account("
        << "Id="                << getId()
        << ", Description="     << getDescription()
        << ", Balance="         << getBalance()
        << ", LastTransactionId=" << getLastTransactionId()
        << ", CustomerId="      << getCustomerId()
        << ')';
    }

virtual size32_t hashCode() const
    {
    return (size32_t) getId();
    }
};
```

Overall, the code isn't much different from the original. Let's go through the differences one by one.

Understanding specifications

Perhaps, the strangest looking bit is the inheritance statement:

```
public cloneable_spec<Account>
```

This is part of the object model, and is called a "spec"-based class definition, where spec is short for specification. Specs do a fair amount of boiler-plate code injection to make the authoring of new managed classes easier than it would otherwise be. For instance, the following items (and more) are injected:

- Implied virtual inheritance from Object, making it managed
- Defined Account::Handle/View/Holder nested smart pointer typedefs
- Defined Account::super typedef to parent class

- Added static `create` methods to match `Account`'s constructors, returning `Account::Handle`
- Added `clone()` method implementation that delegates to `Account`'s copy constructor

There is an entire family of specs. In the previous example, we used `cloneable_spec` because the item is going to be stored within a cache and needs to be cloneable. The other types of specs are:

- `class_spec` — the most basic of specs, which just defines a managed class
- `cloneable_spec` — a `class_spec` that supports cloning
- `abstract_spec` — defines a non-instantiable class with a partial implementation
- `interface_spec` — defines a non-instantiable class with all pure virtual methods
- `throwable_spec` — defines a spec-based exception class

All specs will automatically add inheritance from Object. Each will also add in some specific features of its own. Specs take the following template parameters:

```
spec<class, extends<parent>, implements<interface, ...> >
```

The arguments for the spec are:

- *class*: Required, specifies the name of the class being defined
- `extends`<*parent*>: Optional, specifies a class to derive from, defaults to `extends <Object>`, not included for `interface_spec`
- `implements`<*interface1, interface2, ...*>: Optional, the list of interfaces that this class implements, defaults to `implements<>`

Factory methods

The next related part is:

```
friend class factory<Account>;
```

This friend declaration allows the auto-generated `create` methods to access the protected constructors. It is the only bit of boiler-plate that specs cannot inject themselves.

Member variables

Next, we can look at the data member declarations:

```
private:
    const int64_t        m_lId;
    MemberView<String>   m_sDescription;
    MemberHandle<Money>  m_balance;
    int64_t              m_lLastTransactionId;
    const int64_t        m_lCustomerId;
```

First we switch our `long long` data members to use `int64_t`. On most modern C++ compilers, `long long` is a 64-bit integer type, but it is not required to be of a specific size. The `int64_t` is a fixed-sized type, which is guaranteed to be 64 bits wide. It is part of a family of fixed-size types that exist on many systems—for those on which it does not, Coherence adds the definitions. By convention, managed types use fixed-size primitives, though this is not a requirement.

Next, we switch from `std::string` to a Coherence managed `String`, referenced by a `View`. The `Money` class is similarly overhauled, allowing us to reference it via `Handle`. You are not required to change these types—it is done here to improve serialization efficiency by avoiding the need to perform type conversion during serialization later on.

You'll also notice that, for `String` and `Money`, we used `MemberView<String>` and `MemberHandle<Money>` rather than nested `String::View`, and `Money::Handle`. This is done because the nested `Handle/View/Holder` smart pointer types are not thread-safe. As objects stored in a cache could be accessed by multiple threads, it is important that they internally be thread-safe. `MemberHandle/View/Holder` are thread-safe variants and should be used as data member references.

This doesn't mean you should avoid using the nested smart pointer types. In fact, they are what you will use most often. They are used as local variables and function/method parameters, basically anything that is stack allocated. Note that using the nested types for data members would have compiled and appeared to function just fine, but there would have been a memory leak/corruption looming. It is, therefore, highly recommended that you use the thread-safe variants for data members of all managed classes.

There are two additional thread-safe smart pointer variants included with Coherence C++:

- `FinalHandle/View/Holder`—an immutable smart-pointer data member
- `WeakHandle/View/Holder`—a weak reference-style smart pointer3

The `Final` variants are similar in functionality to `const MemberHandle/View/`
`Holder`, but include object model performance benefits based on the awareness that
it is immutable. The `Weak` variants are used in conditions where your object graph
includes cycles. As the object model makes use of reference counting, a cyclical
graph would result in a memory leak. These "weak" smart pointers avoid the leak
by automatically being `NULL`'ed out once they are the sole reference to an object, thus
allowing the object to be collected. The use of these variants is otherwise identical to
the `Member` variants.

Implementing constructors

Moving right along, we get to the constructors:

```
protected:
    Account(int64_t lId, String::View sDesc, Money::View balance,
            int64_t lLastTransId, int64_t lCustomerId)
        : m_lId(lId), m_sDescription(self(), sDesc),
          m_balance(self(), balance),
          m_lLastTransactionId(lLastTransId),
          m_lCustomerId(lCustomerId)
        {
        }

    Account()
        : m_lId(0), m_sDescription(self(), sDesc),
          m_balance(self(), balance), m_lLastTransactionId(0),
          m_lCustomerId(0)
        {
        }

    Account(const Account& that)
        : m_lId(lId), m_sDescription(self(), sDesc),
          m_balance(self(), cast<Money::View>(balance->clone())),
          m_lLastTransactionId(lLastTransId),
          m_lCustomerId(lCustomerId)
        {
        }
```

First we notice that the constructors are now declared as protected, which blocks
both stack-based as well as operator `new`-based allocations, leaving the static `create`
method as the only allocation mechanism.

Next we see that `MemberView` and `MemberHandle` are initialized with `self()`. The thread-safe smart pointers take an optional second parameter, which is the object they are to reference, and if left out, defaults to `NULL`. The `self()` used in initialization is an easy pattern to follow, though perhaps a bit difficult to understand.

Each managed object contains an embedded micro read/write lock, which is used to provide the thread-safety to its smart pointer data members. The smart pointers thus require a reference to their enclosing object, and this is exactly what `self()` returns. Specifically, the `self()` method returns a reference to the base class of the managed object being created. It is conceptually similar to the `this` pointer, except that it references the fully initialized base class, while `this` refers to the partially initialized derived type.

Note that the thread-safe smart pointers can be used outside of managed classes as well. In this case, you will need to provide them a surrogate object that will protect them, as there is no `self`. This surrogate can either be an object you allocate yourself, or you can use one from a pool obtained by calling `System::common()`.

Implementing methods

The next change is that the methods are now all declared as virtual. This is certainly not required, but in general, managed classes are designed to operate like Java where all methods are virtual.

Finally, we override some standard methods declared by `Object`. These allow for hashing, equality testing, and printing of the object.

Implementing the PortableObject interface

This was a bit of a detour, but finally, we can get back to making our class implement `PortableObject`. To do this, we'll simply modify the inheritance statement to indicate that this class implements `PortableObject`, and then implement its methods and register the type:

```
class Account
    : public cloneable_spec<Account,
        extends<Object>,
        implements<PortableObject> >
    {
    ...
    // ----- PortableObject methods ------------------------------

    public:
        virtual void writeExternal(PofWriter::Handle hWriter) const
            {
```

```
            hWriter->writeInt64(0, getId());
            hWriter->writeString(1, getDescription());
            hWriter->writeObject(2, getBalance());
            hWriter->writeInt64(3, getLastTransactionId());
            hWriter->writeInt64(4, getCustomerId());
            }

        virtual void readExternal(PofReader::Handle hReader)
            {
            m_lId = hReader->readInt64(0, getId());
            setDescription(hReader->readString(1));
            setBalance(cast<Money::Handle>(hReader->readObject(2)));
            setLastTransactionId(hReader->readInt64(3));
            m_lCustomerId = hReader->readInt64(4);
            }
    };
COH_REGISTER_PORTABLE_CLASS(
    POF_TYPE_ACCOUNT, Account); // must be in .cpp
```

So after a lot of explanation, the act of making the class POF serializable is quite trivial. You will notice that in `readExternal`, we need to set two `const` data members, which is not allowable. This issue exists because `PortableObject` deserialization occurs after the object has already been instantiated. To achieve `const`-correctness, we would unfortunately need to either remove the `const` modifier from the declaration of these data members, or cast it away within `readExternal`.

Implementing external serializer

The final serialization option available to us is to write an external serializer for our managed data object. Here we'll create one for the non-`PortableObject` version of the managed `Account` class. Note that the serializer-based solution does not exhibit the `const` data member issues we encountered with `PortableObject`.

```
class AccountSerializer
    : public class_spec<AccountSerializer,
        extends<Object>,
        implements<PofSerializer> >
    {
    friend class factory<AccountSerializer>;
    public:
     virtual void serialize(PofWriter::Handle hWriter, Object::View v)
            const
            {
```

```
        Account::View vAccount = cast<Account::View>(v);

        hWriter->writeInt64(0, vAccount->getId());
        hWriter->writeString(1, vAccount->getDescription());
        hWriter->writeObject(2, vAccount->getBalance());
        hWriter->writeInt64(3, vAccount->getLastTransactionId());
        hWriter->writeInt64(4, vAccount->getCustomerId());

        hWriter->writeRemainder(NULL); // mark end of object
        }

    virtual Object::Holder deserialize(PofReader::Handle hReader)
        const
        {
        int64_t      lId         = hReader->readInt64(0);
        String::View sDesc       = hReader->readString(1);
        Money::Handle hBalance   = cast<Money::Handle>(
            hReader->readObject(2));
        int64_t      lTransId    = hReader->readInt64(3);
        int64_t      lCustomerId = hReader->readInt64(4);

        hReader->readRemainder(); // read to end of object

        return Account::create(lId, sDesc, hBalance, lTransId,
            lCustomerId);
        }
    };
COH_REGISTER_POF_SERIALIZER(POF_TYPE_ACCOUNT,
    TypedClass<Account>::create(),
    AccountSerializer::create()); // must be in .cpp
```

All in all, this is pretty much the same as we'd done in Java, the prime difference being the COH_REGISTER statement that registers AccountSerializer and Account class with the Coherence library. The usage of the new managed Account class is somewhat more direct than with Managed<Account>:

```
// construct managed key and value
Account::Handle  hAccount = Account::create(32105, "checking",
    Money::create(7374, 10, "USD"), 55, 62409);
Integer64::Handle hlKey   = Integer64::create(32105);
```

```
// cache hAccount
hCache->put(hlKey, hAccount);

// retrieve the cached value
Account::View vResult = cast<Account::View>(hCache->get(hlKey));

std::cout << "retrieved " << vResult << " from cache for key "
        << vResult->getId() << std::endl;
```

In later sections, we'll make use of specs to write other types of custom classes such as filters and aggregators.

Executing queries

Coherence C++ offers a `QueryMap` interface that closely resembles its Java counterpart:

```
class QueryMap
    : public interface_spec<QueryMap,
        implements<Map> >
    {
    public:
        virtual Set::View keySet(Filter::View vFilter) const;
        virtual Set::View entrySet(Filter::View vFilter) const;
        virtual Set::View entrySet(Filter::View vFilter,
            Comparator::View vComparator) const;

        virtual void addIndex(ValueExtractor::View vExtractor,
            bool fOrdered, Comparator::View vComparator);
        virtual void removeIndex(ValueExtractor::View vExtractor);
    };
```

Executing a query is a simple matter of constructing the filter to identify the record matching criteria, and then supplying it to either the `keySet` or `entrySet` methods. The `Comparator` variants can be used to order the result set if necessary.

Unless operating on a local cache, the supplied filters, extractors, and comparators are only used as serializable stubs, as all processing will be done remotely in Java on the cache servers.

Value extractors

Central to QueryMap is the concept of the ValueExtractor, which is used to extract an embedded value from a cached entry. For instance, you can use a value extractor to extract the balance from our Account data object.

These extractors are used both in expressing the filter criteria and in applying indexes to the cache in order to optimize query performance. Included with Coherence C++ is a ReflectionExtractor implementation, which is suitable for queries against remote caches, so long as the cache server contains a Java version of the data object:

```
hCache->addIndex(ReflectionExtractor::create("getBalance"), false,
    NULL);
```

Extracting values from locally cached objects

As the C++ language does not have reflection support, it should come as no surprise that the ReflectionExtractor throws an UnsupportedOperationExpection if it is used against a C++ local cache. If you intended to perform queries against local caches, it would appear that you would be left with writing your own custom C++ extractors for each of your data objects to obtain embedded values. While this is not terribly difficult, it is also thankfully unnecessary. Coherence C++ includes a TypedExtractor that utilizes a combination of macros, templates, and function pointers to do a fairly decent job of emulating the Java ReflectionExtractor.

```
ValueExtractor::View vExtractor =
    COH_TYPED_EXTRACTOR(Money::View, Account, getBalance);
```

The macro parameters are the type of the extracted value, the class type to perform the extraction on, and finally, the const accessor method used to obtain the value. In the case of accessor methods that return non-managed types, there is a BoxExtractor variant, which will wrap the primitive type back into its corresponding managed type, which is required to implement the ValueExtractor interface.

```
ValueExtractor::View vExtractor =
    COH_BOX_EXTRACTOR(Integer64::View, Account, getId);
```

Note that if you are working with the Managed<> template helper, you need to use a special COH_BOX_MANAGED_EXTRACTOR version instead.

To make things even nicer, these extractors actually extend ReflectionExtractor, and thus can be used against both local and remote caches, so long as the cache server has the corresponding Java version of the class and uses the same method names.

PofExtractor

The final type of built-in extractor included with Coherence C++ is the
`PofExtractor`. As described earlier, `PofExtractor` allows for efficient extraction
on the server side without the need for full de-serialization, or the corresponding
Java classes.

```
ValueExtractor::View vExtractor = PofExtractor::create(typeid(Money),
    Account::BALANCE);
```

When using `PofExtractor`, it is best practice to create static identifiers for the
property indexes. The previous example assumes that we've defined one for the
`BALANCE` field.

In Coherence 3.5, C++ `PofExtractor` can only be applied to remote caches.
This is for two reasons—for one, local caches hold onto data in the object rather
the serialized form, and secondly (largely because of the first reason), the C++
`PofExtractor` is currently implemented as a stub, because its primary use is
to be evaluated on cache servers within the cluster.

Implementing PropertyExtractor in C++

In Java and .NET, we've introduced `PropertyExtractor`, and you might find it
useful to have the same in C++. This can be accomplished easily enough with a
new macro helper around `TypedExtractor`.

```
#define COH_PROPERTY_EXTRACTOR(TYPE, CLASS, PROPERTY) \
  coherence::util::extractor::TypedExtractor< \
      TYPE, CLASS, &CLASS::get##PROPERTY> \
          ::create(COH_TO_STRING("get" << #PROPERTY));
```

This allows usage like the following:

```
ValueExtractor::View vExtractor =
    COH_PROPERTY_EXTRACTOR(Money::View, Account, Balance);
```

We will need an additional version if we wish to handle `Managed<>` data objects,
such as our original `Managed<Account>`:

```
#define COH_MANAGED_PROPERTY_EXTRACTOR(TYPE, CLASS, PROPERTY) \
    coherence::util::extractor::BoxExtractor< \
        TYPE, CLASS, &CLASS::get##PROPERTY, \
            coherence::lang::Managed<CLASS>::Holder> \
                ::create(COH_TO_STRING("get" << #PROPERTY));
```

The usage remains quite similar:

```
ValueExtractor::View vExtractor =
    COH_MANAGED_PROPERTY_EXTRACTOR(Money::View, Account, Balance);
```

Ok, these aren't quite the same as our other `PropertyExtractor` implementations, but they are close enough to be just as useful. The key differences are that property names are capitalized, it assumes a `get` accessor, and that on the Java side it will deserialize and execute as plain old `ReflectionExtractor` rather than a `PropertyExtractor`.

It is certainly possible to create a full fledged C++ `PropertyExtractor` implementation; it would closely follow the pattern laid out in `TypedExtractor` whose source is entirely within the `TypedExtractor.hpp` header.

Filters

Coherence C++ ships with the same built-in filter set as that provided for Java. These filters are capable of executing against both local and remote caches. When chaining together the built-in filters is not sufficient to express your query, you are free to also write custom filters. Unless the filters will only be targeted at a local cache, you will also need to produce a Java version, as that is what will actually do the filtering when running against a remote cache.

While the logic within Java and C++ implementations doesn't have to be identical, it is important that the implementations are compatible, which implies:

- For a given set of inputs, both implementations should produce the same result

- The serialized form of both implementations should be equivalent

Performing a query in C++

Now we can put all these things together and finally perform a query from within C++:

```
// add an index for the description property on the Account class
ValueExtractor::View vExtractor =
    COH_PROPERTY_EXTRACTOR(String::View, Account, Description);
hCache->addIndex(vExtractor, false, NULL);

// query for all "checking" Accounts
Set::View vSetResult =
    hCache->entrySet(LikeFilter::create(vExtractor, "checking%"));

// iterate the result set printing each matching entry
for (Iterator::Handle hIter = vSetResult->iterator();
    hIter->hasNext(); )
    {
```

```
Map::Entry::View vEntry = cast<Map::Entry::View>(hIter->next());
Account::View  vAccount = cast<Account::View>(vEntry->getValue());
std::cout << vAccount << std::endl;
}
```

As you can see, performing the query and iterating the results is quite trivial. All the real work is in defining extractors and filters. Knowing how to implement custom extractors and filters is important, but keep in mind that you can get quite far with the built-in ones.

Executing aggregators and entry processors

Coherence C++ includes full support for aggregators and entry processors via a native `InvocableMap` interface, which closely resembles the Java version described in *Chapters 5* and *6*.

```
class InvocableMap
    : public interface_spec<InvocableMap,
        implements<Map> >
    {
    public:
        virtual Object::Holder invoke(Object::View vKey,
            EntryProcessor::Handle hAgent);
        virtual Map::View invokeAll(Collection::View vCollKeys,
            EntryProcessor::Handle hAgent);
        virtual Map::View invokeAll(Filter::View vFilter,
            EntryProcessor::Handle hAgent);


        virtual Object::Holder aggregate(Collection::View vCollKeys,
            EntryAggregator::Handle hAgent) const;
        virtual Object::Holder aggregate(Filter::View vFilter,
            EntryAggregator::Handle hAgent) const;
    };
```

As you can see, the interface allows for explicit key-and-filter based selection of the entries to be processed or aggregated. The operation to perform is expressed as either an `EntryProcessor` or `Aggregator`, for which there are a number of built-in implementations. You may also supply your own custom implementations.

The InvocableMap interface is supported by both local and remote caches. By far, the more common case is to use them on remote (clustered) caches. If your custom EntryProcessors and Aggregators will be used against remote caches, you will need to have the corresponding Java version in the classpath of your cache servers. Just as with .NET, if you only intend to use them remotely, your C++ implementations need to only contain state and serialization logic, and can skip the actual processing logic.

Implementing DepositProcessor in C++

The following is a entry processor which can be used to deposit funds into our remote Account cache:

```cpp
class DepositProcessor
    : public class_spec<DepositProcessor,
        extends<AbstractProcessor>,
        implements<PortableObject> >
    {
    friend class factory<DepositProcessor>;

    // ----- constructors ---------------------------------------

    protected:
        DepositProcessor()
            : m_vMoney(self()), m_vsDescription(self())
            {}

        DepositProcessor(Managed<Money>::View vMoney,
                        String::View vsDescription)
            : m_vMoney(self(), vMoney),
              m_vsDescription(self(), vsDescription)
            {}

    // ----- InvocableMap::EntryProcessor interface -----------------

    public:
        virtual Object::Holder process(
                InvocableMap::Entry::Handle hEntry) const
            {
            COH_THROW (UnsupportedOperationException::create());
            }

    // ----- PortableObject interface ------------------------------
```

```
public:
    virtual void readExternal(PofReader::Handle hIn)
        {
        initialize(m_vMoney, cast<Managed<Money>::View>(
            hIn->readObject(0)));
        initialize(m_vsDescription, hIn->readString(1));
        }

    virtual void writeExternal(PofWriter::Handle hOut) const
        {
        hOut->writeObject(0, m_vMoney);
        hOut->writeString(1, m_vsDescription);
        }

    // ----- data members ---------------------------------------

protected:
    FinalView<Managed<Money> > m_vMoney;
    FinalView<String>          m_vsDescription;
    };
COH_REGISTER_PORTABLE_CLASS(POF_TYPE_DEPOSIT_PROCESSOR,
    DepositProcessor);
```

As you can see, this stub implementation contains no processing logic. Its only purpose is to convey the operation type and state when serialized and transmitted to the Java cache servers, where the deserialized Java version will handle the processing work.

Aggregators will follow the same pattern of just being client-side state conveying stubs, and an example is omitted here due to their close similarity with the stub entry processor we've just presented.

Listening for cache events

Just as with Java, C++ clients may register event listeners to be notified when cache entries are inserted, updated, or deleted. These event feeds are extremely useful in building real-time non-polling applications based on cached state.

Cache listeners

Coherence C++ follows the Java-style observer pattern, and event registration is performed against methods declared as part of the ObservableMap interface.

```
class ObservableMap
    : public interface_spec<ObservableMap,
        implements<Map> >
    {
    public:
        virtual void addKeyListener(MapListener::Handle hListener,
                Object::View vKey, bool fLite);
        virtual void removeKeyListener(MapListener::Handle hListener,
                Object::View vKey);

        virtual void addFilterListener(MapListener::Handle hListener,
                Filter::View vFilter = NULL, bool fLite = false);
        virtual void removeFilterListener(
                MapListener::Handle hListener,
                Filter::View vFilter = NULL);
    };
```

As you can see, the feature set is the same as that available in the Java version of ObservableMap, including key-and-filter based registrations, and the ability to request lite events. Lite events are free to omit the old and new values in order to avoid the additional resources required to carry them over the network.

When matching events occur, you are notified by a callback on the supplied custom MapListener implementation. The MapListener interface is again similar to the Java version, and the usage is the same as described in *Chapter 7, Processing Data Grid Events*.

```
class MapListener
    : public interface_spec<MapListener,
        implements<EventListener> >
    {
    public:
        virtual void entryInserted(MapEvent::View vEvent);
        virtual void entryUpdated(MapEvent::View vEvent);
        virtual void entryDeleted(MapEvent::View vEvent);
    };
```

```
class VerboseMapListener
    : public class_spec<VerboseMapListener,
        extends<Object>,
        implements<MapListener> >
    {
    friend class factory<VerboseMapListener>;

    public:
        virtual void entryInserted(MapEvent::View vEvent)
            {
            std::cout << "inserted " << vEvent->getKey() << ", "
                    << vEvent->getNewValue() << std::endl;
            }

        virtual void entryUpdated(MapEvent::View vEvent)
            {
            std::cout << "updated " << vEvent->getKey() << " from "
                    << vEvent->getOldValue() << " to "
                    << vEvent->getNewValue() << std::endl;
            }

        virtual void entryDeleted(MapEvent::View vEvent)
            {
            std::cout << "deleted " << vEvent->getKey() << std::endl;
            }
    };
```

Event listener registration is performed just as in Java:

```
hCache->addFilterListener(VerboseMapListener::create());
```

Event notifications occur locally on a dedicated event-dispatching thread associated with the cache. It is thus important to consider pushing any long running listener logic onto application threads so that subsequent events are not blocked or delayed.

Standard type integration

The final Coherence C++ feature we will look at is integration with standard C++ data types. We've already seen that the Coherence-managed String can interoperate with char* and std::string, but there are a number of other type integrations worth considering.

Managed type	Non-managed type
Boolean	bool
Octet	uint8_t, unsigned char
Character16	char16_t, wchar_t
Integer16	int16_t, short
Integer32	int32_t, int
Integer64	int64_t, long long
Float32	float32_t, float
Float64	float64_t, double
String	char*, wchar_t*, std::string, std::wstring
Array<T>	T[], for primitive type T
ObjectArray	Object::Holder[]
RawDateTime	struct tm
Exception	std::exception

For each of these type integrations, the managed type will support some form of assignment from and to the standard type. In most cases, the managed type will be constructable from the standard type, and can be de-referenced and assigned to the standard type:

```
Integer32::View vInt = Integer32::create(5);
int32_t         nInt = *vInt; // assigns 5 to nInt
```

Another integration point is with std::map, or more specifically, the STL pair associative container concept. It is probably quite clear by this point that the Coherence caches do not operate based on std::map, but rather based on coherence::util::Map interface, which mimics java.util.Map. For those who prefer the feel of std::map, or those replacing an existing std::map-based local cache, Coherence includes an adapter to make any Coherence map or cache implementation usable through a std::map-style API.

The adapter class `boxing_map` is an implementation of the `std::map` (pair associative container) concept, which delegates to any `coherence::util::Map` implementation. This includes doing the work of converting the keys and values back to their non-managed C++ types, making for an even stronger traditional C++ feel.

As an example, let's create a `boxing_map` around our `Account` cache, and re-write our original cache access code:

```
boxing_map<Integer64, Managed<Account> >
    cache(CacheFactory::getCache("accounts"));

// construct plain old Account object
Account account(32105, "checking", Money(7374, 10, "USD"), 55, 62409);

// cache account
cache[32105] = account;

// retrieve the cached value
Account accountResult = cache[32105];
```

As you can see, other than the declaration, all the other statements are just as they would be for `std::map`. The `boxing_map` includes all the standard operators and methods you'd expect from `std::map`. This allows for some interesting combinations. For instance, you can make use of STL algorithms to operate on the cache, for example, copying `std::map` into a cache:

```
std::map<int64_t, Account> mapBatch;

// fill up mapBatch with records
// ...

// use std::copy to transfer them to the cache
std::copy(mapBatch.begin(), mapBatch.end(),
    std::inserter(cache, cache.begin()));
```

While the ability to access caches as `std::maps` is useful, it is also limited. Most of the advanced features of Coherence caches are unavailable because the `std::map` API does not have corresponding concepts. Ultimately, the `boxing_map` is really intended for applications that would primarily access the cache in a get/put style, leaving more advanced cache usage to be accessible only through the Coherence cache interfaces.

Summary

This concludes our foray into the land of Coherence C++.

Start playing with the APIs, dig deep, and look for other features we've discussed for the Java version. In general, you'll find that they exist and are in the same basic form. There is a lot there to make use of, so have fun!

12
The Right Tool for the Job

Achieving performance, scalability, and high availability at the same time is very difficult. Coherence is by no means a silver bullet that will solve all these problems for you out of the box. However, it is a great tool that can be used to solve many of the problems involved and can make your job as an architect significantly less difficult.

However, whether you use Coherence or not, you should take away from this book a few general recommendations that will help you design and build scalable systems.

For one, try to avoid your application making a large number of network calls. This includes web requests, database calls, web service calls, calls to remote EJBs or COM+ components, access to shared network resources, and so on. Every network call introduces some latency, and if you are not careful these latencies quickly add up to create non-responsive, poorly performing applications.

One way to minimize the number of network calls is to use caching in every application layer. Coherence provides a great caching solution for your application objects, but is by no means the only cache you should use. You should take advantage of both the page and fragment caching provided by your chosen web server and delivery technology. You should set HTTP expiration headers properly to allow both proxy servers and web browsers to cache the content for as long as possible. If you are building a large public website, you should seriously consider using **Content Delivery Network (CDN)** to cache static content geographically closer to the end users. The sooner you can respond to the user's request, the better your application's performance will be, and the lower the overall load on your servers is going to be.

Even with Coherence, you should keep in mind that access to an object in a partitioned cache involves network calls, and should look for ways to eliminate them. Some of the Coherence features, such as near and continuous query caching, will go a long way to help you achieve that, so look for the opportunities to use them.

Second, try to minimize the amount of data that you need to move across the wire in order to perform some processing. Moving many megabytes of data to answer a few bytes question will take some time no matter how fast your network is, and will put significant load on all components of your applications, from application servers and network hardware, all the way to the database servers. Always ask yourself if a particular piece of functionality is moving more data across the wire than it really needs—you will be surprised how often the answer will be "yes".

To avoid that, look for ways to move the logic to where the data is instead of moving data to where the logic is. If you are using Coherence, use entry processors and parallel aggregators whenever you can. If you are not, look to leverage features of your database, such as stored procedures, that allow you to achieve the same thing.

When you do need to move data, try to do it in batches instead of object by object. Use write behind and batching features of your database when persisting cached objects. Use client-side batching and `putAll` when loading data into Coherence caches.

Last, but not least, make sure that you use the right tool for the job throughout the architecture.

Relational databases were designed to safeguard data on a persistent storage and to answer complex relational queries, not to be used as key-value stores or to be scalable. The same design decisions that were made to ensure ACID properties of relational databases also make them incredibly hard to scale out. While you *can* use sharding to scale relational databases out, you must be aware that it is a kludge we as an industry have come up with to work around their inherent limitations. You will likely loose most of the ACID properties in the process, and even such basic things as queries will become a nightmare. That doesn't qualify as the right tool for the job in my book (no pun intended).

Coherence, on the other hand, was designed from the very beginning to enable massive scale-out and high availability, and we also got improved performance for free as a nice side effect of the decision to store objects in memory. (As far as I know, absolute performance was never a design goal for Coherence—predictable, scalable performance was).

That doesn't mean that relational databases are going to go away, as Patrick pointed out in his chapter. They still have their role if you need persistence (some applications don't) or need to query your data using complex relational joins (many applications don't.) But it does mean that you should use an in-memory data grid in front of them if you need to scale out the data layer.

On a more subjective and personal note, look for technologies that can help you achieve your goals but are also fun to work with. I have had the pleasure of meeting and talking to many Coherence users, and one thing that is consistent, no matter what kind of system they built on top of Coherence, is that they absolutely loved using it. For me personally, working both with and on Coherence has been a great pleasure that I hope will continue for many more years.

A few years ago, Charles Connell wrote an essay *Most Software Stinks!* While I strongly recommend reading the whole essay, which is available at `http://www.chc-3.com/pub/beautifulsoftware.htm`, I would like to end the book by quoting a small excerpt from it:

> *Most software design is lousy. Most software is so bad, in fact, that if it were a bridge, no one in his or her right mind would walk across it. If it were a house, we would be afraid to enter. The only reason we (software engineers) get away with this scam is the general public cannot see inside of software systems. If software design were as visible as a bridge or house, we would be hiding our heads in shame.*

He then goes on to define "beautiful software" and its qualities:

> *Beautiful programs work better, cost less, match user needs, have fewer bugs, run faster, are easier to fix, and have a longer life span.*

> *Beautiful software is achieved by creating a "wonderful whole" which is more than the sum of its parts. Beautiful software is the right solution, both internally and externally, to the problem presented to its designers.*

Coherence is beautiful software. Have fun with it!

Coherent Bank Sample Application

As I mentioned in *Chapter 4, Implementing Domain Objects*, the sample application that accompanies the book is a banking application containing three components.

The central component is an online banking Java application built on top of Coherence. This is where pretty much all of the business logic for the whole solution resides, encapsulated within a set of rich domain objects. It uses Spring MVC (`http://www.springsource.org/`) to expose REST endpoints to an ExtJS (`http://www.extjs.com/`) frontend, and uses H2 database (`http://www.h2database.com/`) as a persistent data store behind Coherence.

These third-party components were chosen by me and the team of my colleagues who helped with the implementation of the sample application, either because we were already familiar with them and found them to be the most appropriate tools for the job, as was the case with Spring and ExtJS, or because they helped simplify the testing and deployment of the application, as was the case with H2. We have also embedded Jetty web server (`http://jetty.codehaus.org/jetty/`) into the application for the same reason.

The second component of the solution is a .NET application that uses WPF for the presentation layer and relies on data binding to **CQC (Continuous Query Cache)** to display account balance changes and a list of account transactions in real time.

The third and last component is a C++ command line application that emulates an ATM. It demonstrates implementation of a parallel domain model in C++, and how you can use entry processors from a C++ client to execute business logic within the cluster.

The remainder of this chapter is a step-by-step guide to get the whole solution up and running and start playing with it. Obviously, the fact that we have to deal with three different platforms introduces some complexity, but we have spent a significant amount of time creating and tuning build scripts that will do most of the heavy lifting for you.

I hope you find the sample applications as interesting to read as they were for us to write.

Huge thanks to the Coherent Bank development team

I'd like to use the opportunity to thank once more to my friends who helped with the development of the sample application. I think they have done a great job on a very tight schedule and I'm very proud of the end result:

Marko Dumić, my colleague from S4HC, implemented the ExtJS frontend for the web application.

Ivan Cikić, **Nenad Dobrilović**, and **Aleksandar Jević**, also from S4HC, all worked on the .NET client at some point. Ivan implemented the C++ client as well.

My guest authors, **Patrick Peralta** and **Marko Falco**, contributed as well—Patrick implemented the persistence layer for the Java application, and Mark helped with the C++ client implementation.

Once again—thank you guys for all the hard work and enthusiasm you have put into this despite my crazy requests to add yet another feature at 3 am ☺. You are the best!

Prerequisites

Before you can build, deploy, and run the various components of the Coherent Bank application, you will need to have several prerequisites in place.

First of all, we strongly suggest that you run all the components of the application on a single Windows XP machine, at least the very first time. There are several reasons for this, but the most important one is that Windows is the only OS where you will be able to run all three applications — while we have tested Java and C++ applications both on Windows and OS X, you will only be able to run .NET application on Windows.

Once you become more familiar with the application architecture and configuration, you can experiment by moving things around and running the Coherence cluster across multiple machines, the web application on OS X, the .NET application on Windows, and the C++ application on Linux, but in the beginning you should keep things simple.

The following sections document other software you will need and any specific configuration settings you need to make.

Sun Java JDK 1.6

If you don't already have it (and my guess is you do), you should download and install the latest release of Sun's JDK 1.6. Make sure that you have the full JDK installed, not just the JRE.

You will also need to set the JAVA_HOME environment variable to point to your JDK. For example, if you installed JDK into the default location, your JAVA_HOME should look similar to the following:

```
JAVA_HOME=C:\Program Files\Java\jdk1.6.0_18
```

Microsoft Visual Studio 2008

You will need Visual Studio 2008 to build the .NET and C++ sample applications. If you don't already have it, you can download express editions of Microsoft Visual C# and Microsoft Visual C++ from http://www.microsoft.com/express/Windows/, but please keep in mind that we have only tested the build process with the full version of Visual Studio 2008.

The .NET application requires .NET Framework 3.5, but if you have Visual Studio 2008 this should already be installed.

Oracle Coherence 3.5.3

The application should work with other Coherence versions as well, but it has been tested with 3.5.3 only, so it is strongly recommended that you use that release.

You will need to download and install several packages:

* Download the Coherence Java release and install it according to the instructions in *Chapter 2, Getting Started*. Set the COHERENCE_HOME environment variable to point to your installation directory containing the bin, lib, and other Coherence folders.

* Download and install Coherence for C++ 32-bit Windows release. You should install it by extracting the coherence-cpp directory from the downloaded archive into the COHERENCE_HOME directory. For example, if your COHERENCE_HOME is C:\coherence, your Coherence for C++ installation should be in C:\coherence\coherence-cpp.

- Download and install Coherence for .NET. Simply run the installer from the download archive and accept the installation defaults when prompted. Make sure that you use the default installation path, as that's the location used to find `Coherence.dll` when building the .NET sample application.

Ant 1.7+

You will need to have Ant installed and in your system path in order to build and deploy the application. If you don't already have it, you can download it from `http://ant.apache.org/`.

Make sure that you set the `ANT_HOME` environment variable to the Ant installation directory and that you add `ANT_HOME\bin` to your `PATH`.

NAnt 0.86

You will need NAnt to build the .NET sample application. NAnt can be downloaded from `http://nant.sourceforge.net/`.

Make sure that you add NAnt's `bin` directory to system `PATH` as well.

Installation

In order to install the sample application, simply download `CoherentBank.zip` from the book's website and unzip it somewhere on your disk.

You should have a `CoherentBank` directory with three subdirectories: `cpp`, `java`, and `net`.

Deploying the Java Application

In order to deploy the Java application, you need to perform several steps:

1. Open a command prompt and navigate to the `CoherentBank\java` directory.
2. Edit `build.properties` file to reflect your environment.
3. Start the H2 database:

   ```
   > ant start-db-server
   ```

   If everything goes well, the H2 console should open in the browser. You can log in by changing the JDBC URL to `jdbc:h2:tcp://localhost/db/coherent-bank-db`, setting the username to **sa**, and clicking the **Connect** button.

There will be no tables there at first, which will be corrected shortly.

4. Start the web application:

    ```
    > ant web-app
    ```

    This should run the SQL script to create necessary tables, build the application, start the embedded Jetty web server, and open up the web browser showing the login screen.

If the web server fails to start make sure that you don't have anything else running on port 8080 and retry (or alternatively, change the `jetty.port` property within the `build.xml` file).

If the browser does not open automatically, make sure that you have specified the correct browser location in the `build.properties` file, or open the browser manually and navigate to `http://localhost:8080/bank/login`.

5. Log in using one of the test users from the following table, or create an account for yourself by clicking on the **register here** link below the login form.

   The test accounts that are set up by default are:

Username	Password
sele	pass
aca	pass
marko	pass
ivan	pass
mark	pass
patrick	pass

6. Play with the application—post some transactions by paying bills, look at the transaction list, edit a user profile, and so on.

7. Start the Coherence Extend proxy server:

   ```
   > ant start-extend-proxy
   ```

   This will allow C++ and .NET clients to connect to the cluster.

Optional: Run independent cache servers

By default, the web application runs as a storage-enabled Coherence node to simplify deployment, even though that is not how you would run it in production.

If you want to simulate a more realistic environment, uncomment the `-Dtangosol.coherence.distributed.localstorage=false` JVM argument within `start-web-server` target in `build.xml`.

However, if you do this you will need to run one or more cache servers before Step 4. You can do that by changing the startup sequence to:

```
> ant start-db-server
> ant start-cache-server (one or more times)
> ant web-app
> ant start-extend-proxy
```

Deploying the C++ Application

In order to build the C++ ATM application, you will need to do the following:

1. Open Visual Studio 2008 Command Prompt and navigate to the
   `CoherentBank\cpp` directory. This will ensure that all environment
   variables necessary to run Microsoft C++ compiler are properly configured.

2. Build the **ATM** application:

   ```
   > build
   ```

   This should compile and link the application and copy the executable and
   necessary configuration files into the `dist` subdirectory.

3. Navigate to the `dist` subdirectory.

4. Run the application with no arguments:

   ```
   > atm
   ```

   This should print out usage instructions:

   ```
   Usage: atm <deposit|withdraw> <account number> <amount> <currency
   code>
   ```

5. Run the application one or more times against one of the accounts you have
   access to (you can see them in the web application when logged in). For
   example, if you want to withdraw $200 from the account with the ID 10
   run the following:

   ```
   > atm withdraw 10 200 USD
   ```

   You should see a response similar to the following:

   ```
   Transaction Details
   -----------------------------------
   Type:        WITHDRAWAL
   Description: ATM withdrawal ($ 200.00 @ 0.6630)
   Amount:      132.6 EUR
   Balance:     20745.4 EUR
   ```

6. Do several withdrawals and deposits against the same account and then
   view the account transactions in the web application.

 Note: The only currencies supported at the moment are USD,
EUR, GBP, CHF, AUD, CAD, and JPY.

Deploying the .NET Application

In order to build and run the .NET application, you need to do the following:

1. Open a command prompt and navigate to the `CoherentBank\net` directory.

2. Build and run the **BranchTerminal** sample application:

   ```
   > nant run-terminal
   ```

   This should build and start the .NET client and display a list of all the accounts, grouped by customer. You can click on an account to see a list of transactions on the right.

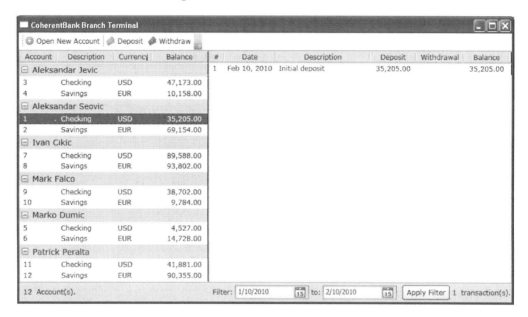

3. Post some transactions by paying bills from the web application and by making ATM withdrawals and deposits using the C++ application and watch how the account balance and transaction list are updated in real time.

Shutting everything down

Shutting down the .NET application is easy (simply close the application window), and the C++ application is even easier—it terminates automatically after each execution, so there is nothing you need to do.

However, shutting down all server-side components is a bit trickier, especially if you started multiple cache servers. At the very least you will need to shut down the web server, Extend proxy server, and database server.

What makes this even more complicated is that all these processes were started in the background using the Ant script, making them almost invisible. However, if you open Task Manager, you will see a number of `java.exe` processes running:

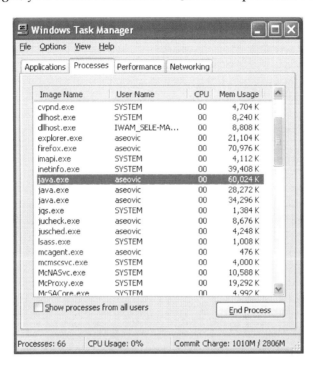

So, in order to shut down everything on the server, you can kill `java.exe` processes one by one in Task Manager.

However, there is an easier way, at least for all processes that are part of the Coherence cluster, which includes the web server, proxy server, and all cache servers you have started.

The Ant build file contains a `stop-cluster` target, which will send an invocable agent (see *Chapter 6, Parallel and In-Place Processing*, if you don't remember what that is) that executes `System.exit()` to all cluster members, effectively shutting them down gracefully.

```
> ant stop-cluster
```

However, before you run this task, **make sure that your sample application cluster is fully isolated from any other clusters you might have on your network**. Otherwise, there is a possibility that the `stop-cluster` task might decide to send the shutdown agent to your production cluster as well! If you are not sure, be safe and kill the processes from the Task Manager instead.

The last thing you need to do is to shut down the database server as well. You can try to do so by running this Ant task:

```
> ant stop-db-server
```

However, my experience so far has been that this task rarely succeeds, so you might need to kill the last remaining `java.exe` process using Task Manager (or if you have multiple `java.exe` processes running even after you have shut down the cluster, look for one that uses approximately 30 MB of memory).

Review the code

The main reason for the sample application's existence is not the functionality it provides (which is fairly limited), but the implementation code behind it that demonstrates some Coherence best practices. By reviewing the sample code while reading the book, you will gain a lot more than by simply reading the book alone.

You should also download the latest Coherence Tools release from `http://code.google.com/p/coherence-tools/`, as that's where most of the base and utility classes used in the sample application are.

Reviewing Coherence Tools code along with the sample application code that depends on it is highly recommended. It will give you the most "bang for the buck", as you'll be better able to leverage Coherence Tools classes and components on your next project.

Enjoy!

Index

Symbols

.NET application
  deploying 368
  shutting down 368-370
.NET client configuration
  about 291, 292
  approaches 298, 300
  Coherence configuration files 292
  resource loading, in Coherence 296
.NET client configuration, approaches
  convention-based configuration 298
  explicit configuration 298, 299
  programmatic configuration 300
<high-units> setting 251
<internal-cache-scheme> 243
 LimitFilter 178, 179

A

AbstractAggregator class 184
AbstractBatchingCacheStore 257, 258
AbstractCacheStore class 252
AbstractCoherenceRepository class 175
AbstractExtractor class 310
AbstractJdbcCacheStore class 245, 246
AbstractMapListener 224
AbstractPofSerializer 149
Account.withdraw method 199
AccountJdbcCacheStore class 253
AccountProcessor class 311
AccountsWindow class 318
ACID 18
Add/RemoveCacheListener methods 318
Add method 301

aggregate, domain model building blocks
  118
aggregate method 189, 195
aggregator
  about 184-187
  AbstractAggregator class 184
  AverageAggregator 187
  built-ins 187, 188
  example 185, 187
  LookupValueExtractor, implementing 189
  using 189
AllFilter class 163
AlwaysFilter class 163
AndFilter class 163
Ant 1.7+ 364
AnyFilter class 163
atomicity, consistency, isolation,
  and durability. *See* **ACID**

B

backing map listener
  about 222
  AbstractMapListener 223, 225
  cavets 222
  low balance listener, implementing 223
  registering 226-228
backing maps
  about 95
  external backing map 96
  local cache 95, 96
  overflow backing map 97
  paged external backing map 97
  partitioned backing map 99
  read-write backing map 98

O

Object@clone() method 339
object serialization, implementing
  about 137
  code, implementing 142-145
  collection serialization 150
  POF, basics 137
  PofSerializer, choosing 145-149
  PortableObject, choosing 145-149
ObservableCollection class 317
operation bundling 240
Optimistic Cache service 81
Oracle Coherence 3.5.3
  about 363
  Coherence for C++ 32-bit Windows release,
    downloading 363
  Coherence Java release, downloading 363
Oracle Technology Network. *See* OTN
OrFilter class 163
OTN 36

P

partitioned cache
  about 86
  data set size 89
  evaluating 86
  fault ignorance 90
  read performance 86, 87
  using 90
  write performance 87-89
PasswordBasedEncryptionFilter class 290
performance objectives, achieving
  about 13
  bandwidth usage, minimizing 15, 16
  Coherence 16
  latency, dealing with 14, 15
  performance 16
persistence ignorance (PI) 137
persistence patterns, Coherence
  cache aside 238
  read through 239
  write behind 254
  write through 252
POF
  about 137

basics 137, 138
context 139
history 138
POF value, type identifier 138
serializer 139
user types 138
POF context
  about 139
  ConfigurablePofContext 140, 142
PofExtractor 168, 303
PofReader.readCollection method 150
PofReader method 143
POF serializer 140
POF value 138
PofWriter method 143
Portable Object Format. *See* POF
PortableObjectSerializer 145
PortfolioPosition class 192
PriorityProcessors 201, 202
process method 193, 195
programmatic registration, map listeners
  about 216
  addMapListener method 216
  MapEventFilter class 216
  map events, transforming 218, 219
  ValueChangeEventFilter 218
PropertyChange event 317
PropertyExtractor
  implementing 347
  implementing in C# 307-310
proxy servers
  about 270
  AuthorizedHostsFilter, implementing 283
  host-address element 282
  host-filter element 282
  host-range element 282
  securing 281, 282, 284
pseudorandom function 288
putAll method 68
put method 68

Q

queries, executing
  filters, implementing 306, 307
  value extractors, implementing 306, 307

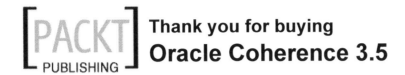

Thank you for buying
Oracle Coherence 3.5

About Packt Publishing

Packt, pronounced 'packed', published its first book "*Mastering phpMyAdmin for Effective MySQL Management*" in April 2004 and subsequently continued to specialize in publishing highly focused books on specific technologies and solutions.

Our books and publications share the experiences of your fellow IT professionals in adapting and customizing today's systems, applications, and frameworks. Our solution based books give you the knowledge and power to customize the software and technologies you're using to get the job done. Packt books are more specific and less general than the IT books you have seen in the past. Our unique business model allows us to bring you more focused information, giving you more of what you need to know, and less of what you don't.

Packt is a modern, yet unique publishing company, which focuses on producing quality, cutting-edge books for communities of developers, administrators, and newbies alike. For more information, please visit our website: www.packtpub.com.

Writing for Packt

We welcome all inquiries from people who are interested in authoring. Book proposals should be sent to author@packtpub.com. If your book idea is still at an early stage and you would like to discuss it first before writing a formal book proposal, contact us; one of our commissioning editors will get in touch with you.

We're not just looking for published authors; if you have strong technical skills but no writing experience, our experienced editors can help you develop a writing career, or simply get some additional reward for your expertise.

Oracle 11g Streams Implementer's Guide

ISBN: 978-1-847199-70-6   Paperback: 352 pages

Design, implement, and maintain a distributed environment with Oracle Streams

1. Implement Oracle Streams to manage and coordinate the resources, information, and functions of a distributed system

2. Get to grips with in-depth explanations of the components that make up Oracle Streams, and how they work together

3. Learn design considerations that help identify and avoid Oracle Streams obstacles – before you get caught in them

Oracle Warehouse Builder 11g: Getting Started

ISBN: 978-1-847195-74-6   Paperback: 368 pages

Extract, Transform, and Load data to build a dynamic, operational data warehouse

1. Build a working data warehouse from scratch with Oracle Warehouse Builder

2. Cover techniques in Extracting, Transforming, and Loading data into your data warehouse

3. Learn about the design of a data warehouse by using a multi-dimensional design with an underlying relational star schema.

Please check **www.PacktPub.com** for information on our titles

**Oracle 10g/11g Data and
Database Management Utilities**

ISBN: 978-1-847196-28-6   Paperback: 432 pages

Master twelve must-use utilities to optimize the
efficiency, management, and performance of your
daily database tasks

1. Optimize time-consuming tasks efficiently using
   the Oracle database utilities

2. Perform data loads on the fly and replace the
   functionality of the old export and import
   utilities using Data Pump or SQL*Loader

3. Boost database defenses with Oracle Wallet
   Manager and Security

4. A handbook with lots of practical content with
   real-life scenarios

**Mastering Oracle Scheduler in
Oracle 11g Databases**

ISBN: 978-1-847195-98-2   Paperback: 240 pages

Schedule, manage, and execute jobs that automate
your business processes

1. Automate jobs from within the Oracle database
   with the built-in Scheduler

2. Boost database performance by managing,
   monitoring, and controlling jobs more
   effectively

3. Contains easy-to-understand explanations,
   simple examples, debugging tips, and
   real-life scenarios

Please check **www.PacktPub.com** for information on our titles

PACKT
PUBLISHING

Oracle Application Express 3.2 – The
Essentials and More

Develop Oracle database centric Web applications quickly and
easily with Oracle Application Express

Arie Geller   Matthew Lyon   PACKT

Oracle Application Express 3.2 – The Essentials and More

ISBN: 978-1-847194-52-7   Paperback: 520 pages

Develop Native Oracle database-centric web
applications quickly and easily with Oracle APEX

1. Grasp the principles behind APEX to develop
   efficient and optimized data-centric native web
   applications, for the Oracle environment

2. Gain a better understanding of the major
   principles and building blocks of APEX, like
   the IDE and its modules

3. Review APEX-related technologies like HTML
   and the DOM, CSS, and JavaScript, which will
   help you to develop better, richer, and more
   efficient APEX applications

Oracle Essbase 9
Implementation Guide

Develop high-performance multidimensional analytic OLAP
solutions with Oracle Essbase

Sarma Anantapantula
Joseph Sydney Gomez   PACKT

Oracle Essbase 9 Implementation Guide

ISBN: 978-1-847196-86-6   Paperback: 444 pages

Develop high-performance multidimensional analytic
OLAP solutions with Oracle Essbase

1. Build multidimensional Essbase database cubes
   and develop analytical Essbase applications

2. Step-by-step instructions with expert tips from
   installation to implementation

3. Can be used to learn any version of Essbase
   starting from 4.x to 11.x

4. For beginners as well as experienced
   professionals; no Essbase experience required

Please check **www.PacktPub.com** for information on our titles

Made in the USA
Lexington, KY
14 May 2010